OUTLINES

of

Doctrinal Theology.

———•❈•———

BY

A. L. GRAEBNER.

St. Louis, Mo.
CONCORDIA PUBLISHING HOUSE.
1910.

PREFACE.

These Outlines of Doctrinal Theology were not originally intended for publication. They were prepared for the students of Concordia Seminary, to be used as a compend for the English lectures on Dogmatic Theology.[1] To avoid the tedious process of dictation, by which they had for several years been transmitted to the classes, the paragraphs and texts were, by the students, printed on the mimeograph. A number of copies, without the author's knowledge, found their way into the hands of brethren in the ministry, and from various quarters the request was made that the work be published in a regular edition. Finally, when the students' supply was exhausted and the Board of Directors of Concordia Publishing House determined on the publication of the book, the author deemed it no longer proper to refuse his consent and cooperation.

In preparing the copy for the press, the author has in no wise changed the character of the work. It remains what, as originally designed, it was to be, not an exhaustive treatise of Dogmatic Theology, but a brief thetical compend of the outlines of Christian doctrine, consisting of concise definitions and an array of texts from which the various points of doctrine are derived as from their theological source, the written Word of God. The chief purpose of the book, too, remains unchanged, and the desire to see his students provided with a well-printed text-book for his lectures to them was foremost

---

1) The leading course of lectures on Dogmatic Theology in said institution is delivered in German and Latin.

in prompting the author to concur in its publication. For the benefit of others who may find the book of some use to them, he would say that his method of instruction comprises, mainly, an analysis of the Paragraphs, an exposition of the texts with a view of substantiating therefrom the points embodied in the Paragraphs, and a demonstration of the incompatibility of the chief antitheses with the texts and the points of doctrine therein set forth. The use of the book in the absence of such comments will be, in a measure, facilitated by the *italics* employed for the purpose of marking the pertinence of each text to the point under consideration. Many texts covering different points have been given repeatedly, in different groups, but differently italicized, and in rare cases references only have been given instead of the texts in full, especially where the words are found on the same or an adjacent page. It may not be entirely superfluous to say in this connection that in a number of instances the pertinence of a text, while not so apparent in the English version, will appear when the original Greek or Hebrew is compared. In other instances, where a divergence of exegesis may tend to impugn the argumentativeness of a text for the purpose in point, care has been taken to cover the same topic by other texts. The reader will also notice that various subjects, *e. g.,* the divinity of Christ, the moral law, the natural state of man, marriage, civil government, the work of redemption, the means of grace, the Church, predestination, temporal death, final judgment, the kingdom of glory, have been repeatedly dealt with under different heads, to point out the various relations of these points of doctrine.

While it has been the author's constant aim to demonstrate the scripturalness of the doctrinal statements set forth in the Paragraphs of this book, he deems it a duty to say that he knows himself also in full accord with the doctrine of the

Lutheran Church as laid down in the Book of Concord, and
that the absence of references to the Symbols of our church,
the *norma normata* of sound Lutheranism, must not be con-
strued into a disparagement of the Lutheran standards or of
any point of doctrine therein contained. With an emphatic
refusal to apologize for having nowhere, from the first point
in Bibliology to the last in Eschatology, progressed beyond the
theology of our orthodox fathers, and with the fervent prayer
that God would graciously keep him and his brethren in the
faith from any such progress, this humble contribution toward
the theological literature of our church in America is dedicated
to the service of our Lord and Savior Jesus Christ and commended to His divine blessing by

THE AUTHOR.

CONTENTS.

OUTLINES OF DOCTRINAL THEOLOGY.

Prolegomena.

DEFINITIONS OF THEOLOGY.

§ 1. Theology is a practical habitude of the mind comprising the knowledge and acceptance of divine truth, together with an aptitude to instruct others towards such knowledge and acceptance, and to defend such truth against its adversaries.

Acts 18, 24—28: And a certain Jew named Apollos, born at Alexandria, an eloquent man, and *mighty in the Scriptures,* came to Ephesus. This man was *instructed in the way of the Lord;* and being *fervent in the Spirit,* he *spake and taught diligently* the things of the Lord, knowing only the baptism of John. And he began *to speak boldly in the synagogue:* whom when Aquila and Priscilla had heard, they took him unto them, *and expounded unto him the way of God more perfectly.* And when he was disposed to pass into Achaia, the brethren wrote, exhorting the disciples to receive him: who, when he was come, *helped them much which had believed* through grace. For he *mightily convinced the Jews,* and that publicly, *showing by the Scriptures that Jesus was Christ.*

2 Tim. 3, 16. 17: All Scripture is given by inspiration of God, and is *profitable for doctrine,* for reproof, for correction, for instruction in righteousness: *that the man of God may be perfect, throughly furnished unto all good works.*

Tit. 1, 9: *Holding fast* the faithful Word *as he hath been taught,* that he may be *able by sound doctrine both to exhort and to convince the gainsayers.*

§ 2. Theology may be viewed as doctrinal, exegetical, historical, and practical Theology.

DOCTRINAL THEOLOGY.

§ 3. Theology is *Doctrinal Theology* inasmuch as it comprises the knowledge and acceptance of the doctrines of divine revelation, and the aptitude to exhibit and substantiate such doctrines in themselves and in their proper relations to each other.

1

EXEGETICAL THEOLOGY.

§ 4. Theology is *Exegetical Theology* inasmuch as it comprises the aptitude to find and expound the true sense of the divinely inspired writings, the Old and the New Testaments, whence all theological truths must be derived as from their only infallible and sufficient source, and the knowledge requisite for such aptitude.

HISTORICAL THEOLOGY.

§ 5. Theology is *Historical Theology* inasmuch as it comprises the knowledge and theological discernment of the rise, progress, and preservation of the Christian Church and of its institutions, and an aptitude to utilize such knowledge in the promulgation, application, and defense of divine truth.

PRACTICAL THEOLOGY.

§ 6. Theology is *Practical Theology* inasmuch as it comprises the knowledge of the proper functions of a minister of the Christian Church and of their underlying principles, together with an aptitude to perform such functions in accordance with such principles.

THEOLOGY IN AN ABSTRACT SENSE.

§ 7. An oral or written exhibition of the truths, doctrines, principles, etc., by virtue of the knowledge, acceptance, maintenance, and practical application of which a theologian is a theologian, is also, in an *abstract sense,* called theology.

Doctrinal Theology.

DEFINITION.

§ 8. Doctrinal Theology, in the abstract sense of the term, is the aggregate of the doctrines laid down in the Holy Scriptures, which should be known, accepted, properly applied, and strenuously defended, by a theologian; and Doctrinal Theology in this sense is outlined in the following chapters and paragraphs.

§ 9. Doctrinal Theology may be divided into Bibliology, Theology Proper, Cosmology, Christology, Soteriology, and Eschatology.

BIBLIOLOGY.

DEFINITION.

§ 10. Bibliology is the doctrine of Holy Scripture concerning the origin, the properties, and the purposes of the Bible.

ORIGIN OF THE BIBLE.

§ 11. By its ORIGIN, the Bible, or Holy Scripture, consisting of the canonical books of the Old and the New Testaments,[1] is in all its parts[2] the Word of God.[3]

1.

John 5, 39: Search *the Scriptures;* for in them ye think ye have eternal life: and they are they which testify of me.

Rom. 3, 2: Much every way: chiefly, because that *unto them* were committed *the oracles of God.*

1 Pet. 1, 25: But the *Word of the Lord* endureth forever. And *this* is *the Word which by the Gospel is preached unto you.*

1 Cor. 14, 37: If any man think himself to be a prophet, or spiritual, let him acknowledge that *the things that I write* unto you are the commandments *of the Lord.*

2.

Gal. 3, 16: Now to Abraham and his seed were the promises made. *He* saith not, And to *seeds,* as of many; but as of one, And to thy *seed,* which is Christ.

John 10, 35: If he called them *gods,* unto whom *the Word of God* came, and the *Scripture* cannot be broken. Cf. Ps. 82, 6.

Hebr. 12, 26: Whose voice then shook the earth: but now He hath promised, saying, *Yet once more* I shake not the earth only, but also heaven.

Hebr. 3, 7: Wherefore as the Holy Ghost saith, *To-day,* if ye will hear His voice, . . . Cf. Ps. 95, 7. 8.

Mark 7, 10. 13: For *Moses said,* Honor thy father and thy mother; and, Whoso curseth father or mother, let him die the death. (13) Making *the Word of God* of none effect through your tradition, which ye have delivered: and many such like things do ye.

3.

2 Pet. 1, 21: For the prophecy came not in old time by the will of man: but holy men of God *spake as they were moved by the Holy Ghost.*

Rom. 3, 2: Much every way: chiefly, because that unto them were committed the *oracles of God.*

1 Pet. 1, 11: Searching what, or what manner of time *the Spirit of Christ* which was in them *did signify,* when *it testified* beforehand the sufferings of Christ, and the glory that should follow.

1 Pet. 1, 25: But the WORD *of the Lord* endureth forever. And this is the *Word* which *by the Gospel* is *preached* unto you.

Matt. 1, 22 f.: Which was *spoken of the Lord by the prophet,* saying, Behold, a virgin shall be with child. Cf. Is. 7, 14.

Gal. 3, 16: Now to Abraham and his *seed* were the promises made. *He saith* not, And to *seeds,* as of many; but as of one, And to thy *seed,* which is Christ.

Matt. 22, 31: But as touching the resurrection of the dead, have ye not *read* that which was *spoken unto you by God?*

Hebr. 3, 7: Wherefore, as the *Holy Ghost saith, To-day,* if ye will hear His voice. . . .

Hebr. 10, 15. 16: Whereof *the Holy Ghost* also is a *witness to us:* for after that He had said before, This is the covenant that I will make with them after those days, saith the Lord, I will put my laws into their hearts, and in their minds will I write them. Cf. Jer. 31, 33 f.

Mark 7, 13: Making the *Word of God* of none effect through your tradition, which ye have delivered; and many such like things do ye. Cf. § 11, 2.

Acts 13, 46: Then Paul and Barnabas waxed bold, and said, It was necessary that *the Word of God* should first have been spoken to you: but seeing ye put it from you, and judge yourselves unworthy of everlasting life, lo, *we* turn to the Gentiles.

Tit. 1, 2: In hope of eternal life, which *God,* that cannot lie, *promised* before the world began. Cf. § 11, 1.

Acts 11, 1: And the apostles and brethren that were in Judea heard that the Gentiles had also received *the Word of God.*

INSPIRATION.

§ 12. The Bible was written by divine inspiration,[1] inasmuch as the inspired penmen[2] performed their work as the personal organs[3] of God,[4] especially of the Holy Spirit,[5] who not only prompted and actuated them toward writing what they wrote,[6] but also suggested to them both the thoughts and the words they uttered as they wrote.[7]

1.

2 Tim. 3, 16: All Scripture is given by inspiration of God, etc.

2.

Rom. 15, 15: Nevertheless, brethren, *I have written* the more boldly unto you in some sort.

1 Cor. 5, 9: *I wrote* unto you in an epistle.

2 Cor. 2, 3. 4. 9: And *I wrote* this same unto you. For out of much affliction and anguish of heart *I wrote* unto you with many

tears; not that ye should be grieved, but that ye might know the love which *I have* more abundantly unto you. (9) For to this end also *did I write,* that *I might know* the proof of you, whether ye be obedient in all things.

Gal. 1, 20: Now the things which *I write* unto you, behold, before God, *I lie not.*

Phil. 3, 1: Finally, my brethren, rejoice in the Lord. To write the same things to you, to me indeed is not grievous, but for you it is safe.

1 Tim. 3, 14: These things *write I* unto thee, hoping to come unto thee shortly.

1 John 1, 4: And these things *write we* unto you, that your joy may be full.

1 John 2, 1. 13: My little children, these things *write I* unto you, that ye sin not. (13) *I write* unto you, fathers, because ye have known Him that is from the beginning. *I write* unto you, young men, because ye have overcome the wicked one. *I write* unto you, little children, because ye have known the Father.

John 5, 46. 47: For had ye believed *Moses,* ye would have believed me: for *he wrote* of me. But if ye believe not *his writings,* how shall ye believe my words?

Luke 3, 4: As it is written in the book *of the words of Esaias,* the prophet.

Matt. 13, 14: And in them is fulfilled *the prophecy of Esaias* which saith, . . .

Matt. 15, 7: Ye hypocrites, well *did Esaias prophesy* of you, saying, . . .

Luke 20, 42: And *David himself saith* in the book of Psalms, The Lord said unto my Lord, Sit Thou on my right hand.

3.

Matt. 2, 5. 17: And they said unto him, In Bethlehem of Judea: for thus it is *written* BY *the prophet.* (17) Then was fulfilled that which was *spoken* BY *Jeremy,* the prophet, saying, . . .

Matt. 8, 17: That it might be fulfilled which was *spoken* BY *Esaias* the prophet, saying, . . .

Matt. 12, 17: That it might be fulfilled which was *spoken* BY *Esaias* the prophet, saying, . . .

Matt. 13, 35: That it might be fulfilled which was *spoken* BY *the prophet,* saying, I will open my mouth in parables; I will utter things which have been kept secret from the foundation of the world.

Matt. 24, 15: When ye therefore shall see the abomination of desolation, *spoken* of BY *Daniel the prophet,* stand in the holy place, (whoso readeth, let him understand).

Matt. 27, 9. 35: Then was fulfilled that which was *spoken* BY *Jeremy the prophet,* saying, . . . (35) That it might be fulfilled which was *spoken* BY *the prophet,* . . .

Acts 2, 16: But this is that which was *spoken* BY *the prophet Joel.*

4.

Matt. 1, 22: Now all this was done, that it might be fulfilled which was spoken OF *the Lord* BY *the prophet,* saying, . . .

Acts 4, 24. 25: And when they heard that, they lifted up their voice to *God* with one accord, and said, *Lord,* Thou art *God,* which hast made heaven, and earth, and the sea, and all that in them is: WHO BY *the mouth of Thy servant David hast* said, Why did the heathen rage, and the people imagine vain things? Cf. Ps. 2, 1. 2.

Hebr. 4, 7: Again, *He* limiteth a certain day, *saying* IN *David,* To-day, after so long a time; as it is said, To-day, if ye will hear His voice, harden not your hearts.

Rom. 9, 25: As HE *saith also* IN *Osee,* I will call them my people which were not my people; and her beloved which was not beloved.

Rom. 1, 2: Which HE *had promised* afore BY *His prophets in the Holy Scriptures.*

5.

Acts 1, 16: Men and brethren, *this scripture* must needs have been fulfilled, which the *Holy Ghost by the mouth of David spake* before concerning Judas, which was guide to them that took Jesus.

Acts 28, 25: Well *spake the Holy Ghost by Esaias the prophet* unto our fathers.

2 Sam. 23, 1. 2: Now these be the last *words of David. David,* the son of Jesse, *said,* and the man who was raised up on high, the anointed of the God of Jacob, and *the sweet psalmist* of Israel, *said,* The *Spirit of the Lord spake by me,* and *His word* was in *my tongue.*

2 Pet. 1, 19—21: We have also a more sure *word of prophecy;* whereunto ye do well that ye take heed, as unto a light that shineth in a dark place, until the day dawn, and the day-star arise in your hearts: knowing this first, that no *prophecy of the Scripture* is of any private interpretation. For *the prophecy* came *not* in old time *by the will of man:* but *holy men of God spake* as they were *moved by the Holy Ghost.*

1 Pet. 1, 11. 12: Searching what, or what manner of time the *Spirit of Christ* which was *in them did signify,* when *it testified* beforehand the sufferings of Christ, and the glory that should follow. Unto whom it was revealed, that not unto themselves, but unto us they did *minister* the things, which are now reported unto you by them that have *preached the Gospel* unto you *with the Holy Ghost sent down from heaven;* which things the angels desire to look into.

Matt. 10, 19: But when they deliver you up, take no thought how or what ye shall speak: for *it shall be given you* in that same hour *what ye shall speak.*

Mark 13, 11: But when they shall lead you, and deliver you up, take no thought beforehand what ye shall speak, neither do ye premeditate: but *whatsoever shall be given you* in that hour, *that speak ye: for it is not ye that speak,* but *the Holy Ghost.*

Luke 12, 12: For the *Holy Ghost* shall teach you in the same hour what ye ought to say.

6.

2 Pet. 1, 21: For the prophecy came not in old time by the will of man: but holy men of God *spake* as they were *moved* by *the Holy Ghost.*

2 Tim. 3, 16: All Scripture is given by *inspiration of God,* and is profitable for doctrine, for reproof, for correction, for instruction in righteousness.

Rom. 15, 18. 19: For *I will not dare to speak of any of those things which ·Christ hath not wrought by me,* to make the Gentiles obedient, by *word* and deed, through mighty signs and wonders, by the *power of the Spirit of God.*

Gal. 1, 11: But I certify you, brethren, that the Gospel which was preached of me is not after man.

Jer. 30, 2: Thus speaketh the Lord God of Israel, saying, Write thee all the words that I have spoken unto thee in a book.

7.

Jer. 30, 2: Thus speaketh the Lord God of Israel, *saying, Write* thee *all* the *words* that *I have spoken* unto thee in a book.

Rom. 15, 18: For *I will not dare* to speak of any of those things which Christ hath not wrought by me, to make the Gentiles obedient by word and deed.

1 Thess. 2, 13: For this cause also thank we God without ceasing, because, when ye received the Word of God which ye heard of us, ye received it *not as the word of men,* but *as it is in truth, the Word of God,* which effectually worketh also in you that believe.

Acts 2, 4: And they were all filled with the Holy Ghost, and began to speak with other tongues, *as the Spirit gave them utterance.*

2 Pet. 1, 19—21: We have also a more sure *word* of prophecy; whereunto ye do well that ye take heed, as unto a light that shineth in a dark place, until the day dawn, and the day-star arise in your hearts: knowing this first, that no prophecy of the *Scripture* is of any private interpretation. For the prophecy *came not* in old time *by the will of man:* but holy men of God *spake as they were moved* by the Holy Ghost.

John 10, 34. 35: Jesus answered them, Is it not *written* in your law, I said, Ye are *gods?* If He called them *gods,* unto whom the Word of God came, and the *Scripture cannot be broken.*

Matt. 22, 43. 44: He saith unto them, How, then, doth *David in spirit* call him *Lord,* saying, The Lord said unto *my Lord,* Sit Thou on my right hand, till I make Thine enemies Thy footstool?

Rom. 15, 9—12: And that the *Gentiles* might glorify God for His mercy; as it is written, For this cause I will confess to Thee among the *Gentiles,* and sing unto Thy name. And again He saith, Rejoice, ye *Gentiles,* with His people! And again, Praise the Lord, all ye *Gentiles;* and laud Him, all ye people! And again, Esaias saith, There shall be a root of Jesse, and He that shall rise to reign over the *Gentiles;* in Him shall the *Gentiles* trust.

Gal. 3, 16: He saith not, And to *seeds,* as of many; but as of one, And to thy *seed,* which is Christ.

Rom. 10, 16: But they have not all obeyed *the Gospel.* For Esaias saith, Lord, who hath *believed* our report?

1 Pet. 3, 6: Even as Sarah obeyed Abraham, calling him *lord.*

Hebr. 12, 27: And *this word, Yet once more,* signifieth the removing of those things that are shaken, as of things that are made, that those things which cannot be shaken may remain.

Hebr. 8, 8. 13: For finding fault with them, He saith, Behold, the days come, saith the Lord, when I will make a *new covenant* with the house of Israel and with the house of Judah. (13) In that He saith, A *new* covenant, He hath made the first old. Now that which decayeth and waxeth old is ready to vanish away.

Hebr. 4, 7: Again, *He* limiteth a certain day, *saying* in David, *To-day,* after so long a time; as it is said, *To-day,* if ye will hear His voice, harden not your hearts.

Hebr. 7, 20. 21: And inasmuch as not without an *oath* He was made priest: (for those priests were made without an oath; but this with an oath by Him that said unto Him, *The Lord sware* and will not repent, Thou art a priest forever after the order of Melchisedec:). Ps. 110, 4.

Rom. 4, 6. 7. 9: Even as David also *describeth the blessedness* of the man unto whom God imputeth righteousness without works, saying, *Blessed* are they whose iniquities are forgiven, and whose sins are covered. (9) Cometh *this blessedness,* then, upon the circumcision only, or upon the uncircumcision also?

Eph. 4, 8. 9: Wherefore he saith, When *He ascended up* on high, He led captivity captive, and gave gifts unto men. Now *that He ascended,* what is it but that He also descended first into the lower parts of the earth? Cf. Ps. 68, 18.

John 7, 42: Hath not *the Scripture said,* That Christ cometh of the seed of *David,* and out of the town of *Bethlehem,* where David was?

Luke 16, 17: And it is easier for heaven and earth to pass than one *tittle of the Law* to fail.

PROPERTIES OF THE BIBLE.

§ 13. The PROPERTIES of the Bible are its divine authority, its perspicuity, its efficacy, and its sufficiency.

AUTHORITY.

§ 14. The *authority* of the Bible is that prerogative by which the Bible justly claims unrestricted acceptance of all its statements,[1] full assent to all its teachings,[2] unwavering confidence in all its promises,[3] and willing observance of all its demands[4] by those whom they concern, the prerogative by which it is the only infallible source and norm of doctrine[5] and rule of life.[6]

1.

Matt. 4, 3: And when the tempter came to Him, he said, *If* Thou be the Son of God, command that these stones be made bread.

Luke 4, 3: And the devil said unto Him, *If* Thou be the Son of God, command this stone that it be made bread.

Gen. 3, 1: Now the serpent was more subtile than any beast of the field which the Lord God had made. And he said unto the woman, *Yea, hath God said,* Ye shall not eat of every tree of the garden?

John 10, 35: If He called them *gods,* unto whom the Word of God came, and the *Scripture* cannot be broken.

Luke 24, 25: Then He said unto them, O fools, and slow of heart to believe *all* that the prophets have spoken!

Ps. 119, 160: Thy *word* is *true from the beginning;* and every one of Thy righteous judgments endureth forever.

Ps. 119, 140: Thy word is *very pure;* therefore Thy servant loveth it.

Ps. 119, 167: My soul hath kept *Thy testimonies;* and I love them exceedingly.

2.

2 Tim. 3, 16: *All Scripture* is given by inspiration of God, and is *profitable for doctrine,* for reproof, for correction, for instruction in righteousness.

2 Thess. 2, 15: Therefore, brethren, stand fast, and hold *the traditions which ye have been taught,* whether by word *or our epistle.*

Luke 24, 25—27: Then He said unto them, O fools, and slow of heart to believe *all that the prophets have spoken: ought* not Christ to have suffered these things, and to enter into His glory? And *beginning* at *Moses* and *all the prophets,* He expounded unto them in *all the Scriptures the things concerning Himself.*

Luke 16, 29—31: Abraham saith unto him, They have *Moses and the prophets; let them hear them.* And he said, Nay, father Abraham: but if one went unto them from the dead, they will repent. And he said unto him, If they hear not Moses and the prophets, neither will they *be persuaded,* though one rose from the dead.

3.

2 Thess. 2, 13: But we are bound to give thanks alway to God for you, brethren beloved of the Lord, because God hath from the beginning chosen you to salvation through sanctification of the Spirit and *belief of the truth.*

2 Cor. 1, 20: For all the *promises* of God in Him are *yea,* and in Him *Amen,* unto the glory of God *by us.*

Tit. 1, 2. 3: In hope of eternal life, which God, that cannot lie, *promised* before the world began; but hath in due times *manifested His Word through preaching,* which is committed *unto me* according to the commandment of God, our Savior.

2 Thess. 2, 15: Therefore, brethren, *stand fast, and hold* the traditions which ye have been taught, whether by word or our epistle.

2 Pet. 1, 19: We have also a *more sure* word of prophecy; whereunto ye do well that ye *take heed.*

4.

Deut. 12, 32: *What thing soever I command* you, *observe to do it:* thou shalt not add thereto, nor diminish from it.

Deut. 5, 9. 10: Thou shalt not bow down thyself unto them, nor serve them: *for* I the Lord, thy God, am a jealous God, visiting the iniquity of the fathers upon the children unto the third and fourth generation of them that hate me, and showing mercy unto thousands of them that love me and *keep my commandments.*

Cf. Exod. 20, 5. 6.

James 2, 10: For whosoever shall *keep the whole Law,* and yet offend in *one* point, he is *guilty of all.*

Josh. 1, 8: This *book* of the Law shall not depart out of thy mouth, but thou shalt meditate therein day and night, *that thou mayest observe to do according to all that is written therein.*

5.

Luke 16, 29: Abraham saith unto him, They have *Moses and the prophets;* let them *hear them.*

2 Tim. 3, 15—17: And that from a child thou hast known the *Holy Scriptures,* which are able to make thee *wise* unto salvation through faith which is in Christ Jesus. *All Scripture* is given by inspiration of God, and is *profitable for doctrine,* for reproof, for correction, for instruction in righteousness, that the man of God may be *perfect,* throughly furnished unto *all good works.*

Jer. 8, 9: The wise men are ashamed, they are dismayed and taken: lo, they have *rejected the Word of the Lord,* and *what wisdom is in them?*

Jer. 23, 16: Thus saith the Lord of hosts, *Hearken not* unto the words of the prophets that prophesy unto you; they make you vain: *they speak* a vision of their own heart, and *not out of the mouth of the Lord.*

Is. 8, 19. 20: And when they shall say unto you, Seek unto them that have familiar spirits, and unto wizards that peep and that mutter: should not a people seek unto their God? for the living to the dead? *To the Law and to the testimony: if they speak not according to this word,* it is because *there is no light in them.*

1 Cor. 14, 37: If any man think himself to be a *prophet,* or spiritual, *let him acknowledge that the things I write unto you are the commandments of the Lord.*

Gal. 1, 8: But *though we,* or *an angel from heaven,* preach *other gospel* unto you *than that which we have preached* unto you, let him *be accursed!*

Acts 17, 11: These were more noble than those in Thessalonica, in that they received the Word with all readiness of mind, *and searched the Scriptures* daily, *whether those things were so.*

Acts 15, 14. 15: *Simeon hath declared* how God at the first did visit the Gentiles, to take out of them a people for His name. *And to this agree the words of the prophets; as it is written.*

6.

Luke 16, 29: Abraham said unto him, They have *Moses and the prophets; let them hear them.*

2 Tim. 3, 16: *All Scripture* is given by inspiration of God, and is *profitable* for doctrine, for reproof, *for correction, for instruction in righteousness.*

PERSPICUITY.

§ 15. The *perspicuity* of the Bible is that clearness of Holy Writ which renders all the doctrines and precepts laid down in the inspired Word freely accessible to every reader or hearer of average human intelligence and sufficient knowledge of the languages employed, and of a mind not in a manner preoccupied by error as to preclude the apprehension of the truths themselves, however clearly set forth in words of human speech.

Ps. 119, 105: *Thy Word* is a *lamp* unto my feet, and a *light* unto my path.

Ps. 119, 130: The entrance of Thy words *giveth light;* it *giveth understanding* unto the *simple.*

2 Pet. 1, 19: We have also a more sure *word of prophecy;* whereunto ye do well that ye take heed, as unto *a light that shineth in a dark place,* until the day dawn, and the day-star arise in your hearts.

Ps. 19, 8: The statutes of the Lord are right, rejoicing the heart: the commandment of the Lord is pure, *enlightening the eyes.*

Eph. 3, 3. 4: How that by revelation He made known unto me the mystery; as *I wrote* afore in few words, whereby, *when ye read, ye may understand* my knowledge in the mystery of Christ.

John 8, 31. 32: Then said Jesus to those Jews which believed on Him, If ye continue in my Word, then are ye my disciples indeed; and *ye shall know the truth,* and the truth shall make you free.

2 Cor. 4, 3. 4: But *if our Gospel be hid,* it is hid *to them that are lost:* in whom the god of this world hath *blinded the minds* of them which believe not, lest the *light of the glorious Gospel* of Christ, who is the image of God, should *shine* unto them.

John 8, 43—45. 47: *Why do ye not understand my speech?* Even because *ye cannot hear my Word.* Ye are of your father, the devil, and the lusts of your father *ye will do.* He was a murderer from the beginning, and abode not in the truth, because there is no truth in him. When he speaketh a lie, he speaketh of his own: for he is a liar, and the father of it. And *because I tell you the truth, ye believe me not.* (47) He that is of God heareth God's words: ye therefore hear them not, *because ye are not of God.*

2 Pet. 3, 15. 16: Even as our beloved brother Paul also according to the wisdom given unto him hath written unto you; as also *in all his epistles,* speaking in them of these things; *in which are some things hard to be understood, which they that are unlearned and unstable wrest, as they do also the other scriptures,* unto their own destruction.

EFFICACY.

§ 16. The *efficacy* of the Bible is that property by which the Bible has indissolubly united[1] with the true and genuine sense[2] expressed in its words the power of the Holy Spirit,[3] who has made it for all times the ordinary means by which He operates[4] on and in the hearts and minds of those who properly hear and read it.[5]

1.

Rom. 1, 16: For I am not ashamed of the Gospel of Christ; for *it is the power of God* unto salvation to every one that believeth.

1 Thess. 2, 13: For this cause also thank we God without ceasing, because, when ye received *the Word of God which ye heard of us,* ye received it not as the word of men, but as it is in truth, the *Word of God, which effectually worketh* also in you that believe.

2.

Eph. 3, 3. 4: How that by revelation He made known unto me the mystery; as I wrote afore in few words, whereby, *when ye read,* ye may *understand my knowledge* in the mystery of Christ.

Acts 8, 30. 31. 34: And Philip ran thither to him, and heard him read the prophet Esaias, and said, *Understandest thou what thou readest?* And he said, How can I, except some man should guide me? And he desired Philip that he would come up and sit with him. (34) And the eunuch answered Philip, and said, I pray thee, *of whom speaketh the prophet this?* of himself, or of some other man?

3.

Rom. 1, 16: For I am not ashamed of the *Gospel of Christ;* for it *is* the *power of God* unto salvation to every one that believeth; to the Jew first, and also to the Greek.

1 Thess. 1, 5: For *our Gospel* came not unto you in word only, but also *in power,* and in the *Holy Ghost,* and in much assurance; as ye know what manner of men we were among you for your sake.

4.

Ps. 19, 8: The statutes of the Lord are right, *rejoicing* the heart: the commandment of the Lord is pure, *enlightening* the eyes.

Ps. 119, 105. 130: Thy Word is a *lamp* unto my feet, and a *light* unto my path. (130) The entrance of Thy words *giveth light;* it *giveth understanding* unto the simple.

2 Pet. 1, 19: We have also a more sure word of prophecy; whereunto ye do well that ye take heed, as unto a light that *shineth* in a dark place, *until the day dawn, and the day-star arise in your hearts.*

2 Tim. 3, 16. 17: All Scripture is given by inspiration of God, and is *profitable* for doctrine, for reproof, for correction, for instruction in righteousness, that the man of God *may be perfect, throughly furnished* unto all good works.

5.

Rev. 1, 3: *Blessed* is he *that readeth, and that hear* the words of this prophecy, *and keep those things* which are *written* therein: for the time is at hand.

Eph. 3, 3. 4: How that by revelation He made known unto me the mystery; (as I *wrote* afore in few words, whereby, *when ye read,* ye may understand my knowledge in the mystery of Christ).

John 7, 17: *If any man will do His will,* he shall know of *the doctrine,* whether it be *of God,* or whether I speak of myself.

SUFFICIENCY.

§ 17. The *sufficiency* of the Bible is that perfection according to which the Bible contains all that is necessary for the achievement of the end and aim of the Holy Scriptures.

Is. 8, 20: To the Law and to the testimony: if they speak not according to this word, it is because there is no light in them.

Luke 16, 29—31: Abraham saith unto him, They have Moses and the prophets; let them hear them. And he said, Nay, father Abraham: but if one went unto them from the dead, they will repent. And he said unto him, If they hear not Moses and the prophets, neither will they be persuaded, though one rose from the dead.

2 Tim. 3, 16. 17: All Scripture is given by inspiration of God, and is profitable for doctrine, for reproof, for correction, for instruction in righteousness, that the man of God may be *perfect, throughly furnished* unto *all* good works.

PURPOSES OF SCRIPTURE.

§ 18. The *purposes* of the Bible are, to convey to the understanding[1] of men the truths and precepts of Holy Writ, to convert[2] the unregenerate, and to preserve and strengthen the faith of the regenerate,[3] to rear them in holiness of life,[4] to afford them consolation in their afflictions,[5] to furnish weapons of offense and defense, wherewith to combat error and falsehood conflicting with God's truth,[6] and all this for the glory of God and man's eternal salvation.[7]

1.

Eph. 3, 3. 4: How that by revelation He made known unto me the mystery; (as I wrote afore in few words, whereby, when ye read, *ye may understand* my knowledge in the mystery of Christ).

Rom. 3, 20: Therefore by the deeds of the Law there shall no flesh be justified in His sight: for by the Law is the *knowledge* of sin.

Luke 24, 25—27: Then He said unto them, O fools, and slow of heart to believe all that the prophets have spoken: *ought* not Christ to have suffered these things, and to enter into His glory? And beginning at Moses and all the prophets, He *expounded* unto them in all the Scriptures the things concerning Himself.

2 Tim. 3, 16: All Scripture is given by inspiration of God, and is profitable for *doctrine*.

Rom. 15, 4: For whatsoever things were written aforetime were written for our *learning*, that we through patience and comfort of the Scriptures might have hope.

2 Tim. 3, 15: And that from a child thou hast *known* the Holy Scriptures, which are able to make thee *wise* unto salvation through faith which is in *Christ Jesus*.

Ps. 119, 104. 113: Through Thy *precepts* I get *understanding;* therefore I hate every false way. (113) *I hate vain thoughts:* but *Thy Law do I love.*

Ps. 19, 8: The statutes of the Lord are right, rejoicing the heart: the commandment of the Lord is pure, *enlightening the eyes.*

2.

Ps. 19, 7: The Law of the Lord is perfect, *converting* the soul: the testimony of the Lord is sure, making wise the simple.

Luke 16, 29—31: Abraham saith unto him, They have Moses and the prophets; let them hear them. And he said, Nay, father Abraham; but if one went unto them from the dead, they *will repent.* And he said unto him, If they hear not Moses and the prophets, neither will they *be persuaded,* though one rose from the dead.

2 Chron. 34, 27: Because thine heart was tender, and thou didst *humble thyself before God, when thou heardest His words* against this place, and against the inhabitants thereof, and humbledst thyself before me, and didst rend thy clothes, and weep before me, I have even heard thee also, saith the Lord.

3.

Luke 24, 25—27: Then He said unto them, O fools, and *slow* of heart to *believe all that the prophets have spoken:* ought not Christ to have suffered these things, and to enter into His glory? And beginning at Moses and all the prophets, He expounded unto them in all the Scriptures the things concerning Himself.

John 20, 31: But these are written, that *ye might believe* that Jesus is the Christ, the Son of God, and that, believing, ye might have life through His name.

4.

2 Tim. 3, 16. 17: All Scripture is given by inspiration of God, and is profitable for doctrine, for reproof, *for correction, for instruction in righteousness,* that the man of God may be *perfect,* throughly furnished unto all *good works.*

John 17, 17: *Sanctify* them through *Thy truth: Thy Word* is truth.

Ps. 119, 9: Wherewithal shall a young man *cleanse his way?* By taking heed thereto according to *Thy Word.*

Ps. 119, 43. 44: And take not the *word of truth* utterly out of my mouth; for I have *hoped in Thy judgments. So shall I keep Thy Law* continually for ever and ever.

5.

Rom. 15, 4: For whatsoever things were written aforetime were written for our learning, that we through patience *and comfort of the Scriptures might have hope.*

Ps. 130, 5: My soul doth *wait,* and in *His Word* do I *hope.*

6.

Acts 18, 24. 28: And a certain Jew named Apollos, born at Alexandria, an eloquent man, and *mighty in the Scriptures,* came to Ephesus. (28) For he mightily *convinced the Jews,* and that publicly, showing *by the Scriptures* that Jesus was Christ.

2 Tim. 3, 16: *All Scripture* is given by inspiration of God, and *is profitable* for doctrine, *for reproof,* for correction, for instruction in righteousness.

7.

John 20, 31: But these are written, that ye might believe that Jesus is the Christ, the Son of God, and that, believing, *ye might have life through His name.*

John 5, 39: Search the Scriptures; for in them ye think *ye have eternal life:* and they are they *which testify of me.*

2 Tim. 3, 15: And that from a child thou hast known the Holy Scriptures, which are able to make thee *wise unto salvation* through faith which is in *Christ Jesus.*

Ps. 138, 1. 2: I will *praise Thee* with my whole heart: before the gods will I sing praise unto Thee. I will *worship* toward Thy holy temple, and *praise Thy name* for Thy loving-kindness and for Thy truth: *for Thou hast magnified Thy Word above all Thy name.*

Ps. 138, 4: All the kings of the earth shall *praise Thee,* O Lord, *when they hear the words of Thy mouth.*

Ps. 119, 171: My lips shall utter *praise,* when Thou hast taught me *Thy statutes.*

THEOLOGY PROPER.

DEFINITION.

§ 19. Theology in the narrower sense of the term is the doctrine of Holy Scripture concerning the true God.

GOD.

§ 20. God is the one indivisible, immutable, infinite Spirit, who is life, intelligence, wisdom, will, holiness, justice, truth, goodness, and power, one God in three Persons, Father, Son, and Holy Ghost.

EXISTENCE OF GOD.

§ 21. The existence of God is not only evidenced by the works of creation[1] and by man's conscience,[2] but is taught wherever God is named and His works are mentioned in Holy Writ.[3]

1.

Rom. 1, 19—21: Because that which may be known of God is manifest in them; for God hath showed it unto them. For the invisible things of Him *from the creation of the world* are clearly seen, being understood *by the things that are made,* even His eternal power and Godhead; so that they are without excuse: because that, when *they knew God,* they glorified Him not as God, neither were thankful, but became vain in their imaginations, and their foolish heart was darkened.

Ps. 19, 1—3: The heavens declare the glory of God, and the firmament showeth His handiwork. Day unto day uttereth speech, and night unto night showeth knowledge. There is no speech nor language where their voice is not heard.

2.

Rom. 2, 15: Which show the work of the Law written in their hearts, their conscience also bearing witness, and their thoughts the mean while accusing or else excusing one another.

3.

Gen. 1, 1: In the beginning *God* created the heaven and the earth.

Rev. 22, 19: And if any man shall take away from the words of the book of this prophecy, *God* shall take away his part out of the book of life, and out of the holy city, and from the things which are written in this book.

Ps. 90, 2: Before the mountains were brought forth, or ever Thou hadst formed the earth and the world, even from everlasting to everlasting, *Thou art God.*

Ps. 14, 1: The *fool* hath said in his heart, There is no God.

SPIRITUALITY AND PERSONALITY.

§ 22. God is not a power subsisting in, or exerted by, a material being or number of beings, nor a material being endowed with, or exerting, power, nor a being composed of a material nature and a spiritual nature, but a spirit complete and subsisting in Himself.

John 4, 24: God is a *Spirit:* and they that worship Him must worship Him in spirit and in truth.

Exod. 3, 14: And God said unto Moses, *I Am That I Am.* And He said, Thus shalt thou say unto the children of Israel, *I Am* hath sent me unto you.

John 5, 26: For as the Father *hath life in Himself,* so hath He given to the Son to have life in Himself.

Is. 41, 4: Who hath *wrought and done it,* calling the generations from the beginning? I the Lord, the first, and with the last; *I am He.*

Is. 48, 12: Hearken unto me, O Jacob and Israel, my called: I am He; I am the first, I also am the last.

Acts 17, 28: For in Him we live, and move, and have our being; as certain also of your own poets have said, For we are also His offspring.

Col. 1, 16. 17: For *by Him were all things created,* that are in heaven, and that are in earth, visible and invisible, whether they be thrones, or dominions, or principalities, or powers: all things were created by Him and for Him. And *He is before all things,* and *by Him all things consist.*

Ps. 104, 24: O Lord, how manifold are Thy works! In *wisdom* hast Thou made them all: the earth is full of Thy riches.

Ps. 90, 2: Before the mountains were brought forth, or ever *Thou hadst formed the earth* and the world, even from everlasting to everlasting, *Thou art God.*

Is. 42, 8: I am the Lord, that is my name: and my glory will I not give to another, neither my praise to graven images.

UNITY OF GOD.

§ 23. God is one,[1] inasmuch as He cannot but be what He is; and there never has been, nor is, nor ever will, nor can be, another being like Him.[2]

1.

Mark 12, 29. 32: And Jesus answered Him, The first of all the commandments is, Hear, O Israel: The Lord, our God, is one Lord. (32) And the scribe said unto Him, Well, Master, Thou hast said the truth: for there is one God; and there is none other but He.

John 17, 3: And this is life eternal, that they might know Thee *the only true God,* and Jesus Christ, whom Thou hast sent.

2

2.

Deut. 4, 35: Unto thee it was showed, that thou mightest know that *the Lord He is God; there is none else beside Him.*

Is. 42, 8: *I am the Lord,* that is *my name:* and my glory will I not give *to another,* neither my praise to graven images.

Is. 48, 11: For mine own sake, even for mine own sake, will I do it: for how should my name be polluted? *And I will not give my glory unto another.*

Exod. 3, 14: And God said unto Moses, *I Am that I Am.* And He said, Thus shalt thou say unto the children of Israel, *I Am* hath sent me unto you.

Is. 44, 6: Thus saith the Lord, the King of Israel, and his Redeemer, the Lord of hosts; I am *the first,* and I am *the last;* and *beside me there is no God.*

Is. 48, 12: Hearken unto me, O Jacob and Israel, my called; *I am He; I am the first, I also am the last.*

TRINITY IN UNITY.

§ 24. In the one Godhead there are three distinct Persons,[1] the Father, the Son, and the Holy Ghost, indissolubly one in the same divine essence,[2] and equal in power and divine glory and majesty.[3]

1.

Gen. 1, 1: In the beginning *God created* (בָּרָא אֱלֹהִים) the heaven and the earth.

Gen. 1, 26. 27: And God said, Let *us* make man in *our* image, after *our* likeness: and let them have dominion over the fish of the sea, and over the fowl of the air, and over the cattle, and over all the earth, and over every creeping thing that creepeth upon the earth. So *God created* man in His own image, in the *image of God* created He him; male and female created He them.

Gen. 3, 22: And the Lord *God* said, Behold, the man is become as one of *us.*

Gen. 11, 7: Go to, let *us* go down, and there confound their language.

Is. 54, 5: For *thy Maker* is thine husband; *the Lord of hosts* is His name; and *thy Redeemer* the Holy One of Israel; *The God of* the whole earth *shall He be called.*

Ps. 110, 1: The *Lord* said *unto my Lord,* Sit *Thou* at *my* right hand, until *I* make *Thine* enemies *Thy* footstool.

Ps. 2, 7: I will declare the decree: the *Lord* hath said unto *me, Thou* art *my* Son; this day have *I* begotten *Thee.*

Ps. 45, 6. 7: *Thy* throne, O *God,* is for ever and ever; the scepter of *Thy* kingdom is a right scepter. *Thou* lovest righteousness and hatest wickedness: therefore *God,* Thy *God,* hath anointed *Thee* with the oil of gladness above Thy fellows.

Is. 48, 12. 13. 16: Hearken unto me, O Jacob and Israel, my called; *I* am He; *I am the first, I also am the last.* Mine hand also hath laid the foundation of the earth, and my right hand hath spanned the heavens: when I call unto them, they stand up together. . . . (16) Come ye near unto me, hear ye this; I have not spoken in secret from the beginning; from the time that it was, *there am I:* and now the *Lord God,* and *His Spirit,* hath sent *me.*

Jer. 23, 5. 6: Behold, the days come, saith the *Lord,* that *I* will raise unto David a righteous Branch, and a King shall reign and prosper, and shall execute judgment and justice in the earth. In His days Judah shall be saved, and Israel shall dwell safely: and this is *His* name whereby He shall be called, *The Lord,* our Righteousness.

Numb. 6, 24—26: The *Lord* bless thee, and keep thee: the *Lord* make His face shine upon thee, and be gracious unto thee: the *Lord* lift up His countenance upon thee, and give thee peace!

Is. 6, 3: And one cried unto another, and said, *Holy, holy, holy,* is *the Lord* of hosts: the whole earth is full of His glory.

Ps. 33, 6: By the *word* of the *Lord* were the heavens made; and all the host of them by *the breath of His mouth.*

Matt. 3, 16. 17: And Jesus, when He was baptized, went up straightway out of the water: and, lo, the heavens were opened unto Him, and He saw the *Spirit* of God descending like a dove, and lighting upon Him: and lo, a voice from heaven, saying, This is *my* beloved *Son,* in whom I am well pleased.

Matt. 28, 19: Go ye therefore, and teach all nations, baptizing them in the name of the *Father,* and of the *Son,* and of the *Holy Ghost.*

John 14, 15—17: If ye love me, keep my commandments. And *I* will pray *the Father,* and He shall give you another Comforter, that He may abide with you forever, even the *Spirit of truth.*

2.

Deut. 6, 4: Hear, O Israel: The Lord, our God, is *one Lord.*

John 10, 30: I and my Father are *one* (not *εἷς, one in person,* but *ἕν, one in essence*).

1 Tim. 3, 16: And without controversy great is the mystery of godliness: *God* was *manifest in the flesh.*

3.

Gen. 1, 1—3: In the beginning *God created* the heaven and the earth. And the earth was without form, and void; and darkness was upon the face of the deep. And the *Spirit of God* moved upon the face of the waters. And *God said,* Let there be light! And there was light.

Ps. 33, 6: By the *word of the Lord* were the *heavens made,* and *all the host of them* by *the breath of His mouth.*

John 1, 1—3: In the beginning was the *Word,* and the Word was with *God,* and *the Word was God. The same* was in the beginning *with God. All things were made by Him;* and without Him was not anything made that was made.

Is. 6, 3: And one cried unto another, and said, *Holy, holy, holy,* is the Lord of hosts: the *whole earth is full of His glory.*

John 5, 23: That all men should *honor the Son,* even *as they honor the Father.* He that honoreth not the Son honoreth not the Father which hath sent Him.

Phil. 2, 10. 11: That *at the name of Jesus every knee should bow,* of things in heaven, and things in earth, and things under the earth; and that 'every tongue should confess that *Jesus Christ is Lord, to the glory of God the Father.*

Rom. 9, 5: Of whom as concerning the flesh *Christ* came, *who is over all, God blessed forever. Amen.*

THE FATHER.

§ 25. The Father, personally so named in Holy Scripture,[1] is from eternity God of Himself and unbegotten,[2] and has by equally eternal generation begotten or filiated the Son from His divine essence,[3] and with the Son by equally eternal spiration spirates the Holy Ghost.[4]

1.

John 3, 35: *The Father* loveth the Son, and hath given all things into His hand.

John 5, 20: *The Father* loveth the Son, and showeth Him all things that Himself doeth.

John 15, 9: As *the Father* hath loved me, so have I loved you.

John 20, 17: Jesus saith unto her, Touch me not, for I am not yet ascended to *my Father.*

1 Pet. 1, 3: Blessed be the *God and Father* of our Lord Jesus Christ.

John 17: (The entire chapter.)

2.

John 5, 26: For as the *Father hath* life in Himself, so hath He *given* to the *Son* to have life in Himself.

3.

2 Sam. 7, 14: *I* will be *His Father,* and *He* shall be *my Son.*

Ps. 2, 7: The Lord hath said unto me, *Thou art my Son; this day have I begotten Thee.*

4.

John 15, 26: When the Comforter is come, *whom I will send* unto you from the Father, even the *Spirit of Truth* which *proceedeth from the Father,* He shall testify of me.

Matt. 10, 20: It is not ye that speak, but the *Spirit of your Father* which speaketh in you.

Gal. 4, 6: *God hath sent forth the Spirit* of His Son into your hearts, crying, Abba, Father!

THE SON.

§ 26. The Son is personally,[1] from eternity,[2] the only-begotten[3] Son of the Father,[4] very God,[5] and equal with the Father in divine essence[6] and thus in divine attributes[7] and glory,[8] and with the Father from eternity spirates the Holy Ghost.[9]

1.

Matt. 17, 5: This is *my* beloved *Son,* in whom *I* am well pleased; hear ye *Him!*

John 20, 17: *I* am not yet ascended to *my Father.* . . . I ascend unto my Father, and your Father; unto my God, and your God.

Ps. 2, 7: The Lord hath said unto me, *Thou* art *my Son;* this day have *I* begotten *Thee.*

2.

Micah 5, 2: Out of thee shall He come forth unto me that is to be the Ruler in Israel; *whose goings-forth have been* from of old, *from everlasting.*

John 8, 58: Before *Abraham* WAS, *I* AM.

John 1, 1: *In the beginning* WAS *the Word,* and the Word was *with God,* and the Word was God.

3.

John 3, 16: For God so loved the world that He gave His *only-begotten Son,* that whosoever believeth in Him should not perish, but have everlasting life.

John 3, 18: He hath not believed in the name of the *only-begotten Son of God.*

1 John 4, 9: *God* sent *His only-begotten Son* into the world.

4.

John 1, 14: The Word was made flesh, and dwelt among us, (and we beheld His glory, the glory as of the Only-Begotten *of the Father,*) full of grace and truth.

John 1, 18: No man hath seen God at any time; the only-begotten *Son,* which is in the bosom *of the Father,* He hath declared Him.

5.

Jer. 23, 6: And this is His name whereby He shall be called, *The Lord,* our Righteousness.

John 20, 28: And Thomas answered and said unto Him, *My Lord and my God!*

John 1, 1. 2: In the beginning was the Word, and the Word was with God, and *the Word was God.* The same was in the beginning with God.

Ps. 110, 1: The *Lord* said unto my *Lord,* Sit Thou at my right hand.

1 Tim. 3, 16: *God* was manifest in the flesh.

1 John 5, 20: We are in Him that is true, even in *His Son Jesus Christ.* This *is the true God,* and eternal life.

6.

John 10, 30: *I* and my *Father* are ONE.

John 14, 9: He that hath seen *me* hath seen *the Father.*

Cf. texts sub 5.

7.

John 1, 2. 3: (Eternal existence, omnipotence.)

Matt. 18, 20: Where two or three are gathered together in my name, there am I in the midst of them.

Matt. 28, 20: Lo, I am with you alway, even unto the end of the world. (Omnipresence.)

Eph. 1, 23: Which is His body, the fullness of Him that filleth all in all.

John 1, 18: No man hath seen God at any time; the only-begotten Son, which is in the bosom of the Father, He hath declared Him.

John 2, 25: He knew what was in man.

Col. 2, 3: In whom are hid all the treasures of wisdom and knowledge. (Omniscience.)

Acts 3, 14: Ye denied the Holy One and the Just.

8.

John 5, 23: That all men should *honor* the Son, even as they honor the Father. He that honoreth not the Son honoreth not the Father which hath sent Him.

Phil. 2, 11: That every tongue should confess that Jesus Christ is Lord, to the glory of God the Father.

Hebr. 1, 6: When He bringeth in the First-Begotten into the world, He says, And let all the angels of God *worship* Him!

John 17, 5: And now, O Father, glorify Thou me with Thine own self with the *glory* which I had with Thee before the world was. (Cf. John 1, 1.)

9.

Cf. § 25, 4.

THE HOLY GHOST.

§ 27. The Holy Ghost is from eternity personally[1] spirated by, and proceeds from, the Father and the Son,[2] very God, equal with the Father and the Son in divine essence,[3] and attributes,[4] and glory.[5]

1.

2 Sam. 23, 2: The *Spirit of the Lord spake* by me, and His word was in my tongue.

Job 33, 4: The *Spirit of God* hath *made me,* and the *breath* of the Almighty hath *given me life.*

Matt. 3, 16: (The baptism of Jesus.) Cf. Luke 3, 22.

John 14, 26: But the Comforter, which is the *Holy Ghost,* whom the Father will send in my name, He *shall teach* you all things.

2.

John 15, 26: The Spirit of Truth, which *proceedeth from the Father,* He shall testify of me.

Gal. 4, 6: God hath *sent forth* the *Spirit of His Son into* your hearts, crying, Abba, Father!

Rom. 8, 9: If so be that the *Spirit of God* dwell in you. Now if any man have not the *Spirit of·Christ,* he is none of His.

1 Pet. 1, 11: Searching what, or what manner of time the *Spirit of Christ* which was in them did signify.

3.

Acts 5, 3. 4: Why hath Satan filled thine heart to lie to the *Holy Ghost?* . . . Thou hast not lied unto men, but unto *God.*

1 Cor. 3, 16: Know ye not that ye are the temple of *God,* and that the *Spirit of God* dwelleth in you?

2 Cor. 3, 17: Now the *Lord* is *that Spirit;* and where the Spirit of the Lord is, there is liberty.

Matt. 28, 19: Baptizing them in the name of the Father, and of the Son, and of the Holy Ghost.

4.

Ps. 139, 7. 8: Whither shall I go from *Thy Spirit?* or whither shall I flee from Thy presence? If I ascend up into heaven, Thou art there; if I make my bed in hell, behold, Thou art there. (Omnipresence.)

1 Cor. 2, 10. 11: God hath revealed them unto us by His Spirit; for the Spirit searcheth all things, yea, the deep things of God. For what man knoweth the things of a man, save the spirit of man which is in him? Even so the things of God knoweth no man but the Spirit of God. (Omniscience.)

5.

1 Pet. 4, 14: The *Spirit of glory* and of God resteth upon you.

Is. 6, 3: Holy, holy, *holy,* is the Lord of hosts; the whole earth is full of *His glory.*

ATTRIBUTES OF GOD.

§ 28. The attributes of God are Indivisibility, Immutability, Infinity,[1] Life, Intelligence, Wisdom, Will, Holiness, Justice, Truth, Goodness, and Power.[2]

1.

Negative, intransitive, quiescent attributes.

2.

Positive, transitive, operative attributes.

INDIVISIBILITY.

§ 29. God is indivisible, inasmuch as He is not a compound being made up of component parts, not of a substance and qualities inherent in such substance, but absolutely simple in His divine essence.

Exod. 3, 14: And God said unto Moses, *I Am that I Am.* And He said, Thus shalt thou say unto the children of Israel, *I Am* hath sent me unto you.
1 John 4, 16: God is Love.
Deut. 6, 4: The Lord, our God, is one Lord.
Ps. 139, 8: If I ascend up into heaven, Thou art there; if I make my bed in hell, behold, Thou art there.

IMMUTABILITY.

§ 30. God is immutable, inasmuch as in His essence and attributes[1] there never has been, nor ever will be, nor ever can be, any increase or decrease,[2] any development or evolution,[3] any improvement or deterioration,[4] or any change of whatever kind.[5]

1.

James 1, 17: Every good gift and every perfect gift is from above, and cometh down from the Father of lights, with whom is *no variableness,* neither shadow of turning.
Mal. 3, 6: For I *am* the Lord, *I change not.*

2.

Ps. 121, 4: Behold, He that keepeth Israel shall *neither slumber nor sleep.*
Is. 40, 28: Hast thou not known? Hast thou not heard that the *everlasting* God, the Lord, the Creator of the ends of the earth, *fainteth not, neither is weary?* There is no searching of His understanding.

3.

Exod. 3, 14: And God said unto Moses, *I Am That I Am.*

4.

Ps. 102, 26. 27: They shall perish, but *Thou shalt endure:* yea, all of them shall wax old like a garment; as a vesture shalt Thou change them, and they shall be changed. But *Thou art the same,* and Thy years shall have no end.
Rom. 1, 23: And changed the glory of *the uncorruptible God* into an image made like to corruptible man.
1 Tim. 1, 17: Now unto the *King eternal, immortal,* invisible, the only wise God, be honor and glory *forever and ever!* Amen.

1 Tim. 6, 16: Who *only hath immortality,* dwelling in the light which no man can approach unto; whom no man hath seen, nor can see: to whom be *honor and power everlasting!* Amen.

5.

Ps. 33, 11: The counsel of the Lord *standeth forever,* the thoughts of His heart *to all generations.*

1 Sam. 15, 29: And also the Strength of Israel will *not lie nor repent;* for He is *not a man, that He should repent.*

Ps. 110, 4: The Lord hath sworn, and *will not repent,* Thou art a *priest forever* after the order of Melchizedek.

Ps. 90, 4: For a thousand years in Thy sight are but as yesterday when it is passed, and as a watch in the night.

2 Pet. 3, 8: But, beloved, be not ignorant of this one thing, that one day is with the Lord as a thousand years, and a thousand years as one day.

INFINITY.

§ 31. God is infinite, inasmuch as He is not limited by space[1] or time,[2] there being in Him no distinction of here and there,[3] sooner or later,[4] His essence being immeasurable,[5] or, in relation to the universe, omnipresent,[6] and in duration eternal.[7]

1.

1 Kings 8, 27: But will God indeed dwell on the earth? Behold, *the heaven and heaven of heavens cannot contain Thee,* how much less this house that I have builded?

Jer. 23, 24: Can any hide himself in secret places that I shall not see him? saith the Lord. Do not I *fill heaven and earth?* saith the Lord.

Eph. 1, 23: Which is His body, the fullness of Him *that filleth all in all.*

Ps. 103, 19: The Lord hath prepared His *throne in the heavens;* and His kingdom ruleth *over all.*

2 Chron. 2, 6: But who is able to build Him an house, seeing the *heaven and heaven of heavens cannot contain Him?* Who am I, then, that I should build Him an house, save only to burn sacrifice before Him?

2.

Ps. 90, 2: Before the mountains were brought forth, or ever Thou hadst formed the earth and the world, even *from everlasting to everlasting,* Thou art God.

Ps. 102, 25—27: Of old hast Thou *laid the foundation* of the earth: and the heavens are the work of Thy hands. They shall perish, but *Thou shalt endure:* yea, all of them shall wax old like a garment; as a vesture shalt Thou change them, and they shall be changed. But Thou *art the same,* and *Thy years shall have no end.*

3.

Is. 57, 15: For thus saith the High and Lofty One that *inhabiteth eternity,* whose name is Holy: I dwell *in the high and holy place,* with him *also that is of a contrite and humble spirit.*

Ps. 139, 7—12: Whither shall I go from Thy Spirit or whither shall I flee from *Thy presence?* If I ascend up into *heaven,* Thou art there: if I make my bed in *hell,* behold, Thou art there. If I take the wings of the morning, and dwell in the *uttermost parts of the sea,* even there shall Thy hand lead me, and Thy right hand shall hold me. If I say, Surely the darkness shall cover me, even the night shall be light about me. Yea, the darkness hideth not from Thee; but the night shineth as the day: the darkness and the light are both alike to Thee.

Job 11, 7: Canst thou *by searching find out God?* Canst thou find out the Almighty unto perfection?

Amos 9, 2: Though they dig into *hell,* thence shall mine hand take them; though they climb up to *heaven,* thence will I bring them down.

4.

Is. 41, 4: Who hath wrought and done it, calling *the generations from the beginning?* I the Lord, the *first* and with the *last;* I am He.

Is. 44, 6: Thus saith the Lord, the King of Israel, and his Redeemer, the Lord of hosts; I am the *first,* and I am the *last;* and beside me there is no God.

Is. 43, 10: I am He: *before* me there was no God formed, *neither* shall there be *after* me.

2 Pet. 3, 8: One day is with the Lord as a thousand years, and a thousand years as one day.

Rev. 1, 8: I am *Alpha* and *Omega,* the *beginning* and the *ending,* saith the Lord, which *is,* and which *was,* and which *is to come,* the Almighty.

Ps. 2, 7: I will declare the decree: the Lord hath said unto me Thou art my Son; *this day* have I begotten Thee.

5.

Job 11, 8. 9: It is as *high as heaven;* what canst thou do? *deeper than hell;* what canst thou know? The measure thereof is *longer than the earth, and broader than the sea.*

1 Tim. 6, 16: Who only hath immortality, dwelling in the light *which no man can approach unto;* whom no man hath seen, nor can see: to whom be honor and power everlasting!

6.

Ps. 115, 3: But our God is *in the heavens:* He hath done whatsoever He hath pleased.

Luke 11, 2: And He said unto them, When ye pray, say, *Our Father* which art *in heaven.*

Exod. 8, 22: I am the Lord in *the midst of the earth.*

Exod. 14, 24: The *Lord* looked unto the host of the Egyptians through *the pillar of fire and of the cloud.*

Exod. 19, 18: And *Mount Sinai* was altogether on smoke, because *the Lord descended upon it* in fire.

Acts 17, 27: That they should seek the Lord, if haply they might feel after Him, and find Him, though He be *not far from every one of us.*

Rom. 8, 9. 11: But ye are not in the flesh but in the Spirit, if so be that the *Spirit of God dwell in you.* Now if any man have not the Spirit of Christ, he is none of His. (11) But if the *Spirit* of Him that raised up Jesus from the dead *dwell in you,* He that raised up Christ from the dead shall also quicken your mortal bodies by *His Spirit that dwelleth in you.*

1 Cor. 3, 16: Know ye not that *ye are the temple of God,* and that the *Spirit of God dwelleth in you?*

2 Cor. 6, 16: And what agreement hath the temple of God with idols? for *ye are the temple of the living God,* as God hath said, I will dwell in them, and walk in them, and I will be their God, and they shall be my people.

Is. 57, 15: For ·thus saith the High and Lofty One that *inhabiteth eternity,* whose name is Holy; I dwell *in the high and holy place,* with him also *that is of a contrite and humble spirit,* to revive the spirit of the humble, and to revive the heart of the contrite ones.

John 14, 23: Jesus answered and said unto him, If a man love me, he will keep my words: and my Father will love him, and *we will come unto him, and make our abode with him.*

Is. 40, 12: Who hath measured the waters in the hollow of his hand, and meted out heaven with the span, and comprehended the dust of the earth in a measure, and weighed the mountains in scales, and the hills in a balance?

Ps. 36, 6. 7: Thy righteousness is like the great mountains; Thy judgments are a great deep; O Lord, Thou preservest man and beast. How excellent is Thy loving-kindness, O God! Therefore the children of men put their trust under the shadow of Thy wings.

Ps. 33, 8: Let all the earth fear the Lord: let all the inhabitants of the world stand in awe of Him!

Ps. 103, 19—22: The Lord hath prepared His throne in the heavens; and His kingdom ruleth over all. Bless the Lord, ye His angels that excel in strength, that do His commandments, hearkening unto the voice of His word. Bless ye the Lord, all ye hosts; ye ministers of His, that do His pleasure. Bless the Lord, all His works in all places of His dominion: bless the Lord, O my soul!

See also the texts sub 1 and 3.

7.

Is. 40, 28: Hast thou not known? Hast thou not heard that the *everlasting God,* the Lord, the Creator of the ends of the earth, fainteth not, neither is weary? There is no searching of His understanding.

1 Tim. 1, 17: Now unto the *King eternal,* immortal, invisible, the only wise God, be *honor and glory forever and ever!* Amen.

Hebr. 13, 8: Jesus Christ the same yesterday, and to-day, and forever.

Gen. 21, 33: And Abraham planted a grove in Beer-sheba, and called there on the name of the Lord, the *everlasting God.*

Ps. 102, 26. 27: They shall perish, but Thou shalt endure. . . . Thou art the same, and Thy years shall have no end.

See also the texts sub 2 and 4.

LIFE.

§ 32. God is life,[1] inasmuch as He has His being of Himself,[2] and of Himself knows, wills, and does whatever He knows, wills, and does.[3]

1.

Josh. 3, 10: And Joshua said, Hereby ye shall know that the *living God* is among you.

Jer. 10, 10: But the Lord is the true God; He is *the living God* and an everlasting king.

Ps. 84, 2: My heart and my flesh crieth out for *the living God.*

Acts 14, 15: We also are men of like passions with you, and preach unto you that ye should turn from these vanities unto *the living God,* which made heaven, and earth, and the sea, and all things that are therein.

1 Tim. 6, 16: Who only hath *immortality.*

Rom. 1, 23: And changed the glory of the *uncorruptible* God into an image made like to corruptible man.

1 Tim. 1, 17: Now unto the King eternal, *immortal,* invisible, the only wise God, be honor and glory forever and ever! Amen.

Deut. 32, 40: For I lift up my hands to heaven, and say, *I live forever.*

Ezek. 33, 11: Say unto them, *As I live,* saith the Lord God.

John 1, 4: In Him was *life;* and *the Life* was the light of men.

John 11, 25: Jesus said unto her, *I am* the Resurrection, and *the Life:* he that believeth in me, though he were dead, yet shall he live.

1 John 1, 2: For *the Life was manifested,* and we have seen it, and bear witness, and show unto you *that eternal Life,* which was with the Father, and was manifested unto us.

2.

John 5, 26: For as the Father hath *life in Himself,* so hath He given to the Son to have *life in Himself.*

3.

John 5, 17: But Jesus answered them, My Father *worketh hitherto, and I work.*

John 5, 19—21: Then answered Jesus and said unto them, Verily, verily. I say unto you, The Son can do nothing of Himself, but what He seeth the Father do: for *what things soever He doeth, these also doeth the Son likewise.* For the Father loveth the Son, and *showeth Him all things· that Himself doeth:* and He will show Him greater works than these, that ye may marvel. For as *the Father raiseth up the dead, and quickeneth them,* even so *the Son quickeneth whom He will.*

Acts 17, 28: For in Him we live, and move, and have our being.

INTELLIGENCE.

§ 33. Intelligence[1] is an attribute of God, inasmuch as He beholds or perfectly knows Himself[2] and all that beside Him is, has been, will be, can be, or might be.[3]

1.

1 Sam. 2, 3: The Lord is a *God of knowledge,* and by Him actions are weighed.

2.

John 1, 18: No man hath *seen God* at any time; the *only-begotten Son,* which is in the bosom of the Father, *He hath declared Him.*

1 Cor. 2, 10. 11: But God hath revealed them unto us by His Spirit: for the *Spirit searcheth all things,* yea, *the deep things of God.* For what man knoweth the things of a man, save the spirit of man which is in him? Even so *the things of God knoweth* no man but *the Spirit of God.*

3.

1 John 3, 20: For if our heart condemn us, *God* is greater than our heart, *and knoweth all things.*

1 Kings 8, 39: Then hear Thou in heaven, Thy dwelling-place, and forgive, and do, and give to every man according to his ways, *whose heart Thou knowest;* for Thou, even *Thou* only, *knowest the hearts of all the children of men.*

Ps. 34, 15: The *eyes of the Lord* are upon the righteous, and His ears are open unto their cry.

Ps. 139, 1—4: O Lord, *Thou hast searched me, and known me.* Thou *knowest* my downsitting and mine uprising; Thou *understandest my thought afar off.* · Thou compassest my path and my lying down, and *art acquainted with all my ways.* For there is *not a word* in my tongue, but, lo, O Lord, *Thou knowest it altogether.*

Prov. 15, 3: The *eyes* of the Lord are *in every place,* beholding the evil and the good.

Hebr. 4, 13: *All things* are *naked and opened* unto the eyes of Him with whom we have to do.

Ps. 147, 5: Great is our Lord and of great power; His *understanding is infinite.*

Matt. 10, 30: The very hairs of your head are all numbered.

Matt. 11, 21: Woe unto thee, Chorazin! woe unto thee, Bethsaida! for if the mighty works which were done in you had been done in Tyre and Sidon, they would have repented long ago in sackcloth and ashes.

WISDOM.

§ 34. Wisdom is that attribute of God by which He devises, disposes, and directs the proper means to proper ends,[1] an attribute exhibited chiefly in the plan of creation[2] and in the plan of salvation.[3]

1.

Job 12, 13: With Him is *wisdom* and strength; He hath *counsel* and understanding.

1 Tim. 1, 17: Now unto the King eternal, immortal, invisible, *the only wise God,* be honor and glory forever and ever! Amen.

Is. 40, 13: *Who hath* DIRECTED *the Spirit of the Lord,* or, being *His counselor,* hath taught Him? *With whom took He counsel,* and who instructed Him, and *taught Him in the path* of judgment, and taught Him knowledge, and *showed to Him the way of understanding?*

Is. 46, 9. 10: I am God, and there is none like me, declaring *the end from the beginning,* and from ancient times the things that are not yet done, saying, *My counsel shall stand,* and I will *do all my pleasure.*

Is. 55, 8. 9: My thoughts are not your thoughts, neither are your ways *my ways,* saith the Lord. For as the heavens are higher than the earth, so are *my ways higher* than your ways, and my thoughts than your thoughts.

2.

Ps. 104, 24: O Lord, how manifold are Thy works! In wisdom hast Thou made them all. The earth is full of Thy riches.

Job 28, 20—27: Whence, then, cometh *wisdom?* and where is the place of understanding? . . . (23) God understandeth the *way* thereof, and He knoweth the *place* thereof. For He looketh to the ends of the earth, and seeth under the whole heaven; to make the *weight* for the winds; and He weigheth the waters by *measure.* When He made a *decree* for the rain, and a *way* for the lightning of the thunder, then did He see it, and declare it; He *prepared* it, yea, and *searched it out.*

3.

Eph. 1, 7. 8: In whom we have redemption through His blood, the forgiveness of sins, according to the riches of His grace, wherein He hath abounded toward us in *all wisdom* and prudence.

Eph. 3, 10. 11: That now unto the principalities and powers in heavenly places might be known *by the Church* the *manifold wisdom* of God, according to the *eternal purpose* which He purposed in Christ Jesus, our Lord.

Rom. 11, 33—36: O the *depth* of the riches, both of the *wisdom* and knowledge of God! How unsearchable are His judgments, and *His ways* past finding out! For who hath known the mind of the Lord, or *who hath been His counselor?* . . . (36) For of Him, and through Him, and *to Him,* are all things: *to whom be glory forever!* Amen.

WILL.

§ 35. Will[1] is an attribute of God, inasmuch as He consciously prompts His own acts,[2] and is intent upon the execution of His purposes, the accomplishment of His designs, the realization of His counsels, and the fufillment of His ordinances.[3] — Hidden will[4] and revealed will;[5] antecedent will[6] and consequent will.[7]

1.

Rom. 9, 19: Thou wilt say, then, unto me, Why doth He yet find fault? For who hath resisted His *will?*

2.

Ps. 135, 6: Whatsoever the Lord *pleased, that did He* in heaven, and in earth, in the seas, and all deep places.

Rom. 11, 34: For who hath known the mind of the Lord? or who hath been His *counselor?*

Job 36, 23: *Who hath enjoined* Him His way?

James 1, 18: *Of His own will* begat He us with the word of truth, that we should be a kind of firstfruits of His creatures.

3.

Ps. 33, 9. 10: For He spake, and it was done; He *commanded, and it stood fast.* The Lord *bringeth the counsel of the heathen to naught:* He maketh the devices of the people of none effect.

Is. 46, 11: I have *purposed it,* I will also *do it.*

Is. 65, 2: I have *spread out my hands all the day* unto a *rebellious people,* which walketh in a way that was not good, after their own thoughts.

Matt. 23, 37: O Jerusalem, Jerusalem, thou that killest the prophets, and stonest them which are sent unto thee, *how often would I* have gathered thy children together, even as a hen gathereth her chickens under her wings, and ye would not!

Rom. 10, 16—21: But they have not all obeyed the Gospel. For Esaias saith, Lord, who hath believed our report? So, then, faith cometh by hearing, and hearing by the Word of God. But I say, Have they not heard? Yes, verily, their sound went into all the

earth, and their words unto the ends of the world. But I say, Did
not Israel know? First Moses saith, I will provoke you to jealousy
by them that are no people, and by a foolish nation I will anger you.
But Esaias is very bold, and saith, I was found of them that sought
me not; I was made manifest unto them that asked not after me.
But to Israel He saith, All day long I have stretched forth my hands
unto a disobedient and gainsaying people.

4.

Deut. 29, 29: The secret things belong unto the Lord, our God:
but those things which are revealed belong unto us and to our children forever, that we may do all the words of this Law.

Rom. 11, 33. 34: O the depth of the riches both of the wisdom
and knowledge of God! How unsearchable are His judgments, and
His ways past finding out! For who hath known the mind of the
Lord?

5.

John 1, 18: No man hath seen God at any time; the only-
begotten Son, which is in the bosom of the Father, He hath declared Him.

1 Tim. 3, 16: And without controversy great is the mystery of
godliness: God was manifest in the flesh, justified in the Spirit,
seen of angels, preached unto the Gentiles, believed on in the world,
received up into glory.

Ps. 147, 19. 20: He showeth His word unto Jacob, His statutes
and His judgments unto Israel. He hath not dealt so with any
nation: and as for His judgments, they have not known them.
Praise ye the Lord!

1 Cor. 2, 9. 10: But as it is written, Eye hath not seen, nor ear
heard, neither have entered into the heart of man the things which
God hath prepared for them that love Him. But God hath revealed
them unto us by His Spirit: for the Spirit searcheth all things, yea,
the deep things of God.

Eph. 3, 4—11: Whereby, when ye read, ye may understand my
knowledge in the mystery of Christ, which in other ages was not
made known unto the sons of men, as it is now revealed unto His
holy apostles and prophets by the Spirit; that the Gentiles should
be fellow-heirs, and of the same body, and partakers of His promise
in Christ by the Gospel: whereof I was made a minister, according
to the gift of the grace of God given unto me by the effectual working of His power. Unto me, who am less than the least of all saints,
is this grace given, that I should preach among the Gentiles the
unsearchable riches of Christ, and to make all men see what is the
fellowship of the mystery, which from the beginning of the world
hath been hid in God, who created all things by Jesus Christ: to the
intent that now unto the principalities and powers in heavenly places
might be known by the Church the manifold wisdom of God, according to the eternal purpose which He purposed in Christ Jesus,
our Lord.

6.

Ezek. 33, 11: Say unto them, As I live, saith the Lord God, I have no pleasure in the death of the wicked, but that the wicked turn from his way and live. Turn ye, turn ye, from your evil ways; for why will ye die, O house of Israel?

1 Tim. 2, 4: Who will have all men to be saved, and to come unto the knowledge of the truth.

Prov. 1, 24: Because I have called, and ye refused; I have stretched out my hand, and no man regarded.

7.

Matt. 23, 37. 38: O Jerusalem, Jerusalem, thou that killest the prophets, and stonest them which are sent unto thee, how often would I have gathered thy children together, even as a hen gathereth her chickens under her wings, and ye would not! *Behold, your house is left unto you desolate!*

Prov. 1, 25—31: But ye have set at naught all my counsel, and would none of my reproof: I also will laugh at your calamity: I will mock when your fear cometh; when your fear cometh as desolation, and your destruction cometh as a whirlwind; when distress and anguish cometh upon you. Then shall they call upon me, but I will not answer; they shall seek me early, but they shall not find me: for that they hated knowledge, and did not choose the fear of the Lord: they would none of my counsel: they despised all my reproof. Therefore shall they eat of the fruit of their own way, and be filled with their own devices.

Jer. 5, 29: Shall I not visit for these things? saith the Lord; shall not my soul be avenged on such a nation as this?

HOLINESS.

§ 36. Holiness is the absolute purity of God, according to which His affections, thoughts, will, and acts are in perfect consistency and harmony with His own nature, and in energetic opposition to everything that is not in conformity therewith.

Lev. 19, 2: Speak unto all the congregation of the children of Israel, and say unto them, *Ye shall be holy:* for *I the Lord,* your God, *am holy.*

Job 15, 14. 15: What is man that he should be *clean?* and he which is born of a woman, that he should be righteous? Behold, He putteth no trust in His *saints;* yea, *the heavens are not clean in His sight.*

(Eph. 5, 27: That He might present it to Himself a glorious Church, *not having spot, or wrinkle, or any such things,* but that it should be *holy* and *without blemish.*

3

2 Cor. 7, 1: Let us *cleanse* ourselves *from all filthiness* of the flesh and spirit, perfecting *holiness* in the fear of God.)

Is. 6, 3: And one cried unto another, and said, *Holy, holy, holy,* is the Lord of hosts: the whole earth is full of His glory.

Exod. 15, 11: Who is *like unto Thee,* O Lord, among the gods? Who is like Thee, glorious in *holiness,* fearful in praises, doing wonders?

1 Pet. 1, 15. 16: But as He which hath called you *is holy,* so be ye holy in all manner of conversation, because it is written, *Be ye holy; for I am holy.*

Ps. 89, 35: Once have I *sworn by my holiness* that *I will not lie* unto David.

Rev. 4, 8: And the four beasts had each of them six wings about him; and they were full of eyes within: and they rest not day and night, saying, *Holy, holy, holy, Lord God* Almighty, which was, and is, and is to come.

Rev. 15, 4: Who shall not fear Thee, O Lord, and *glorify Thy name?* For *Thou only art holy:* for all nations shall come and worship before Thee; for *Thy judgments are made manifest.*

Ps. 145, 17: The Lord is *righteous* in all His ways, and *holy in all His works.*

Is. 41, 20: That they may see, and know, and consider, and understand together, that the hand of the Lord hath done this, and the *Holy One* of Israel hath *created it.*

Josh. 24, 19. 20: Ye cannot serve the Lord: for He is *an holy God;* He is a jealous God; He will not forgive your transgressions nor your sins. If ye forsake the Lord, and serve strange gods, then He will *turn and do you hurt, and consume you.*

Amos 4, 2: The Lord God hath sworn *by His holiness,* that, lo, the days shall come upon you that He will take you away with hooks.

Rom. 1, 18: The *wrath of God* is revealed from heaven *against all ungodliness* and unrighteousness of men.

JUSTICE.

§ 37. God is just, inasmuch as He is His own perfect ethical norm,[1] a legislator whose laws are true utterances of His holy will,[2] a judge whose judgments are in perfect conformity with His laws,[3] an executor whose retribution is in full consistency with His judgments,[4] and a father who executes His gracious and good will upon His children according to His promise.[5]

1.

Deut. 32, 4: He is the Rock, *His work is perfect:* for *all His ways are judgment: a God* of truth and *without iniquity, just and right is He.*

Ps. 145, 17: The Lord is *righteous* in *all His ways,* and holy in all His works.

Ps. 89, 14: *Justice and judgment* are the habitation of Thy throne: mercy and truth shall go before Thy face.

Ps. 92, 15: To show that the *Lord is upright:* He is my rock, and there is *no unrighteousness in Him.*

Rom. 3, 5: *Is God unrighteous who taketh vengeance?* (I speak as a man.)

Is. 5, 16: The Lord of hosts shall be exalted in judgment, and God that is holy shall be sanctified in righteousness.

2.

Ps. 111, 7: All His commandments are sure.

Ps. 119, 86: All Thy commandments are faithful.

Ps. 119, 151: All Thy commandments are truth.

Ps. 119, 172: All Thy commandments are righteousness.

Ps. 19, 7: The Law of the Lord is perfect.

Ps. 19, 8: The statutes of the Lord are right, rejoicing the heart: the commandment of the Lord is pure, enlightening the eyes.

3.

Ps. 19, 9: The fear of the Lord is clean, enduring forever: the *judgments of the Lord are true and righteous altogether.*

Rom. 2, 5. 6: But after thy hardness and impenitent heart treasurest up unto thyself wrath against the day of wrath and revelation of *the righteous judgment of God;* who will render to every man according to his deeds.

1 Pet. 1, 17: And if ye call on the Father, who *without respect of persons judgeth* according to every man's work, pass the time of your sojourning here in fear.

Rom. 2, 11: There is no respect of persons with God.

Gal. 3, 10: For as many as are of the works of the Law are under the curse; for it is written, *Cursed* is every one that continueth not in *all things which are written in the book of the Law* to do them.

Gen. 18, 20. 21: And the Lord said, Because the cry of Sodom and Gomorrah is great, and because their sin is very grievous, I will go down now, and see whether they have done altogether according to the cry of it, which is come unto me; and if not, *I will know.*

4.

Rom. 2, 8. 9: But unto them that are contentious, and do not obey the truth, but obey unrighteousness: indignation and wrath, tribulation and anguish, upon *every soul of man that doeth evil,* of the Jew first, and also of the Gentile.

Is. 3, 11: Woe unto the *wicked!* It shall be *ill* with him: for *the reward of his hands* shall be given him.

Gen. 2, 17: But of the tree of the knowledge of good and evil, thou shalt not eat of it; for in the day that thou eatest thereof *thou shalt surely die.*

Rom. 5, 12: Wherefore, as *by one man sin entered* into the world, *and death by sin.*

2 Thess. 1, 6—8: Seeing it is a righteous thing with God to recompense tribulation to them that trouble you; and to you who are troubled rest with us, when the Lord Jesus shall be revealed from heaven with His mighty angels, in flaming fire taking vengeance on them that know not God, and that obey not the Gospel of our Lord Jesus Christ.

Rev. 16, 5. 6: And I heard the angel of the waters say, Thou art righteous, O Lord, which art, and wast, and shalt be, because Thou hast judged thus. For they have shed the blood of saints and prophets, and Thou hast given them blood to drink; for they are worthy.

Rom. 12, 19: Vengeance is mine; I will repay, saith the Lord.

Ezek. 18, 4: The soul that sinneth, it shall die.

Rom. 6, 23: The wages of sin is death.

Ps. 11, 6: Upon the wicked He shall rain snares, fire and brimstone, and an horrible tempest: this shall be the portion of their cup.

Luke 12, 5: Fear Him, which, after He hath killed, hath power to cast into hell; yea, I say unto you, Fear Him!

Hebr. 2, 2: Every transgression and disobedience received a just recompense of reward.

Is. 53, 5. 8: He was wounded for our transgressions, He was bruised for our iniquities: the chastisement of our peace was upon Him; and with His stripes we are healed. (8) He was cut off out of the land of the living; for the transgression of my people was He stricken.

5.

Micah 7, 20: Thou wilt *perform the truth* to Jacob, *and the mercy* to Abraham, which *Thou hast sworn* unto our fathers from the day of old. Cf. Is. 54, 10.

2 Chron. 6, 15: Thou which hast *kept* with Thy servant David, my father, that *which Thou hast promised* him, and *spakest* with Thy mouth, and hast *fulfilled it* with Thine hand, as it is this day.

Matt. 25, 21: His lord said unto him, Well done, thou good and faithful servant! Thou hast been faithful over a *few* things, I will make thee ruler over *many* things: enter thou into the joy of thy Lord!

Matt. 25, 34: Then shall the King say unto them on His right hand, Come, *ye blessed of my Father, inherit* the kingdom prepared *for* you from the foundation of the world!

1 Cor. 4, 7: For who maketh thee to differ from another? and what hast thou that thou didst not receive? Now if thou didst receive it, why dost thou glory, as if thou hadst not received it?

1 Chron. 29, 14: But who am I, and what is my people, that we should be able to offer so willingly after this sort? For all things come of Thee, and of Thine own have we given Thee.

John 17, 25: O *righteous Father,* the world hath not known Thee: but I have known Thee, and these have known that Thou hast sent me.

1 John 1, 9: If we confess our sins, He is *faithful* and *just* to *forgive us our sins,* and to *cleanse us* from all unrighteousness.

2 Tim. 4, 8: Henceforth there is laid up for me a crown of righteousness, which the Lord, *the righteous Judge,* shall give me at that day: and not to me only, but unto all them also that *love His appearing.*

TRUTH.

§ 38. God is truth, inasmuch as He really is as He manifests Himself,[1] wills what He professes to will,[2] and does what He has promised to do,[3] His works being in full agreement with His words.[4]

1.

Jer. 10, 10. 11: But the Lord is *the true God;* He is the living God, and an everlasting King. At His wrath the earth shall tremble, and the nations shall not be able to abide His indignation. Thus shall ye say unto them, *The gods that have not made the heavens and the earth,* even they shall perish from the earth, and from under these heavens.

John 5, 18—21: Therefore the Jews sought the more to kill Him, because He not only had broken the Sabbath, but *said* also that God was His Father, *making Himself equal with God.* Then answered Jesus and said unto them, *Verily, verily,* I say unto you, The Son can do nothing of Himself, but what He seeth the Father do; for what things soever He doeth, *these also doeth the Son likewise.* For the Father loveth the Son, and showeth Him all things that Himself doeth: and He will show Him greater works than these, that ye may marvel. For *as the Father* raiseth up the dead, and quickeneth them, *even so the Son* quickeneth whom He will.

Rom. 3, 3. 4: For what if some did not believe? Shall their unbelief make the faith of God without effect? God forbid! Yea, *let God be true,* but every man a liar; as it is written, That Thou mightest be *justified in Thy sayings,* and mightest overcome when Thou art judged.

2 Tim. 2, 13: If we believe not, yet He abideth faithful: *He cannot deny Himself.*

2.

2 Sam. 7, 28: And now, O Lord God, Thou art that God, and *Thy words be true,* and Thou hast promised this goodness unto Thy servant.

Ps. 25, 10: All the paths of the Lord are *mercy* and *truth* unto such as keep His covenant and His testimonies.

Numb. 23, 19: God is *not* a man, that He should *lie,* neither the son of man, that He should *repent.* Hath He *said,* and shall He not *do* it? or hath He *spoken,* and shall He not *make it good?*

1 Sam. 15, 29: And also the Strength of Israel will *not lie nor repent;* for He is not a man, that He should repent.

Hebr. 6, 17. 18: Wherein God, willing more abundantly to show unto the heirs of promise the *immutability* of His *counsel,* confirmed it *by an oath:* that by two immutable things, in which it was *impossible for God to lie,* we might have a strong consolation, who have fled for refuge to lay hold upon the hope set before us.

3.

Tit. 1, 2: In hope of eternal life, which God, that *cannot lie, promised* before the world began.

Ps. 146, 6: Which made heaven, and earth, the sea, and all that therein is: which *keepeth truth forever.*

4.

Numb. 23, 19: Hath He *said,* and shall He not *do* it? or hath He *spoken,* and shall He not *make it good?*

Ps. 33, 4: For the *Word* of the Lord is right; and all His *works* are done in *truth.*

GOODNESS.

§. 39. The goodness of God is His Love, Benevolence, Grace, and Mercy.

LOVE.

§ 40. God is Love, inasmuch as He longs for and delights in union and communion with the objects of His holy desire.

1 John 4, 16: And we have known and believed the love that God hath to us. God is Love; and he that dwelleth in love dwelleth in God, and God in him.

John 3, 16: For God so *loved* the world that He *gave* His only-begotten Son, that whosoever believeth in Him should not perish, but *have everlasting life.*

Jer. 31, 3: The Lord hath appeared of old unto me, saying, Yea, I have loved thee with an everlasting love: therefore with loving-kindness *have I drawn thee.*

Deut. 33, 3: Yea, He *loved* the people; all *His saints are in Thy hand:* and they sat down *at Thy feet:* every one *shall receive* of Thy words.

Is. 1, 2—5: Hear, O heavens, and give ear, O earth: for the Lord hath spoken, I have nourished and brought up children, and they have rebelled against me. The ox knoweth his owner, and the ass his master's crib: but Israel doth not know, my people doth not consider. Ah, sinful nation, a people laden with iniquity, a seed of evildoers, children that are corrupters: they have forsaken the Lord; they have provoked the Holy One of Israel unto anger; they are gone away backward. Why should ye be stricken any more? Ye will revolt more and more: the whole head is sick, and the whole heart faint.

Is. 7, 14: Therefore the Lord Himself shall give you a sign; behold, a virgin shall conceive, and bear a son, and shall call his name *Immanuel.*

Matt. 1, 23: Behold, a virgin shall be with child, and shall bring forth a son, and they shall call his name Immanuel, which being interpreted is, *God with us.*

Is. 43, 1: I have redeemed thee, I have called thee by thy name; *thou art mine.*

Is. 49, 15. 16: Can a woman forget her sucking child, that she should not have compassion on the son of her womb? Yea, they may forget, yet will I *not forget* thee. Behold, I have graven thee *upon the palms of my hands;* thy walls are *continually before me.*

Jer. 31, 20: Is Ephraim my dear son? Is he a pleasant child? For since I spake against him, I do *earnestly remember him* still: therefore my bowels are *troubled for him:* I will surely have mercy upon him, saith the Lord.

Jer. 31, 33: I will be *their God,* and they shall be *my people.*

Hos. 2, 19. 20: And I will *betroth thee unto me* forever; yea, I will betroth thee unto me in righteousness, and in judgment, and in loving-kindness, and in mercies. I will even betroth thee unto me in *faithfulness:* and *thou shalt know the Lord.*

BENEVOLENCE.

§ 41. God is benevolent, inasmuch as He is desirous of blessing the objects of His love.

Tit. 3, 4—7: But after that the *kindness* and love of God, our Savior, toward man appeared. Not by works of righteousness which we have done, but according to His mercy *He saved us,* by the washing of regeneration and renewing of the Holy Ghost, which He shed on us abundantly through Jesus Christ, our Savior, that, being justified by His grace, *we should be made heirs* according to the hope of *eternal life.*

1 John 4, 9: In this was manifested the love of God toward us, because that God sent His only-begotten Son into the world, *that we might live through Him.*

Ps. 37, 4: Delight thyself also in the Lord; and He shall *give* thee the desires of thine heart.

Ps. 104, 27. 28: These wait all upon Thee, that Thou mayest *give* them their meat in due season. That Thou givest them they gather: Thou openest Thine hand, they are filled with good.

GRACE.

§ 42. God is gracious, inasmuch as He offers and con-
fers His blessings regardless of the merits or demerits of the
objects of His benevolence.

Ps. 103, 10: He hath *not* dealt with us *after our sins,* nor rewarded us according to our iniquities.

Rom. 3, 23. 24: For *all have sinned,* and come short of the glory
of God, being justified *freely by His grace,* through the redemption
that is in Christ Jesus.

Rom. 4, 5: But to him that *worketh not,* but believeth on Him
that justifieth the ungodly, his faith is counted for righteousness.

Rom. 6, 23: For the *wages* of sin is *death;* but the *gift* of God
is *eternal life* through Jesus Christ, our Lord.

Rom. 5, 8: But God commendeth His love toward us, in that,
while we were yet sinners, Christ died for us.

Rom. 11, 6: And if by *grace,* then is it *no more of works:* otherwise grace is no more grace. But if it be of works, then is it no
more grace: otherwise work is no more work.

Gal. 3, 18: For if the inheritance be of the *Law,* it is no more of
promise: but God gave it to Abraham by promise.

Eph. 2, 8. 9: For by *grace* are ye saved through faith, and that
not of yourselves; it is the *gift of God: not of works,* lest any man
should boast.

MERCY.

§ 43. God is merciful, inasmuch as He has compassion
with the afflicted and bestows His benefits upon the miserable.

Ps. 18, 27: Thou wilt save the afflicted people.

Job 34, 28: He heareth the cry of the afflicted.

Job 36, 15: He delivereth the poor in his affliction, and openeth
their ears in oppression.

Ps. 68, 5: A Father of the fatherless, and a Judge of the widows,
is God in His holy habitation.

Is. 49, 13: The Lord has comforted His people, and will have
mercy upon His afflicted.

Ezek. 16, 6: And when I passed by thee, and saw thee polluted in
thine own blood, I said unto thee when thou wast in thy blood, Live!
Yea, I said unto thee when thou wast in thy blood, Live!

Luke 1, 54: He hath *holpen* His servant Israel, in remembrance
of His mercy.

Luke 6, 36: Be ye therefore merciful, as your Father also is
merciful.

Eph. 2, 4: But God, who is rich in mercy, for His great love
wherewith He loved us.

James 5, 11: Behold, we count them happy which endure. Ye

have heard of the patience of Job, and have seen the end of the Lord; that the Lord is very *pitiful* and of tender *mercy.*

Exod. 34, 6: The Lord, the Lord God, merciful and gracious, long-suffering, and abundant in goodness and truth.

POWER.

§ 44. Power is a divine attribute, inasmuch as God can do and does whatever He purposes to do. — Omnipotence.

Mark 10, 27: And Jesus, looking upon them, saith, With men it is impossible, but not with God: for with God all things are possible.

Mark 14, 36: And He said, Abba, Father, all things are possible unto Thee.

Luke 1, 37: For with God nothing shall be impossible.

Rom. 4, 21: And being fully persuaded that, what He had promised, He was *able* also *to perform.*

Eph. 3, 20: Now unto Him that is *able to do* exceeding abundantly above all that we ask or think, according to the *power* that worketh in us.

Ps. 33, 9: For He spake, and it was *done;* He commanded, and it stood fast.

Ps. 115, 3: But our God is in the heavens: He hath *done* whatsoever He hath *pleased.*

Ps. 135, 6: Whatsoever the Lord *pleased,* that *did* He in *heaven,* and in *earth,* in the seas, and all deep places.

Is. 40, 10: Behold, the Lord God will come with *strong hand,* and His *arm* shall rule for Him: behold, His reward is with Him, and His work before Him.

Is. 14, 27: The Lord of hosts hath *purposed,* and who shall *disannul* it? and His *hand* is stretched out, and who shall *turn it back?*

Is. 46, 10. 11: Declaring the end from the beginning, and from ancient times the things that are not yet done, saying, My counsel shall *stand,* and I will *do* all my pleasure: calling a ravenous bird from the east, the man that executeth my counsel from a far country: yea, I have spoken it, I will also bring it to pass; I have *purposed* it, I will also *do* it.

Eph. 1, 19: And what is the *exceeding greatness of His power* to us-ward who believe, according to the *working* of His *mighty power.*

ACTS OF GOD.

§ 45. The Acts of God are of two kinds, internal and external — *opera ad intra, opera ad extra.*

INTERNAL ACTS.

§ 46. The internal acts of God are again of two kinds, personal and essential.

PERSONAL INTERNAL ACTS.

§ 47. The personal internal acts of God are those acts which terminate within the Godhead and pertain to the divine Person or Persons by whom they are performed as peculiar to such Person or Persons. Acts of this class are the eternal generation of the Son[1] and the eternal spiration of the Holy Ghost.[2]

1.

Cf. §§ 25. 26.

2.

Cf. §§ 26. 27.

ESSENTIAL INTERNAL ACTS.

§ 48. The essential internal acts of God are such exertions of essential attributes of God as terminate within the Godhead, but in which the three persons of the Trinity concur. Such acts are the eternal decrees of God, the decrees of creation,[1] of redemption,[2] and of predestination.[3]

1.

Cf. § 49.

2.

Cf. § 50.

3.

Cf. § 51.

DECREE OF CREATION.

§ 49. The decree of creation is an essential internal act of God,[1] by which He purposed to create in the beginning of time heaven and earth and all creatures,[2] for the manifestation of His wisdom, goodness, and power.[3]

1.

Acts 15, 18: Known unto God are all His works from the beginning of the world.

Job 28, 26. 27: When He made a decree for the rain, and a way for the lightning of the thunder; then did He see it, and declare it; He prepared it, yea, and searched it out.

Acts 17, 26: And hath made of one blood all nations of men for to dwell on all the face of the earth, and hath *determined* the times *before appointed,* and the bounds of their habitation.

2.

Gen. 1, 26: And God *said, Let us make* man in our image after our likeness. Cf. Gen. 1 and 2.

3.

Ps. 104, 24: O Lord, how manifold are Thy works! In *wisdom* hast Thou made them all. The earth is full of Thy riches.

Ps. 136, 5—9: To Him that *by wisdom* made the heavens: for His *mercy* endureth forever. To Him that stretched out the earth above the waters: for His mercy endureth forever. To Him that made great lights: for His mercy endureth forever: the sun to rule by day: for His mercy endureth forever: the moon and stars to rule by night: for His mercy endureth forever.

DECREE OF REDEMPTION.

§ 50. The decree of redemption is an eternal act of God,[1] whereby He graciously and with divine wisdom purposed to work, in the fullness of time, through the Son made manifest in the flesh, a redemption of mankind,[2] and to prepare a way of salvation for the whole human race,[3] whose fall He had foreseen, but not decreed.[4]

1.

1 Pet. 1, 20: Who verily was foreordained before the foundation of the world, but was manifest in these last times for you.

Eph. 1, 7—10: In whom we have *redemption* through His blood, the forgiveness of sins, according to the riches of His *grace;* wherein He hath abounded toward us in all *wisdom and prudence;* having made known unto us the mystery of His *will,* according to His *good pleasure* which He hath *purposed in Himself:* that in the dispensation of the fullness of times He might gather together in one all things in Christ.

Acts 2, 23: Him, being delivered *by the determinate counsel and foreknowledge* of God, ye have taken, and by wicked hands have crucified and slain.

Acts 4, 28: For to do whatsoever Thy hand and *Thy counsel determined before* to be done.

2.

Luke 2, 30—32: For mine eyes have seen Thy salvation, which Thou hast prepared before the face of all people: a light to lighten the Gentiles and the glory of Thy people Israel.

Gal. 4, 4. 5: But when the *fullness of the time* was come, God sent forth His Son, made of a woman, made under the Law, to redeem them that were under the Law.

3.

John 3, 16: For God so *loved the world* that He gave His only-begotten Son, that whosoever believeth in Him should not perish, but have everlasting life.

4.

Hos. 13, 9: O Israel, thou hast destroyed thyself; but in me is thine help.

DECREE OF PREDESTINATION.

§ 51. The decree of predestination is an eternal act of God,[1] who for His goodness' sake,[2] and because of the merit of the foreordained Redeemer of all mankind,[3] purposed to lead into everlasting life,[4] by the way and means of salvation designated for all mankind,[5] a certain number[6] of certain persons,[7] and to procure, work, and promote what would pertain to their final salvation.[8]

1.

Eph. 1, 4: According as He hath chosen us in Him *before the foundation of the world,* that we should be holy and without blame before Him in love.

Eph. 3, 11: According to the *eternal* purpose.

2 Thess. 2, 13: Because God hath *from the beginning* chosen you to salvation.

2 Tim. 1, 9: Who hath saved us, and called us . . . according to His own purpose and grace, which was given us in Christ Jesus *before the world began.*

2.

2 Tim. 1, 9: Who hath saved us, and called us with an holy calling, not according to our works, but *according to His own purpose and grace,* which was given us in Christ Jesus before the world began.

Rom. 9, 11: For the children being not yet born, neither having done any good or evil, that the purpose of God according to election might stand, *not of works,* but of *Him that calleth.*

Rom. 11, 5: Even so, then, at this present time also there is a remnant according to the *election of grace.*

3.

2 Tim. 1, 9: Who hath saved us, and called us with an holy calling, not according to our works, but according to His own purpose and grace, which was given us *in Christ Jesus* before the world began.

Eph. 1, 4: According as He hath chosen us *in Him* before the foundation of the world, that we should be holy and without blame before Him.

Eph. 3, 11: According to the eternal purpose which He purposed *in Christ Jesus, our Lord.*

4.

Acts 13, 48: And as many as were ordained to *eternal life* believed.

2 Tim. 1, 9: Who hath *saved us,* and called us with an holy calling, not according to our works, but according to His own purpose and grace, which was given us in Christ Jesus before the world began.

2 Tim. 2, 10: Therefore I endure all things for the elect's sake, that they may also obtain *the salvation* which is in Christ Jesus *with eternal glory.*

Rom. 8, 28. 29: And we know that all things work together for good to them that love God, to them who are the called according to His purpose; for whom He did foreknow, He also did predestinate *to be conformed to the image of His Son, that He might be the firstborn among many brethren.*

5.

Eph. 1, 4. 5: According as He hath chosen us in Him before the foundation of the world, that we should be *holy and without blame* before Him in love: having predestinated us unto the *adoption of children by Jesus Christ* to Himself, according to the good pleasure of His will.

Rom. 8, 29. 30: For whom He did foreknow, He also did predestinate to be conformed to the image of His Son. . . . Moreover, whom He did predestinate, them He also *called;* and whom He called, them He also *justified:* and whom He justified, them He also *glorified.*

1 Pet. 1, 2: Elect according to the foreknowledge of God the Father, *through sanctification of the Spirit,* unto *obedience and sprinkling of the blood of Jesus Christ.*

6.

Acts 13, 48: And *as many* as were ordained to eternal life believed.

Matt. 20, 16: *Many* be called, but *few* chosen.

Matt. 22, 14: Many are called, but few are chosen.

7.

2 Tim. 2, 19: Nevertheless, the foundation of God standeth sure, having this seal, The Lord *knoweth them that are His.*

1 Pet. 1, 2: *Elect* according to the foreknowledge of God.

John 13, 18: I know whom I have chosen.

8.

Rom. 8, 30: Moreover, whom He did *predestinate,* them He also *called:* and whom He called, them He also *justified:* and whom He justified, them He also *glorified.*

Eph. 1, 11: In whom also we have obtained an *inheritance,* being predestinated according to *the purpose of Him who worketh all things* after the *counsel of His own will.*

Eph. 3, 10. 11: To the intent that now unto the principalities and powers in heavenly places might be *known by the Church* the manifold wisdom of God, according to *the eternal purpose* which He purposed in Christ Jesus, our Lord.

Mark 13, 20. 22: And except that the Lord had shortened those days, no flesh should *be saved:* but *for the elect's sake,* whom He hath *chosen, He hath shortened the days.* (22) For false Christs and false prophets shall rise, and shall show signs and wonders, to seduce, *if it were possible,* even the elect.

EXTERNAL ACTS.

§ 52. The external acts of God are either immediate or mediate.

IMMEDIATE EXTERNAL ACTS.

§ 53. The immediate external acts of God are concurrent acts of the three Persons in the Trinity terminating in objects not within the Godhead, and performed without the employment of intermediate or instrumental causes. Acts of this kind are the creation of heaven and earth out of nothing, the immediate revelation of divine truth to the prophets, the suggestion of concepts and words to the inspired penmen, etc.

Ps. 33, 6: By the word of the Lord were the heavens made; and all the host of them by the breath of His mouth.

MEDIATE EXTERNAL ACTS.

§ 54. The mediate external acts of God are concurrent acts of the three Persons in the Trinity terminating in extra-divine objects and performed with the employment of intermediate or instrumental causes. Of this class are the production of plants, animals, and human beings in the course of nature, the work of regeneration or conversion through the means of grace, etc.

See the respective paragraphs.

COSMOLOGY.

DEFINITION.

§ 55. Cosmology is the doctrine of the Holy Scriptures concerning the genesis, nature, and estates of created things, and may be divided into Cosmology in a restricted sense, Pneumatology, or Angelology, and Anthropology.

Cosmology Proper.

COSMOS.

§ 56. Cosmos, or the world, in a narrower sense of the term, is the aggregate of inanimate and irrational things which God made in the beginning of time[1] to provide for rational beings an abode where,[2] the conditions under, and the means by which, they might subsist and fulfill the purposes for which they have their being.[3]

1.

Hebr. 11, 3: Through faith we understand that the *worlds* were framed by the word of God, so that *things which are seen* were not made of things which do appear.

2.

Acts 17, 26: And hath made of one blood all nations of men for to *dwell on all the face of the earth,* and hath determined the times before appointed, and the *bounds of their habitation.*

3.

Gen. 1, 28. 29: And God blessed them, and God said unto them, Be fruitful, and multiply, and replenish the earth, and subdue it: and have dominion over the fish of the sea, and over the fowl of the air, and over every living thing that moveth upon the earth. And God said, Behold, I have given you every herb bearing seed, which is upon the face of all the earth, and every tree, in the which is the fruit of a tree yielding seed; to you it shall be for meat.

Gen. 8, 22: While the earth remaineth, seedtime and harvest, and cold and heat, and summer and winter, and day and night, shall not cease.

Gen. 9, 3: Every moving thing that liveth shall be meat for you; even as the green herb have I given you all things.

CREATION OF THE COSMOS.

§ 57. The creation of the inanimate and irrational world was begun and completed by the Triune God[1] within six consecutive days[2] by the exertion and for the manifestation and glory of His power,[3] wisdom,[4] and goodness.[5]

1.

Gen. 1, 1: In the beginning *God* created the heaven and the earth.

Ps. 33, 6: By the *word* of the *Lord* were the heavens made; and all the host of them by the *breath of His mouth.*

Col. 1, 15. 16: Who is the image of the invisible God, the First-Born of every creature: for by Him were all things created, that are in heaven, and that are in earth, visible and invisible.

See the record of creation Gen. 1 and 2.

2.

Gen. 1, 5: And the evening and the morning were the first day. Cf. vv. 8. 13. 19. 23. 31.

Exod. 20, 9. 11: *Six days* shalt thou labor, and do all thy work. (11) For in *six days* the *Lord made* heaven and earth, the sea, and all that in them is.

Exod. 31, 17: In six days the Lord made heaven and earth.

3.

Jer. 32, 17: Ah, Lord God! behold, Thou hast made the heaven and the earth by Thy great *power.*

4.

Ps. 104, 24: O Lord, how manifold are Thy works! In *wisdom* hast Thou made them all.

Ps. 136, 5: To Him that by *wisdom* made the heavens: for His mercy endureth forever.

5.

Ps. 136, 5: To Him that by wisdom made the heavens: for His *mercy* endureth forever.

Rev. 4, 11: Thou art worthy, O Lord, to receive glory and honor and power; for Thou hast created all things, and *for Thy pleasure* they are and were created.

PRESERVATION.

§ 58. The continuous preservation of the inanimate and irrational world is, as its first creation was, a work of the Triune God, who by immediate[1] and mediate[2] action preserves and continues what He created in the beginning.

1.

Hebr. 1, 3: Who being the brightness of His glory, and the express image of His person, and *upholding* all things *by the word* of His power.

Col. 1, 17: And He is before all things, and *by Him* all things *consist.*

2.

Acts 14, 17: He did good, and gave us *rain* from heaven, and fruitful seasons.

Acts 17, 25: He giveth to all life, and breath, and all things.

Gen. 1, 11. 12: And God said, Let the *earth* bring forth grass, the herb yielding seed, and the fruit-tree yielding fruit after his kind, whose seed is in itself, upon the earth: and it was so.

Gen. 8, 22: While the earth remaineth, *seed*time and *harvest,* and cold and heat, and summer and winter, and day and night, shall not cease.

Pneumatology, or Angelology.

CREATION OF ANGELS.

§ 59. Within the six days of creation[1] God made a great multitude[2] of angels.

1.

Gen. 2, 2: And on the seventh day God ended His work which He had made; and He rested on the seventh day from *all His work* which He had made. Cf. v. 3.

Exod. 20, 11: For in six days the Lord made *heaven and earth,* the sea, and *all* that in them is.

2.

Dan. 7, 10: Thousand thousands ministered unto Him, and ten thousand times ten thousand stood before Him.

Rev. 5, 11: And I beheld and I heard the voice of *many* angels round about.the throne and the beasts and the elders: and the number of them was ten thousand times ten thousand, and thousands of thousands.

Luke 2, 13: And suddenly there was with the angel a *multitude* of the heavenly host.

NATURE OF ANGELS.

§ 60. Angels are finite spirits,[1] without bodies, and complete in their spiritual nature,[2] personal,[3] rational,[4] and moral[5] beings of great but limited[6] wisdom[7] and power,[8] and of various ranks and orders.[9]

1.

Ps. 104, 4: Who maketh His angels *spirits.*

Hebr. 1, 14: Are they not all ministering *spirits,* sent forth to minister for them who shall be heirs of salvation?

2.

Luke 24, 39: A spirit hath not flesh and bones as ye see me have.

4

3.

Luke 1, 19: And the angel, answering, said unto Him, *I am Gabriel,* that stand in the presence of God.

Dan. 8, 16: Gabriel, make this man to understand the vision.

4.

Luke 15, 10: Likewise I say unto you, There is *joy* in the presence of the angels of God over one sinner that repenteth.

1 Pet. 1, 12: Which things the angels *desire* to *look into.*

5.

Matt. 25, 31: When the Son of Man shall come in His glory, and all the *holy* angels *with Him.*

1 Tim. 5, 21: I *charge thee* before God, and the Lord Jesus Christ, and the elect *angels,* that thou *observe these things* without preferring one before another, doing nothing by partiality.

6.

Mark 13, 32: But of that day and that hour *knoweth* no man, no, *not the angels* which are in heaven, neither the Son, but the Father.

7.

2 Sam. 14, 20: My lord is wise, according to the *wisdom* of an angel of God.

8.

2 Thess. 1, 7: The Lord Jesus shall be revealed from heaven with His *mighty* angels.

Ps. 103, 20: Bless the Lord, ye His angels, that excel in *strength.* Cf. 1 Kings 19, 32—35.

9.

1 Pet. 3, 22: Angels and *authorities* and *powers* being made *subject* unto Him.

1 Thess. 4, 16: For the Lord Himself shall descend from heaven with a shout, with the voice of the *archangel.*

FIXED NUMBER OF ANGELS.

§ 61. Angels, being sexless,[1] do not propagate their kind, and being also immortal and incorruptible,[2] their number is neither increased nor diminished.

1.

Matt. 22, 30: For in the resurrection they neither marry, nor are given in marriage, but are as the angels of God in heaven. Cf. Mark 12, 25.

2.

Luke 20, 36: Neither *can they die* any more, for they are *equal unto the angels.*

GOOD ANGELS.

§ 62. All angels were created perfectly good and holy,[1] but a part only of their number remained in their original estate.[2]

1.

Gen. 1, 31: And God saw *everything* that He made, and behold, it was *very good.*

Matt. 25, 31: When the Son of Man shall come in His glory, and all the *holy angels* with Him.

2.

1 Tim. 5, 21: I charge thee before God and the Lord Jesus Christ and *the elect angels.*

Jude 6: And the angels which kept not their first estate, but left their own habitation, He hath reserved in everlasting chains under darkness unto the judgment of the great day.

2 Pet. 2, 4: God spared not the angels that sinned.

CONFIRMED STATE OF GOOD ANGELS.

§ 63. Those angels who persevered in their primeval state were, in accordance with divine election,[1] confirmed[2] in holiness[3] and in the enjoyment of everlasting bliss and communion with God[4] in a state of glory.[5]

1.

1 Tim. 5, 21: I charge thee before God and the Lord Jesus Christ and the *elect* angels.

2.

Matt. 18, 10: In heaven their angels *do always* behold the face of my Father which is in heaven.

3.

Matt. 25, 31: The Son of Man shall come in His glory, and all the *holy angels* with Him.

4.

Matt. 18, 10: In heaven their angels do always *behold the face of my Father* which is *in heaven.*

Luke 20, 36: *Neither can they die* any more, for they are equal unto the *angels.*

5.

Matt. 25, 31: The Son of Man shall come in *His glory,* and all the holy *angels with Him.* Cf. Luke 2, 9; Matt. 28, 2. 3.

OCCUPATION OF GOOD ANGELS.

§ 64. The good angels serve God in worshiping Him,[1] doing His pleasure, and executing His commandments as His messengers and ministers[2] for the promotion of His purposes,[3] especially in the Church and for the protection and guidance of the heirs of salvation.[4]

1.

Dan. 7, 10: Thousand thousands *ministered* unto Him, and ten thousand times ten thousand *stood before Him.* Cf. Rev. 4, 8—11.

2.

Ps. 103, 21: Bless ye the Lord, all ye His hosts, ye *ministers* of His, that *do His pleasure!*

3.

Matt. 1, 20: Behold, the angel of the Lord appeared unto him in a dream, *saying,* Joseph, thou son of David, fear not to take unto thee Mary, thy wife. Cf. Luke 1, 11; Luke 2, 9—14; Matt. 2, 13. 19; Mark 16, 6. 7.

Matt. 28, 2: The angel of the Lord descended from heaven, and came and rolled back the stone from the door. Cf. John 20, 12; Acts 1, 10. 11.

Matt. 4, 11: And behold, angels came and ministered unto Him.

Luke 22, 43: And there appeared an angel unto Him from heaven strengthening Him. Cf. Matt. 25, 31; 1 Thess. 4, 16.

4.

Hebr. 1, 14: Are they not all *ministering spirits,* sent forth to *minister* for them who shall be *heirs of salvation?*

Matt. 18, 10: Take heed that ye despise not one of *these little ones;* for I say unto you, That in heaven *their angels* do always behold the face of my Father which is in heaven. Cf. § 62, 2.

Ps. 34, 7: The angel of the Lord encampeth round about *them that fear Him,* and *delivereth them.*

Ps. 91, 11: For He shall give His angels charge over thee to keep thee in all thy ways.

Matt. 24, 31: And He shall send His angels with a great sound of a trumpet, and they shall gather together *His elect* from the four winds, from one end of heaven to the other.

Matt. 13, 39: The harvest is the end of the world, and the reapers are the angels.

Luke 16, 22: The beggar died and was carried by the angels into Abraham's bosom.

EVIL ANGELS.

§ 65. A multitude[1] of angels[2] left their first estate and, making the beginning of sin,[3] became evil spirits,[4] or devils,[5] with perverted and depraved intellectual and moral faculties.[6]

1.

Mark 5, 9: And He asked him, What is thy name? And he answered, saying, My name is *Legion:* for we are *many.*

2.

Jude 6: And the *angels* which *kept not their first estate,* but *left their own habitation,* He hath reserved in everlasting chains.

3.

1 John 3, 8: He that committeth sin is of the devil; for the devil *sinneth from the beginning.*

2 Pet. 2, 4: God spared not the *angels that sinned.*

4.

Mark 1, 23: And there was in their synagogue a man with an *unclean* spirit. Cf. v. 26. Matt. 10, 1.

Eph. 6, 12: For we wrestle not against flesh and blood, but against principalities, against powers, against the rulers of the *darkness* of this world, against *spiritual wickedness* in high places.

5.

1 Cor. 10, 20: The things which the Gentiles sacrifice they sacrifice to *devils.*

Mark 5, 12: And all the *devils* besought Him, saying, Send us into the swine.

6.

Matt. 4, 6: And *saith* unto Him, *If Thou be* the Son of God, *cast Thyself down: for it is written,* He shall give His angels charge concerning thee: and in their hands they shall bear thee up, lest at any time thou dash thy foot against a stone.

John 8, 44: Ye are of your father, the devil, and the *lusts of your father* ye will do. He was a *murderer* from the beginning, and *abode not in the truth,* because there is *no truth in him.* When he speaketh a lie, he speaketh of his own: for he is a *liar,* and the *father of it.*

Gen. 3, 4: And the serpent *said* unto the woman, *Ye shall not surely die.* Cf. v. 5.

CONFIRMED STATE OF EVIL ANGELS.

§ 66. The evil angels were by the just judgment of God condemned to everlasting punishment in a confirmed state of wrath.

Matt. 25, 41: Depart from me, ye cursed, into *everlasting* fire, prepared for the devil and his angels.

2 Pet. 2, 4: God spared not the angels that sinned, but cast them down to hell, and delivered them into *chains* of darkness, *to be reserved unto judgment.*

Jude 6: The angels which kept not their first estate, but left their own habitation, He hath reserved in *everlasting chains* under darkness unto the judgment of the great day.

OCCUPATION OF EVIL ANGELS.

§ 67. The evil angels, being since their fall enemies of God and of His children,[1] are under their princes[2] ever bent upon destroying the works of God,[3] counteracting His purposes,[4] doing and promoting evil,[5] and, though subject to God's supreme dominion and control and confined within the bounds of His permission,[6] they are in various ways occupied in strengthening their kingdom[7] and exerting their power in the minds[8] and bodies of men.[9]

1.

Matt. 13, 25. 39: But while men slept, his *enemy* came and sowed tares among the wheat. (39) The enemy that sowed them is the devil.

1 Pet. 5, 8: *Your adversary,* the devil, as a roaring lion, walketh about.

Eph. 6, 11. 12: Put on the whole armor of God, that ye may be able to *stand against* the wiles of the *devil.* For we *wrestle* not against flesh and blood, but against principalities, against powers, against the rulers of darkness of this world, against *spiritual wickedness in high places.*

2.

Matt. 25, 41: Depart from me, ye cursed, into everlasting fire, prepared for *the devil and his angels.* Cf. Eph. 6, 12 supra.

3.

1 Pet. 5, 8: Your adversary, the devil, as a roaring lion, walketh about, *seeking whom he may devour.*

Cf. Gen. 3, 1—6; Matt. 15, 22; Luke 9, 39.

4.

Matt. 13, 19: Then cometh the wicked one, and catcheth away that which was sown in his heart. Cf. Luke 4, 8.

Matt. 13, 25. 26. 38: But while men slept, his enemy came and *sowed tares among the wheat,* and went his way. But when the blade was sprung up, and brought forth fruit, then *appeared the tares also.* (38) The tares are the *children of the wicked one.*

5.

John 13, 2: The devil having now *put into the heart of Judas* Iscariot, Simon's son, *to betray Him.*

Eph. 2, 2: The spirit that now *worketh* in the children of *disobedience.*

2 Thess. 2, 9: Whose coming is after the *working of Satan.* Cf. 1 Chron. 21, 1; Acts 5, 3. 4.

6.

Job 1, 12: The Lord said unto Satan, Behold, all that he hath is in thy power; *only upon himself put not forth thine hand.*

Job 2, 6: And the Lord said unto Satan, Behold, he is in thine hand; *but save his life!* Cf. Matt. 8, 31. 32.

7.

Luke 11, 18: If Satan also be divided against himself, how shall *his kingdom stand?*

Luke 11, 24—26: When the unclean spirit is gone out of a man, he walketh through dry places, seeking rest; and finding none, he saith, I will return *unto my house* whence I came out. And when he cometh, he findeth it swept and garnished. Then goeth he, and taketh to him seven other spirits more wicked than himself; and they enter in, and dwell there: and the *last state of that man is worse than the first.*

8.

Acts 5, 3: Why hath *Satan filled thine heart to lie* to the Holy Ghost?

2 Cor. 4, 4: The *god of this world* hath *blinded the minds* of them which believe not. Cf. Luke 11, 26; Eph. 2, 2; John 13, 2; Judas; see sub **5.**

9.

2 Cor. 12, 7: There was given to me a thorn in *the flesh,* the *messenger of Satan* to buffet me.

Luke 13, 16: Ought not this woman, being a daughter of Abraham, *whom Satan hath bound,* lo, these eighteen years, be loosed? Cf. Matt. 9, 17. 18. 20.

Cf. Job 1 and 2.

Anthropology.

CREATION OF MAN.

§ 68. On the sixth day of creation[1] God created man[2] in His image,[3] forming the body of one mature male,[4] Adam, of the dust of the earth[5] and breathing into his nostrils the breath of life,[6] and making one mature woman,[7] Eve, of a rib taken from Adam.[8]

1.

Gen. 1, 27. 31: So God *created man* in His own image, in the image of God created He him; male and female created He them. (31) And God saw everything that He had made, and, behold, it was very good. And the evening and the morning were the *sixth day.*

2.

Gen. 1, 26. 27: And God said, Let us *make man* in our image, after *our likeness:* and let them have dominion over the fish of the sea, and over the fowl of the air, and over the cattle, and over all the earth, and over every creeping thing that creepeth upon the earth. So God created man *in His own image,* in the image of God created He him; male and female created He them.

Matt. 19, 4: And He answered and said unto them, Have ye not read that He which made them at the beginning made them male and female?

3.

Gen. 1, 26. 27: see sub 2.

4.

Gen. 1, 28: And God blessed them, and God said unto them, *Be fruitful,* and multiply, and replenish the earth, and subdue it: and have dominion over the fish of the sea, and over the fowl of the air, and over every living thing that moveth upon the earth.

Gen. 2, 15. 18. 23: And the Lord God took *the man,* and put him into the garden of Eden *to dress it and to keep it.* (18) And the Lord said, It is not good that *the man* should be alone; I will make him an help meet for him. (23) And *Adam said,* This is now bone of my bones, and flesh of my flesh: she shall be called Woman, because she was taken *out of Man.*

5.

Gen. 2, 7: And the Lord God formed man *of the dust of the ground.*

Gen. 3, 19: In the sweat of thy face shalt thou eat bread, till thou return unto *the ground;* for out of it wast thou taken: for *dust thou art,* and unto dust shalt thou return.

1 Cor. 15, 47: The first man is *of the earth,* earthy: the second man is the Lord from heaven.

Eccl. 12, 7: Then shall the dust return to the earth as it was: and the spirit shall return unto God who gave it.

6.

Gen. 2, 7: And the Lord God formed man of the dust of the ground, and *breathed into his nostrils the breath of life;* and man became a *living soul.*

7.

Gen. 1, 27. 28: So God created man in His own image, in the image of God created He him; male and female created He them. And God blessed them, and God said unto them, *Be fruitful,* and multiply, and replenish the earth, and subdue it, etc.

Gen. 2, 22. 25: And the rib, which the Lord God had taken from man, made He *a woman,* and brought her unto the man. (25) And they were both naked, the man and *his wife,* and were not ashamed.

8.

Gen. 2, 21. 22: And the Lord God caused a deep sleep to fall upon Adam, and he slept: and He took *one of his ribs,* and closed up the flesh instead thereof; *and the rib,* which the Lord God had taken from man, *made He a woman,* and brought her unto the man.

NATURE OF MAN.

§ 69. Man, as created by his Maker, was an intelligent[1] and moral[2] being, consisting of body and soul[3] united in one complete person.[4]

1.

Gen. 2, 19. 20: And out of the ground the Lord God formed every beast of the field, and every fowl of the air; and brought them unto Adam to see *what he would call them:* and *whatsoever Adam called every living creature,* that was the *name thereof.* And Adam *gave names* to all cattle, and to the fowl of the air, and to every beast of the field; but for Adam there was not found an help meet for him.

Gen. 2, 23. 24: And Adam said, This is now bone of my bones, and flesh of my flesh: she shall be called Woman, because she was taken out of Man. Therefore shall a man leave his father and his mother, and shall cleave unto his wife: and they shall be one flesh.

2.

Gen. 2, 16. 17: And the Lord God *commanded* the man, saying, Of every tree of the garden thou mayest freely eat: but of the tree of the knowledge of good and evil, *thou shalt not eat of it:* for in the day that thou eatest thereof thou shalt surely die.

3.

Gen. 2, 7: And the Lord God *formed* man *of the dust of the ground,* and breathed *into his nostrils* the *breath of life;* and man became a living *soul.*

Eccl. 12, 7: Then shall the *dust* return to the earth as it was: and the *spirit* shall return unto God who gave it.

4.

Gen. 2, 4. 7. 8. 15: These are the generations of the heavens and of the earth when they were created, in the day that the Lord God made the earth and the heavens. (7) And the Lord God formed *man* of the dust of the ground, and breathed into his nostrils the breath of life; and *man* became *a living soul.* (8) And the Lord God planted a garden eastward in Eden; and there He put *the man whom He had formed.* (15) And the Lord God took *the man,* and put him into the garden of Eden *to dress it and to keep it.*

PRIMEVAL STATE OF MAN.

§ 70. In his original state, man was not only sound in body and soul, without a germ of disease or death,[1] or a taint of sin,[2] but endowed with concreated[3] spiritual wisdom and knowledge,[4] and with perfect natural righteousness, goodness, and holiness,[5] in the image and likeness of the Triune God.[6]

1.

Gen. 2, 17: But of the tree of the knowledge of good and evil, thou shalt not eat of it: for *in the day* that thou eatest thereof *thou shalt* surely *die.*

Rom. 5, 12: Wherefore, as by one man *sin* ENTERED into the world, and *death* BY SIN; and so death passed upon all men, for that all have sinned.

Rom. 6, 23: For the *wages of sin* is *death.*

2.

Gen. 1, 31: And God saw *everything* that He had made, and, behold, it was *very good.*

Gen. 2, 25: And they were both naked, the *man* and his *wife,* and were *not ashamed.*

3.

Gen. 1, 31: And God saw everything that *He had* MADE, and, behold, it was *very good.*

4.

Col. 3, 10: And have put on the new man, which is renewed in *knowledge* after the *image of Him that created him.*

5.

Eccl. 7, 29: Lo, this only have I found, that God hath *made* man *upright;* but they have sought out many inventions.

Eph. 4, 24: And that ye put on the new man, which *after God* is *created* in *righteousness* and true *holiness.*

6.

Gen. 1, 26. 27: And God said, Let us make man in our image, after our likeness. So God created man in His own image, in the image of God created He him; male and female created He them.

Gen. 5, 1. 2: This is the book of the generations of Adam. In the day that God *created* man, *in the likeness of God made* He him; male and female created He them; and blessed them, and called their name Adam, in the day when they were created.

Eph. 4, 24: And that ye put on the new man, which *after God* is created in righteousness and true holiness.

Col. 3, 10: And have put on the new man, which is renewed in knowledge after *the image of Him that created him.*

PROPAGATION.

§ 71. The two human persons whom God made in the beginning, one man and one woman, were thus created and joined in wedlock by the Creator[1] with a view to the preservation and propagation of the human race by mediate action of the creative power of God[2] in the procreation of children from the substance[3] and in the likeness[4] of their parents.

1.

Gen. 2, 18. 21—24: And the Lord God said, It is not good that the man should be alone; I will *make* him an *help meet for him.* (21—24) And the Lord God caused a deep sleep to fall upon Adam, and he slept: and He took one of his ribs, and closed up the flesh instead thereof; and the rib, which the Lord God had taken from man, made He a woman, and *brought her unto the man.* And Adam said, This is now bone of my bones, and flesh of my flesh: she shall be called Woman, because she was taken out of Man. Therefore shall a man leave his father and his mother, and shall *cleave unto his wife:* and they shall *be one flesh.*

2.

Gen. 1, 27. 28: Male and female created He them. And God *blessed them,* and God said unto them, *Be fruitful, and multiply and replenish the earth,* and subdue it: and have dominion over the fish of the sea, and over the fowl of the air, and over every living thing that moveth upon the earth.

Gen. 2, 24: Therefore shall a man leave his father and his mother, and shall *cleave unto his wife:* and they shall *be one flesh.*

Job 33, 4: The *Spirit of God* hath *made me,* and the *breath of the Almighty* hath *given me life.*

Ps. 139, 14: I will praise Thee; for *I am fearfully and wonderfully made:* marvelous are THY *works;* and that my soul knoweth right well.

3.

Gen. 2, 24: And they shall be *one flesh.*

John 1, 13: Which were born, not *of blood,* nor of the will of *the flesh,* nor of the will of man, but of God.

John 3, 6: That which is *born of the flesh is flesh;* and that which is born of the Spirit is spirit.

4.

Gen. 5, 3: And Adam lived an hundred and thirty years, and begat a son *in his own likeness, after his image;* and called his name Seth.

1 Cor. 15, 49: And as we have borne the *image of the earthy,* we shall also bear the image of the heavenly.

FALL OF MAN.

§ 72. Before the conception of their first offspring,[1] our first parents, Eve tempted by Satan,[2] and Adam, voluntarily transgressed a commandment of God,[3] and by this sin they fell from their primeval state,[4] lost the image of God,[5] became entirely depraved in spiritual death[6] and obnoxious to temporal death[7] and eternal damnation.[8]

1.

Gen. 4, 1: And Adam knew Eve, his wife; and *she conceived,* and bare Cain, and said, I have gotten a man from the Lord.

2.

Gen. 3, 13: And the Lord God said unto the woman, What is this that thou hast done? And the woman said, *The serpent beguiled me,* and I did eat. Cf. Gen. 3, 1—6.

Rev. 12, 9: And the great dragon was cast out, that old serpent, called the Devil, and Satan, which deceiveth the whole world.

1 Tim. 2, 14: And Adam was not deceived, but the woman, being deceived, was in the transgression.

3.

Gen. 3, 6: And when the woman *saw* that the tree was *good for food,* and that it was *pleasant to the eyes,* and a tree *to be desired* to make one wise, she took of the fruit thereof, and *did eat,* and gave also unto her husband with her; and he did eat. Cf. Gen. 2, 17; 3, 2. 3.

Rom. 5, 19: For as by one man's *disobedience* many were made sinners, so by the obedience of One shall many be made righteous.

Rom. 5, 12: By one man *sin* entered into the world.

4.

Gen. 3, 7—10: And the *eyes of them both were opened,* and they knew that they were *naked;* and they sewed fig leaves together, and made themselves aprons. And they heard the voice of the Lord God walking in the garden in the cool of the day: and Adam and his wife *hid themselves* from the presence of the Lord God amongst the trees of the garden. And the Lord God called unto Adam, and said unto him, Where art thou? And he said, I heard Thy voice in the garden, and *I was afraid,* because *I was naked;* and I hid myself.

5.

Gen. 3, 10: And he said, I heard Thy voice in the garden, and I was afraid, because *I was naked:* and I hid myself.

Rom. 5, 12: Wherefore, as by one man *sin* entered into the world, and *death by sin;* and so death passed upon all men, for that all have sinned.

6.

Gen. 2, 17: But of the tree of the knowledge of good and evil, thou shalt not eat of it: for *in the day* that thou eatest thereof *thou shalt surely die.*

Rom. 5, 16: For the judgment was by one *to condemnation.*

Eph. 2, 1. 3: And you hath He quickened, who *were dead in trespasses and sins.* (3) Among whom also we all had our conversation in times past *in the lusts of our flesh,* fulfilling the desires of the flesh and of the mind; and were *by nature the children of wrath,* even as others.

7.

Gen. 3, 19: In the sweat of thy face shalt thou eat bread, till thou *return unto the ground;* for out of it wast thou taken: for dust thou art, and *unto dust shalt thou return.*

Rom. 5, 12: Wherefore, as by one man sin entered into the world, and *death by sin;* and so death passed upon all men, for that all have sinned.

Rom. 6, 23: For the *wages of sin is death.*

8.

Rom. 5, 18: Therefore, as *by the offense of one judgment came* upon all men *to condemnation.*

HEREDITARY GUILT AND SIN.

§ 73. Not only was the guilt of Adam imputed to his descendants,[1] but his children and children's children have inherited from their first ancestor his corrupt nature,[2] being flesh born of the flesh,[3] wholly depraved,[4] totally blind of understanding in spiritual things,[5] of perverse appetites,[6] their will opposed to the will of God and only prone to evil,[7] all their faculties enslaved in the service of sin,[8] without any ability in any measure to work their own spiritual restoration.[9]

1.

Rom. 5, 12—21: Wherefore, as by one man sin entered into the world, and death by sin; and so death passed upon all men, for that all have sinned, etc.

Rom. 5, 18: By the *offense of* ONE *judgment came upon* ALL *men* to condemnation.

2.

Gen. 4, 1. 8: And Adam knew Eve, his wife; and *she conceived, and bare Cain,* and said, I have gotten a man from the Lord. (8) *Cain* rose up against Abel, his brother, and *slew him.*

Gen. 6, 5: And God saw that the wickedness of *man* was great in the earth, and that *every* imagination of the thoughts of *his heart* was *only* evil *continually.*

Gen. 8, 21: The imagination of man's *heart* is evil *from his youth.*

Eph. 2, 3: Among whom also we all had our conversation in times past in the *lusts* of our *flesh,* fulfilling the desires of the *flesh* and of the 'mind; and were BY NATURE the *children of wrath,* even as others.

Rom. 1, 18: For the *wrath of God* is revealed from heaven against all *ungodliness and unrighteousness of men,* who hold the truth in unrighteousness.

3.

John 3, 6: That which is born of the flesh is flesh.

4.

Rom. 3, 23: For all have sinned, and come short of the glory of God.

Rom. 7, 18: For I know that in me (that is, *in my flesh,*) dwelleth NO *good thing.*

Luke 11, 13: Ye then, *being evil,* know how to give good gifts unto your children.

Job 14, 4: Who can bring a clean thing out of an unclean? Not one.

5.

Eph. 4, 18: Having the *understanding darkened,* being alienated from the life of God through the *ignorance* that is in them, because of the *blindness of their heart.*

1 Cor. 2, 14: But the *natural* man *receiveth not the things of the Spirit of God:* for they are *foolishness* unto him: *neither CAN he know them,* because they are spiritually discerned.

2 Cor. 3, 5: Not that we are sufficient of ourselves to *think anything* as of ourselves; but our sufficiency is of God.

Eph. 5, 8: For ye were sometimes *darkness,* but now are ye light in the Lord.

6.

Gen. 6, 5: And God saw that the wickedness of man was great in the earth, and that every imagination of the thoughts of his heart was only evil continually.

Gen. 8, 21: The imagination of man's heart is evil from his youth.

Rom. 6, 12: Let not sin therefore reign in your mortal body, that ye should obey it in the *lusts thereof.*

Eph. 2, 3: Among whom also we all had our conversation in times past in the *lusts* of our *flesh,* fulfilling the *desires* of the *flesh* and of the mind; and were by nature the children of wrath, even as others.

Eph. 4, 22: That ye put off concerning the former conversation the *old man,* which is *corrupt* according to the *deceitful lusts.*

7.

Rom. 8, 7: Because the *carnal mind* is *enmity against God:* for it is not subject to the Law of God, neither indeed can be.

Rom. 5, 10: For if, when we were *enemies,* we were reconciled to God by the death of His Son.

Col. 1, 21: And you, that were sometime *alienated* and *enemies* in your mind by wicked works, yet now hath He reconciled.

Ps. 14, 3: They are *all* gone aside, they are *altogether become filthy:* there is *none* that doeth good, no, *not one.*

8.

Rom. 7, 14: For we know that the Law is spiritual: but *I am carnal, sold under sin.*

Rom. 7, 23. 24: But I see another law in my members, *warring* against the law of my mind, and bringing me into *captivity* to the *law of sin* which is *in my members.* O wretched man that I am! who shall deliver me from the body of this death?

Rom. 6, 17: But God be thanked, that ye were the *servants of sin,* but ye have *obeyed* from the heart that form of doctrine which was delivered you.

Rom. 6, 6: Knowing this, that our old man is crucified with Him, that *the body of sin* might be destroyed, that henceforth we should not *serve sin.*

Rom. 6, 20: For when ye were the *servants of sin,* ye were free from righteousness.

Rom. 3, 9. 10: What then? *Are we better than they?* No, in no wise: for we have before proved both Jews and Gentiles, that they are *all under sin,* as it is written, There is *none righteous,* no, *not one.*

9.

Eph. 2, 1: And you hath He quickened, who were *dead in trespasses and sins.*

Eph. 2, 5: Even when we were *dead in sins,* hath quickened us together with Christ.

Col. 2, 13: And you, being *dead in your sins* and the uncircumcision of your flesh, hath He quickened together with Him.

2 Cor. 3, 5: *Not* that we are *sufficient of ourselves* to *think* anything as of ourselves; but our sufficiency is of God.

ACTUAL SINS.

§ 74. Original sin, or the natural depravity of man, is productive of manifold actual sins,[1] both of commission[2] of that which God forbids, and of omission[3] of that which God demands, internal[4] and external[5] sins, voluntary[6] and involuntary[7] sins, dominant sins,[8] sins committed directly against God,[9] and sins committed indirectly against God[10] and directly against the sinner's self[11] or against his neighbor,[12] sins committed by ourselves[13] and sins of others in which we participate.[14]

1.

Rom. 8, 13: For if ye *live after the flesh,* ye shall die; but if ye through the Spirit do mortify the deeds of the body, ye shall live.

Col. 3, 9: Lie not one to another, seeing that ye have put off the *old man* with *his deeds.*

Gal. 5, 19: Now the *works of the flesh* are manifest, which are these: Adultery, fornication, uncleanness, lasciviousness.

Eph. 5, 11: And have no fellowship with the unfruitful *works of darkness,* but rather reprove them.

2.

Rom. 3, 13—15: Their *throat* is an open sepulcher; with their *tongues* they have *used deceit;* the poison of asps is under their *lips:* whose mouth is full of *cursing* and *bitterness:* their *feet* are swift to *shed blood.*

Rom. 1, 23: And *changed the glory of the uncorruptible God* into an image made like to corruptible man, and to birds, and four-footed beasts, and creeping things.

Gal. 5, 19—21: Now the works of the flesh are manifest, which are these: Adultery, fornication, uncleanness, lasciviousness, idolatry, witchcraft, hatred, variance, emulations, wrath, strife, seditions, heresies, envyings, murders, drunkenness, revelings, and such like.

3.

James 4, 17: Therefore to him that knoweth to do good, and *doeth it not,* to him it *is sin.*

Rom. 1, 21: Because that, when they knew God, they *glorified Him not* as God, *neither were thankful.*

Rom. 3, 12: They are all gone out of the way, they are together become *unprofitable:* there is *none that doeth good,* no, not one.

Dan. 9, 6. 13: *Neither have we hearkened* unto Thy servants, the prophets, which spake in Thy name to our kings, our princes, and our fathers, and to all the people of the land. (13) As it is written in the law of Moses, all this evil is come upon us: yet *made we not our prayer* before the Lord, our God, that we might turn from our iniquities, and understand Thy truth.

4.

Gen. 8, 21: The *imagination* of man's *heart* is *evil* from his *youth.*

Jer. 17, 9: The *heart* is *deceitful* above all things, and desperately *wicked.*

Matt. 5, 28: But I say unto you, That whosoever looketh on a woman to *lust after her* hath committed *adultery* with her already in his heart.

Matt. 7, 21. 22: Not every one that *saith* unto me, Lord, Lord! shall enter into the kingdom of heaven, but he that doeth the will of my Father which is in heaven. Many will *say* to me in that day,

Lord, Lord, have we not prophesied in Thy name? and in Thy name have cast out devils? and in Thy name done many wonderful works?

Acts 8, 21: Thy *heart is not right* in the sight of God.

1 John 3, 15: Whosoever *hateth* his brother is a *murderer:* and ye know that no murderer hath eternal life abiding in him.

5.

Ps. 37, 12: The wicked plotteth against the just, and *gnasheth upon him* with his *teeth.*

Matt. 27, 39. 40: And they that passed by reviled Him, *wagging their heads,* and *saying,* Thou that destroyest the temple, and buildest it in three days, save Thyself!

Matt. 12, 34: Out of the abundance of the heart the mouth *speaketh.*

Matt. 12, 36: But I say unto you, That every idle *word* that men shall *speak,* they shall give account thereof in the day of judgment.

Matt. 5, 21. 22: Ye have heard that it was said by them of old time, Thou shalt not *kill;* and whosoever shall kill shall be in danger of the judgment: but I say unto you, That whosoever is angry with his brother without a cause shall be in danger of the judgment: and whosoever shall *say* to his brother, Raca, shall be in danger of the council: but whosoever shall *say,* Thou fool, shall be in danger of hell fire.

Gal. 5, 19—21: Now the *works of the flesh* are manifest, which are these: *Adultery, fornication,* uncleanness, lasciviousness, idolatry, *witchcraft,* hatred, variance, emulations, wrath, *strife, seditions, heresies,* envyings, *murders, drunkenness, revelings,* and such like: of the which I tell you before, as I have also told you in time past, that they which *do* such things shall not inherit the kingdom of God.

6.

Is. 3, 9: The show of their countenance doth witness against them; and they *declare* their sin as Sodom; they *hide it not.* Woe unto their soul! for they have rewarded evil unto themselves.

Rom. 1, 32: Who, *knowing the judgment* of God, that they which *commit* such things are worthy of death, not only do the same, but *have pleasure* in them that do them.

7.

Numb. 15, 22. 24: And if ye have *erred,* and not observed all these · commandments, which the Lord hath spoken unto Moses. (24) Then it shall be, if aught be committed *by ignorance* without the knowledge of the congregation, etc.

8.

Rom. 6, 12: Let not sin therefore *reign* in your mortal body, that ye should *obey* it in the lusts thereof.

Ps. 19, 13: Keep back Thy servant also from presumptuous sins; let them not *have dominion* over me!

5

9.

Ps. 14, 1: The fool hath said in his heart, *There is no God.* They are corrupt; they have done abominable works; there is none that doeth good.

Rom. 1, 21—23: Because that, when they knew *God,* they *glorified Him not as God,* neither were *thankful,* but became vain in their imaginations, and their foolish heart was darkened. Professing themselves to be wise, they became fools, and *changed the glory of the uncorruptible God* into an image made like to corruptible man, and to birds, and fourfooted beasts, and creeping things.

Exod. 20, 3. 7: Thou shalt have no other gods before me. (7) Thou shalt not take the name of the Lord, thy God, in vain; for the Lord will not hold him guiltless that taketh His name in vain.

Prov. 8, 36: But he that sinneth *against me* wrongeth his own soul: all they that *hate me* love death.

10.

Gen. 39, 9: There is none greater in this house than I; neither hath he kept back anything from me but thee, because *thou art his wife.* How, then, can I do this great wickedness, and *sin against God?*

Acts 5, 2. 3: (Ananias) *kept back part of the price,* his wife also being privy to it, and brought a certain part, and laid it at the apostles' feet. But Peter said, Ananias, why hath Satan filled thine heart to *lie to the Holy Ghost,* and to keep back part of the price of the land?

11.

1 Cor. 6, 18: Flee *fornication!* Every sin that a man doeth is without the body; but he that committeth fornication *sinneth against his own body.*

Eph. 5, 18: And be not *drunk* with wine, wherein is excess; but be filled with the Spirit.

12.

Exod. 20, 12—16: Honor thy *father and thy mother,* that thy days may be long upon the land which the Lord, thy God, giveth thee. Thou shalt not *kill.* Thou shalt not *commit adultery.* Thou shalt not *steal.* Thou shalt not *bear false witness* against thy *neighbor.*

13.

2 Sam. 12, 7: And Nathan said to David, *Thou* art the man.

Gen. 3, 12. 13: . . . She gave me of the tree, and *I did eat.* . . . And the woman said, The serpent beguiled me, and *I did eat.*

14.

1 Tim. 5, 22: Lay hands suddenly on no man, neither be *partaker of other men's sins.* Keep thyself pure.

Eph. 5, 7: Be not ye therefore *partakers with them.*

Eph. 5, 11: And have no *fellowship* with the unfruitful works of darkness, but rather reprove them.

Rev. 18, 4: And I heard another voice from heaven, saying, Come out of her, my people, that ye be not *partakers of her sins,* and that ye receive not of her plagues.

STATE OF WRATH.

§ 75. Inasmuch as God neither was the cause of Adam's sin,[1] nor is the cause of man's original sin or actual sins,[2] nor of his inability to work his own regeneration,[3] all the children of Adam are, as their ancestor was, in consequence of the fall, justly under the wrath of God and deserving of temporal and eternal punishment.[4]

1.

Gen. 1, 31: And God saw everything that *He had made,* and, behold, it was *very good.*

Gen. 2, 16. 17: And the Lord God commanded.the man, saying, Of every tree of the garden *thou* mayest freely eat: but of the tree of the knowledge of good and evil, *thou* shalt not eat of it: for in the day that *thou* eatest thereof thou shalt surely die.

Gen. 3, 12. 17: And the man said, *The woman* whom Thou gavest to be with me, she gave me of the tree, and I did eat. (17) And unto Adam He said, Because thou hast hearkened unto the *voice of thy wife,* and hast eaten of the tree, of which I commanded thee, saying, Thou shalt not eat of it: cursed is the ground *for thy sake;* in sorrow shalt thou eat of it all the days of thy life.

2.

Rom. 5, 12: Wherefore, as *by one man* sin entered into the world, and death by sin; and so death passed upon all men, *for that all have sinned.*

John 8, 44: Ye are of *your father, the devil,* and the lusts *of your father* ye will do. He was a *murderer from the beginning,* and abode not in the truth, because there is no truth in him. When he speaketh a lie, he speaketh of *his own;* for he is a liar, and the father of it.

2 Cor. 4, 4: In whom the *god of this world* hath *blinded the minds* of them which believe not.

1 John 1, 5: This, then, is the message which we have heard of Him, and declare unto you, that *God is light,* and in Him is no darkness at all.

James 1, 13. 14: *Let no man say* when he is tempted, *I am tempted of God;* for God cannot be tempted with evil, *neither tempteth He any man;* but every man is tempted when he is drawn away *of his own lust,* and enticed.

Ps. 5, 5: The foolish shall not stand in Thy sight: Thou *hatest* all workers of iniquity.

Rom. 7, 8: But *sin,* taking occasion by the commandment, *wrought in me all manner of concupiscence.* For without the Law sin was dead.

Rom. 7, 11: For *sin,* taking occasion by the commandment, *deceived* me, and by it *slew* me.

3.

Eph. 2, 1—3: And you hath He quickened, who were *dead in trespasses and sins,* wherein in time past ye walked according to the course of this world, according to the prince of the power of the air, the spirit that now worketh in the *children of disobedience:* among whom also we all had our conversation in times past in *the lusts of our flesh,* fulfilling the *desires of the flesh* and of the mind; and were *by nature* the children of wrath, even as others.

John 3, 5. 6: Jesus answered, Verily, verily, I say unto thee, Except a man be born of water and of the Spirit, he cannot enter into the kingdom of God. That which is born of the flesh is flesh, and that which is born of the Spirit is spirit.

4.

Eph. 2, 3: And were by nature the *children of wrath,* even as others.

Gal. 6. 8: For he that soweth to his flesh shall of the flesh reap corruption; but he that soweth to the Spirit shall of the Spirit reap life everlasting.

THE LAW.

§ 76. To convince the sinner of his innate sinfulness and of his manifold offenses against the holy will of God,[1] of the guilt[2] incurred by original and actual sin, and of the righteous wrath of God,[3] is, since the fall of man, a chief purpose of the divine Law.

1.

Rom. 7, 7: What shall we say, then? Is the Law sin? God forbid! Nay, *I had not known sin but by the Law;* for *I had not known lust,* except the *Law* had said, *Thou shalt not covet.*

Rom. 3, 20: Therefore by the deeds of the Law there shall no flesh be justified in His sight; *for by the Law is the knowledge of sin.*

Dan. 9, 5: We have *sinned,* and have committed iniquity, and have done wickedly, and have *rebelled,* even by *departing from Thy precepts* and from Thy judgments.

2.

Rom. 2, 12. 14. 15: For as many as have sinned without Law shall also perish without Law: and as many as have sinned in *the Law* shall be judged *by the Law.* (14) For when the Gentiles, which have not the Law, do by nature the things contained in the Law, these, having not the Law, are *a law unto themselves:* which show the *work of the Law written in their hearts,* their conscience also bearing witness, and their thoughts the meanwhile *accusing* or else excusing one another.

Rom. 3, 19: Now we know that what things soever the *Law* saith it saith to them who are under the *Law,* that *every mouth may be stopped,* and *all the world may become* GUILTY before God.

3.

Dan. 9, 10. 11: Neither have we obeyed the voice of the Lord, our God, to walk in *His laws,* which He set before us by His servants, the prophets. Yea, all Israel have transgressed *Thy Law,* even by departing, that they might not obey Thy voice; THEREFORE *the curse is poured upon us,* and the oath that is written in *the law* of Moses, the servant of God, *because we have sinned* against Him.

Ps. 51, 3. 4: For I acknowledge my transgressions, and my sin is ever before me. Against Thee, Thee only, have I sinned, and done this evil in Thy sight, that *Thou mightest be justified* when Thou speakest, and be *clear when Thou judgest.*

Exod. 20, 5: Thou shalt not bow down thyself to them, nor serve them; for I the Lord, thy God, am a jealous God, visiting the iniquity of the fathers upon the children unto the third and fourth generation of them that hate me.

Rom. 3, 19: Now we know that what things soever the *Law saith* it saith to them who are under the Law, that *every mouth may be stopped,* and all the world may become *guilty before God.*

FIRST COMMANDMENT.

§ 77.. The Law condemns all who have other gods before the true God,[1] especially those who are ignorant of, or deny, the true God,[2] or who do not fear,[3] love,[4] or trust in[5] God above all things, or who worship a creature as God,[6] or fear, love, or trust in a creature as we should fear, love, or trust in God alone.[7]

1.

Exod. 20, 2: I am the Lord, thy God.
Deut. 5, 7: Thou shalt have none other gods before me.

2.

John 17, 3: And this is life eternal, that they might *know* Thee *the* ONLY *true God,* and Jesus Christ, whom Thou hast sent.

Jer. 9, 23. 24: Thus saith the Lord, Let not the wise man glory in his wisdom, neither let the mighty man glory in his might, let not the rich man glory in his riches: but let him that glorieth glory in this, that he *understandeth and knoweth me, that I am the Lord.*

Ps. 14, 1: The *fool* hath said in his heart, *There is no God.* They are *corrupt,* they have done abominable works, there is none that doeth good.

1 John 2, 23: Whosoever *denieth* the Son, the same hath not the Father; but he that acknowledgeth the Son hath the Father also.

3.

Ps. 33, 8: Let all the earth *fear* the Lord: let all the inhabitants of the world *stand in awe of Him.*

Gen. 39, 9: How, then, can I do this great wickedness, and sin against God?

Deut. 10, 20: Thou shalt *fear* the Lord, thy God; Him shalt thou serve, and to Him shalt thou cleave.

Ps. 67, 7: God shall bless us; and all the ends of the earth shall *fear* Him.

Ps. 147, 11: The Lord taketh pleasure in them that *fear* Him.

Eccl. 12, 13: Let us hear the conclusion of the whole matter: *Fear God,* and keep His commandments; for this is the whole duty of man.

4.

Deut. 6, 5: And thou shalt *love* the Lord, thy God, with all thine heart, and with all thy soul, and with all thy might.

Matt. 22, 37: Jesus said unto him, Thou shalt *love* the Lord, thy God, with all thy heart, and with all thy soul, and with all thy mind.

5.

Prov. 3, 5: *Trust* in the Lord with all thine heart, and *lean not* unto thine own understanding.

Is. 26, 4: *Trust* ye in the Lord forever: for in the Lord Jehovah is everlasting strength.

Jer. 17, 5. 7: Thus saith the Lord, *Cursed* be *the man that trusteth in man,* and maketh flesh his arm, and whose heart departeth from the Lord! (7) Blessed is the man that *trusteth* in the Lord, and whose *hope* the Lord is!

Ps. 146, 5: Happy is he that *hath* the God of Jacob *for his help,* whose *hope* is in the Lord, his God.

Ps. 147, 11: The Lord taketh pleasure in them that fear Him, in those that *hope in* His mercy.

6.

Matt. 4, 10: Thou shalt *worship the Lord, thy God,* and *Him only* shalt thou serve.

Is. 42, 8: *I am the Lord:* that is my name; and *my glory will I not give to another, neither my praise to graven images.*

Rev. 19, 10: And I fell at his feet to *worship him.* And he said unto me, See thou *do it not: I am thy fellow-servant,* and of thy brethren that have the testimony of Jesus: *worship God!*

7.

Matt. 10, 28: *Fear not them which kill the body,* but are not able to kill the soul: but rather *fear Him* which is able to destroy both soul and body in hell.

Matt. 10, 37: He that *loveth father or mother more than me* is not worthy of me: and he that *loveth son or daughter more than me* is not worthy of me.

Ps. 62, 11: God hath spoken once; twice have I heard this; that *power belongeth unto God.*

Col. 3, 5: Mortify therefore your members which are upon the earth: fornication, uncleanness, inordinate affection, evil *concupiscence,* and *covetousness, which is idolatry.*

Eph. 5, 5: For this ye know, that no whoremonger, nor unclean person, nor *covetous man, who is an idolater,* hath any inheritance in the kingdom of Christ and of God.

Phil. 3, 19: Whose end is destruction, whose *god is their belly,* and whose glory is in their shame, who mind earthly things.

Jer. 17, 5: Thus saith the Lord, *Cursed* be the man *that trusteth in man,* and *maketh flesh his arm,* and whose heart departeth from the Lord!

Job 31, 24: If I have *made gold my hope,* or have said to the *fine gold, Thou art my confidence.*

Ps. 146, 3: *Put not your trust in princes,* nor in the son of man, in whom there is no help.

SECOND COMMANDMENT.

§ 78. The Law condemns all those who take the name of God in vain,[1] especially by blaspheming,[2] cursing,[3] false or irreverent swearing,[4] witchcraft,[5] false doctrine,[6] religious hypocrisy,[7] or open denial of the true faith,[8] or by refusing or neglecting to sanctify God's name by prayer,[9] praise,[10] thanksgiving,[11] and the confession of the true faith.[12]

1.

Exod. 20, 7: Thou shalt not take the name of the Lord, thy God, in vain; for the Lord will not hold him guiltless that taketh His name in vain.

Cf. Deut. 5, 11.

2.

Lev. 19, 12: And ye shall not *swear by my name falsely,* neither shalt thou *profane* the name of thy God: I am the Lord.

Lev. 24, 16: And he that *blasphemeth* the name of the Lord, he shall surely be put to death, and all the congregation shall certainly stone him: as well the stranger, as he that is born in the land, when he *blasphemeth* the name of the Lord, shall be put to death.

Ps. 74, 10: O God, how long shall the adversary reproach? Shall the enemy *blaspheme* Thy name forever?

Gal. 6, 7: Be not deceived; *God is not mocked.*

3.

James 3, 9. 10: Therewith bless we God, even the Father, and therewith *curse* we men, which are made after the similitude of God. Out of the same mouth proceedeth blessing and *cursing.* My brethren, these things ought not so to be.

Rom. 12, 14: Bless them which persecute you: bless, and *curse not.*

4.

Ps. 24, 3. 4: Who shall ascend into the hill of the Lord? or who shall stand in His holy place? He that hath clean hands, and a pure heart; who hath not lifted up his soul unto vanity, nor *sworn deceitfully.*

Lev. 19, 12: And ye shall not *swear by my name falsely,* neither shalt thou profane the name of thy God: I am the Lord.

Zech. 8, 17: And let none of you imagine evil in your hearts against his neighbor, and love no *false oath;* for all these are things that I hate, saith the Lord.

Matt. 5, 33—36: Again, ye have heard that it hath been said by them of old time, Thou shalt not *forswear* thyself, but shalt *perform unto the Lord thine oaths.* But I say unto you, Swear not at all: neither *by heaven;* for it is *God's throne:* nor *by the earth;* for it is *His footstool:* neither by *Jerusalem;* for it is the city of *the great King.* Neither shalt thou swear by thy head, because thou canst not make one hair white or black.

5.

Deut. 18, 10—12: There shall not be found among you any one that maketh his son or his daughter to *pass through the fire,* or that useth *divination,* or any *observer of times,* or an *enchanter,* or a *witch,* or a *charmer,* or a consulter with *familiar spirits,* or a *wizard,* or a *necromancer.* For all that do these things are an abomination unto the Lord.

Lev. 19, 31: Regard not them that have *familiar spirits,* neither seek after *wizards,* to be defiled by them: I am the Lord, your God.

Rev. 22, 15: For without are dogs, and *sorcerers,* and whoremongers, and murderers, and idolaters, and whosoever loveth and maketh a lie.

6.

Jer. 23, 31. 32: Behold, I am against the prophets, saith the Lord, that use their tongues, and say, He saith. Behold, I am against them that *prophesy false dreams,* saith the Lord, and do tell them, and *cause my people to err by their lies,* and by their lightness; yet I sent them not, nor commanded them: therefore they shall not profit this people at all, saith the Lord.

Ezek. 13, 19: And will ye pollute me among my people for handfuls of barley and for pieces of bread, to slay the souls that should not die, and to save the souls alive that should not live, by *your lying to my people that hear your lies?*

Ps. 50, 16. 17: But unto the wicked God saith, What hast thou to do to declare my statutes, or that thou shouldest take my covenant in thy mouth? seeing thou *hatest instruction,* and *castest my words behind thee.*

Rev. 22, 18. 19: For I testify unto every man that heareth the words of the prophecy of this book, If any man shall *add unto these things,* God shall add unto him the plagues that are written in this book; and if any man shall *take away from the words* of the book of this prophecy, God shall take away his part out of the book of life, and out of the holy city, and from the things which are written in this book.

Matt. 5, 19: Whosoever therefore shall *break one of these least commandments,* and shall *teach men* so, he shall be called the least in the kingdom of heaven; but whosoever shall do and teach them, the same shall be called great in the kingdom of heaven.

7.

Matt. 15, 8: This people draweth nigh unto me with their *mouth,* and honoreth me with their *lips;* but their *heart is far from me.*

Matt. 7, 21: Not every one that *saith* unto me, Lord, Lord! shall enter into the kingdom of heaven, but he that doeth the will of my Father which is in heaven.

8.

Matt. 10, 33: But whosoever shall *deny me before men,* him will I also deny before my Father which is in heaven.

Mark 8, 38: Whosoever therefore shall be *ashamed of me and of my words* in this adulterous and sinful generation, of him also shall the Son of Man be ashamed, when He cometh in the glory of His Father with the holy angels.

1 Pet. 3, 15: But sanctify the Lord God in your hearts; and be ready always to *give an answer* to every man that asketh you a reason of the hope that is in you with meekness and fear.

9.

Ps. 50, 15: And *call upon me* in the day of trouble: I will deliver thee, and thou shalt glorify me.

1 Thess. 5, 17: *Pray* without ceasing!

10.

Col. 3, 16: Let the Word of Christ dwell in you richly in all wisdom; teaching and admonishing one another in *psalms* and hymns and spiritual songs, *singing* with grace in your hearts *to the Lord.*

Ps. 103, 1. 2: *Bless the Lord,* O my soul: and all that is within me, *bless His holy name. Bless the Lord,* O my soul, and forget not all His benefits!

11.

Ps. 50, 14: Offer unto God *thanksgiving,* and pay thy vows unto the Most High.

Ps. 106, 1: Praise ye the Lord. O *give thanks* unto the Lord; for He is good; for His mercy endureth for ever.

12.

1 Pet. 3, 15: But sanctify the Lord God in your hearts; and be ready always to give an *answer to every man that asketh you* a reason of the hope that is in you with meekness and fear.

Matt. 10, 32: Whosoever therefore shall *confess me before men,* him will I confess also before my Father which is in heaven.

Rom. 10, 10: For with the heart man believeth unto righteousness, and with the mouth *confession is made unto salvation.*

THIRD COMMANDMENT.

§ 79. The Law condemns all those who neglect the proper use of the Word of God and the Sacraments, especially when and where they are publicly administered, or who fail to contribute toward the maintenance of the church and the furtherance of its purposes.

John 5, 39: *Search the Scriptures;* for in them ye think ye have eternal life: and they are they which testify of me.

John 8, 47: He that is of God *heareth God's words:* ye therefore hear them not, because ye are not of God.

Col. 3, 16: Let the *Word of Christ dwell in you richly* in all wisdom; teaching and admonishing one another in psalms and hymns and spiritual songs, singing with grace in your hearts to the Lord.

Eccl. 5, 1: Keep thy foot when thou *goest to the house of God,* and be more *ready to hear* than to give the sacrifice of fools; for they consider not that they do evil.

Ps. 26, 6—8: So will *I compass Thine altar,* O Lord, that I may publish with the voice of thanksgiving, and tell of all Thy wondrous works. Lord, *I have loved the habitation of Thy house,* and the *place where Thine honor dwelleth.*

1 Thess. 2, 13: For this cause also thank we God without ceasing, because, when ye *received the Word of God,* which ye heard of us, ye received it *not as the word of men,* but as it is in truth, *the Word of God.*

James 1, 21: Wherefore lay apart all filthiness and superfluity of naughtiness, and *receive with meekness the engrafted Word,* which is able to save your souls.

Hebr. 10, 25: *Not forsaking the assembling of ourselves together,* as the manner of some is, but exhorting one another, and so much the more as ye see the day approaching.

Luke 11, 28: But He said, Yea, rather, *blessed are they that hear the Word of God, and keep it.*

Luke 10, 16: He that *heareth you heareth me;* and he that *despiseth you despiseth me;* and he that despiseth me despiseth Him that sent me.

Luke 16, 29: Abraham saith unto him, They have *Moses and the prophets; let them hear them.*

Gal. 6, 6: Let him that is taught in the Word *communicate unto him that teacheth* in all good things.

1 Cor. 11, 24. 25: And when He had given thanks, He brake it, and said, *Take, eat:* this is my body, which is broken for you; *this do* in remembrance of me. After the same manner also He took the cup, when He had supped, saying, This cup is the new testament in my blood: *this do* ye, as oft as ye drink it, in remembrance of me.

Matt. 28, 19: Go ye therefore, and *teach all nations,* baptizing them in the name of the Father, and of the Son, and of the Holy Ghost.

Mark 16, 15: And He said unto them, *Go ye into all the world,* and *preach the Gospel* to every creature.

Col. 2, 16. 17: *Let no man therefore judge you* in meat, or in drink, or *in respect of an holyday,* or of the new moon, *or of the Sabbath days:* which are a shadow of things to come; but the body is of Christ.

Rom. 14, 5. 6: One man esteemeth one day above another; another *esteemeth every day alike.* Let every man be fully persuaded in his own mind. He that regardeth the day regardeth it unto the Lord; and he that *regardeth not the day, to the Lord he doth not regard it.*

FOURTH COMMANDMENT.

§ 80. The Law condemns all those who refuse or neglect to honor and duly[1] obey those whom God has endowed with authority over them in the family,[2] the church,[3] and the state,[4] or who, being in authority, refuse or neglect to perform the duties incumbent upon them according to their authority.[5]

1.

Acts 5, 29: Then Peter and the other apostles answered and said, We ought to *obey God rather than men.*

Matt. 22, 21: Then saith He unto them, Render therefore unto *Caesar* the things which are *Caesar's,* and unto *God* the things that are *God's.*

Matt. 20, 25. 26: But Jesus called them unto Him, and said, Ye know that the princes of the Gentiles exercise dominion over them, and they that are great exercise authority upon them. But it shall not be so *among you;* but whosoever will be great among you, let him be your minister.

1 Pet. 5, 3: *Neither as being lords over God's heritage,* but being ensamples to the flock.

2.

Exod. 20, 12: Honor thy father and thy mother, that thy days may be long upon the land which the Lord, thy God, giveth thee.

Deut. 5, 16: Honor thy father and thy mother, as the Lord, thy God, hath commanded thee, that thy days may be prolonged, and that it may go well with thee.

Mal. 1, 6: A son honoreth his father, and a servant his master. If, then, I be a father, where is mine honor? and if I be a master, where is my fear? saith the Lord of hosts unto you, O priests, that despise my name. And ye say, Wherein have we despised Thy name?

Eph. 6, 2. 3: Honor thy father and mother, which is the first commandment with promise, that it may be well with thee, and thou mayest live long on the earth.

Col. 3, 20: Children, obey your parents in all things; for this is well pleasing unto the Lord.

Eph. 6, 1: Children, obey your parents in the Lord; for this is right.

Prov. 23, 22: Hearken unto thy father that begat thee, and despise not thy mother when she is old.

Prov. 30, 17: The eye that mocketh at his father, and despiseth to obey his mother, the ravens of the valley shall pick it out, and the young eagles shall eat it.

3.

Luke 10, 16: He that heareth you heareth me, and he that despiseth you despiseth me; and he that despiseth me despiseth Him that sent me.

1 Thess. 5, 12. 13: And we beseech you, brethren, to know them which labor among you, and are over you in the Lord, and admonish you; and to esteem them very highly in love for their work's sake. And be at peace among yourselves.

1 Tim. 5, 17—19: Let the elders that rule well be counted worthy of double honor, especially they who labor in the Word and doctrine. For the Scripture saith, Thou shalt not muzzle the ox that treadeth out the corn. And, The laborer is worthy of his reward. Against an elder receive not an accusation, but before two or three witnesses.

Hebr. 13, 17: Obey them that have the rule over you, and submit yourselves: for they watch for your souls as they that must give account, that they may do it with joy, and not with grief; for that is unprofitable for you.

Gal. 6, 6: Let him that is taught in the Word communicate unto him that teacheth in all good things.

4.

Matt. 22, 21: Then saith He unto them, Render therefore unto Caesar the things which are Caesar's, and unto God the things that are God's.

Rom. 13, 6. 7: For for this cause pay ye tribute also; for they are God's ministers, attending continually upon this very thing.

Render therefore to all their dues: tribute to whom tribute is due; custom to whom custom; fear to whom fear; honor to whom honor.

Rom. 13, 1: Let every soul be subject unto the higher powers. For there is no power but of God: the powers that be are ordained of God.

Tit. 3, 1: Put them in mind to be subject to principalities and powers, to obey magistrates, to be ready to every good work.

1 Pet. 2, 13. 14: Submit yourselves to every ordinance of man for the Lord's sake: whether it be to the king, as supreme; or unto governors, as unto them that are sent by him for the punishment of evil-doers, and for the praise of them that do well.

5.

Eph. 6, 4: And, ye fathers, provoke not your children to wrath, but bring them up in the nurture and admonition of the Lord.

1 Tim. 5, 8: But if any provide not for his own, and especially for those of his own house, he hath denied the faith, and is worse than an infidel.

1 Pet. 5, 2. 3: Feed the flock of God which is among you, taking the oversight thereof, not by constraint, but willingly; not for filthy lucre, but of a ready mind; neither as being lords over God's heritage, but being ensamples to the flock.

Acts 20, 28: Take heed therefore unto yourselves, and to all the flock, over the which the Holy Ghost hath made you overseers, to feed the Church of God which He hath purchased with His own blood.

John 21, 15—17: So when they had dined, Jesus saith to Simon Peter, Simon, son of Jonas, lovest thou me more than these? He said unto Him, Yea, Lord; Thou knowest that I love Thee. He saith unto him, Feed my lambs! He saith to him again, the second time, Simon, son of Jonas, lovest thou me? He saith unto Him, Yea, Lord; Thou knowest that I love Thee. He saith unto him, Feed my sheep! He saith unto him the third time, Simon, son of Jonas, lovest thou me? Peter was grieved because He said unto him the third time, Lovest thou me? And he said unto Him, Lord, Thou knowest all things; Thou knowest that I love Thee. Jesus saith unto him, Feed my sheep!

Rom. 12, 7. 8: Or ministry, let us wait on our ministering: or he that teacheth, on teaching; or he that exhorteth, on exhortation: he that giveth, let him do it with simplicity; he that ruleth, with diligence; he that showeth mercy, with cheerfulness.

Rom. 13, 4: For he is the minister of God to thee for good. But if thou do that which is evil, be afraid; for he beareth not the sword in vain; for he is the minister of God, a revenger to execute wrath upon him that doeth evil.

Gen. 9, 6: Whoso sheddeth man's blood, by man shall his blood be shed; for in the image of God made He man.

1 Tim. 2, 2: For kings, and for all that are in authority, that we may lead a quiet and peaceable life in all godliness and honesty.

Deut. 1, 16. 17: And I charged your judges at that time, saying, Hear the causes between your brethren, and judge righteously between every man and his brother, and the stranger that is with him. Ye shall not respect persons in judgment, but ye shall hear the small as well as the great. Ye shall not be afraid of the face of man; for the judgment is God's. And the cause that is too hard for you, bring it unto me, and I will hear it.

FIFTH COMMANDMENT.

§ 81. The Law condemns every one who neglects to have the welfare and safety of his neighbor's life and health at heart,[1] or who maliciously harms or desires to harm his own or another's life or health,[2] or is evilly disposed toward any one.[3]

1.

Is. 58, 7: Is it not to deal thy bread to the hungry, and that thou bring the poor that are cast out to thy house? when thou seest the naked, that thou cover him, and that thou hide not thyself from thine own flesh?

James 2, 15. 16: If a brother or sister be naked, and destitute of daily food, and one of you say unto them, Depart in peace, be ye warmed and filled; notwithstanding ye give them not those things which are needful to the body, what doth it profit?

Rom. 12, 20: Therefore, if thine enemy hunger, feed him; if he thirst, give him drink; for in so doing thou shalt heap coals of fire on his head.

Hebr. 13, 16: But to do good and to communicate forget not, for with such sacrifices God is well pleased.

2.

Exod. 20, 13: Thou shalt not kill. Deut. 5, 17.

Gen. 9, 6: Whoso sheddeth man's blood, by man shall his blood be shed; for in the image of God made He man.

Matt. 5, 21: Ye have heard that it was said by them of old time, Thou shalt not kill; and whosoever shall kill shall be in danger of the judgment.

Matt. 26, 51. 52: And, behold, one of them which were with Jesus stretched out his hand, and drew his sword, and struck a servant of the high priest's, and smote off his ear. Then said Jesus unto him, Put up again the sword into his place; for all they that *take* the sword shall perish with the sword.

Rom. 13, 9: Thou shalt not kill.

Matt. 15, 19: For out of the heart proceed evil thoughts, *murders,* . . .

3.

1 John 3, 15: Whosoever *hateth* his brother is a murderer; and ye know that no murderer hath eternal life abiding in him.

Matt. 5, 22: But I say unto you, That whosoever *is angry* with his brother without a cause shall be in danger of the judgment; and whosoever shall *say* to his brother, Raca, shall be in danger of the council; but whosoever shall *say,* Thou fool, shall be in danger of hell fire.

Matt. 5, 25: Agree with thine adversary quickly, whiles thou art in the way with him, lest at any time the adversary deliver thee to the judge, and the judge deliver thee to the officer, and thou be cast into prison.

Col. 3, 12. 13: Put on therefore, as the elect of God, holy and beloved, bowels of *mercies, kindness,* humbleness of mind, *meekness, longsuffering, forbearing one another,* and forgiving one another, if any man have a quarrel against any: even as Christ *forgave* you, so also *do ye.*

SIXTH COMMANDMENT.

§ 82. The Law condemns every one who carnally knows himself,[1] or a brute,[2] or another person of the same sex,[3] or a person of the other sex with whom he is not[4] or, because of a prohibited degree of consanguinity or affinity,[5] or because of an existing marriage of either party with a third person,[6] cannot be joined in lawful wedlock, or who, without a sufficient cause,[7] refuses to live with[8] or to love and honor his lawful spouse,[9] or who annuls a valid betrothal,[10] or who, by any manner of lewdness or indecency in deed,[11] word,[12] or desire,[13] defiles his body or soul. (See, also, § 92.)

1.

Rom. 1, 26. 27: For this cause God gave them up unto vile affections; for even their women did change the natural use into that which is *against nature:* and likewise also the men, . . . receiving *in themselves* that recompense of their error which was meet.

2.

Lev. 18, 23: Neither shalt thou lie with any beast to defile thyself therewith: neither shall any woman stand before a beast to lie down thereto: it is confusion. Cf. Lev. 20, 15. 16.

3.

1 Cor. 6, 9. 10: Be not deceived: neither fornicators, nor idolaters, nor adulterers, nor *effeminate,* nor *abusers of themselves with mankind,* . . . shall inherit the kingdom of God.

Lev. 18, 22: Thou shalt not lie with mankind, as with womankind: it is abomination.

Rom. 1, 27: And likewise also the *men,* leaving the natural use of the woman, burned in their lust *one toward another; men with men* working that which is unseemly.

4.

1 Cor. 6, 15. 18: Know ye not that your bodies are the members of Christ? Shall I, then, take the members of Christ, and make them the members of an *harlot?* (18) Flee fornication! Every sin that a man doeth is without the body, but he that committeth *fornication* sinneth against his own body.

Gen. 39, 9: There is none greater in this house than I; neither hath he kept back anything from me but thee, because *thou art his wife.* How, then, can I do this great wickedness, and sin against God?

5.

Lev. 18, 6 ff.: None of you shall approach to any that is near of kin to him to uncover their nakedness: I am the Lord. . . .

Lev. 20, 11 ff.: And the man that lieth with his father's wife hath uncovered his father's nakedness: both of them shall surely be put to death; their blood shall be upon them. . . .

1 Cor. 5, 1: It is reported commonly that there is fornication among you, and such fornication as is not so much as named among the Gentiles, that one should have his father's wife.

6.

Luke 18, 20: Thou knowest the commandments, Do not commit adultery, Do not kill, Do not steal, Do not bear false witness, Honor thy father and thy mother.

Matt. 19, 9: And I say unto you, Whosoever shall put away his wife, except it be for fornication, and shall *marry another,* committeth adultery; and whoso *marrieth her which is put away* doth commit adultery.

7.

Matt. 5, 32: Whosoever shall put away his wife, *saving for the cause of fornication,* causeth her to commit adultery. See also Matt. 19, 9 sub **6.**

8.

Matt. 19, 3—6: The Pharisees also came unto Him, tempting Him, and saying unto Him, Is it lawful for a man *to put away his wife for every cause?* And He answered and said unto them, Have ye not read that He which made them at the beginning made them male and female, and said, For this cause shall a man leave father and mother, and shall *cleave to his wife:* and *they twain shall be one flesh?* Wherefore they are no more twain, but one flesh. What, therefore, God hath joined together *let no man put asunder.*

Gen. 2, 24: Therefore shall a man leave his father and his mother, and shall *cleave unto his wife;* and *they shall be one flesh.*

Eph. 5, 31: For this cause shall a man leave his father and mother, and shall be joined unto his wife, and they two shall be one flesh.

1 Cor. 7, 3—5: Let the husband render unto the wife due benevolence; and likewise also the wife unto the husband. The wife hath not power of her own body, but the husband: and likewise also the husband hath not power of his own body, but the wife. Defraud ye not one the other, except it be with consent for a time, that ye may give yourselves to fasting and prayer; and come together again, that Satan tempt you not for your incontinency.

1 Cor. 7, 15: But if the *unbelieving depart,* let him depart. A brother or a sister is not under bondage in such cases. But God hath called us to peace.

9.

Eph. 5, 25. 28. 33: Husbands, *love* your wives, even as Christ also loved the Church, and gave Himself for it. (28) So ought men to *love* their wives as their own bodies. He that *loveth* his wife loveth himself. (33) Nevertheless, let every one of you in particular so *love* his wife even as himself; and the wife see that she *reverence* her husband.

1 Pet. 3, 7: Likewise, ye husbands, dwell with them *according to knowledge, giving honor* unto the wife, as unto the weaker vessel, and as being heirs together of the grace of life, that your prayers be not hindered.

Col. 3, 19: Husbands, *love* your wives, and *be not bitter* against them.

10.

Matt. 1, 18—20: Now the birth of Jesus Christ was on this wise: When as His mother Mary was *espoused* to Joseph, before they came together, she was found with child of the Holy Ghost. Then Joseph, *her husband,* being a just man, and not willing to make her a public example, was minded to put her away privily. . . . Joseph, thou son of David, fear not to take unto thee Mary, *thy wife.*

11.

Eph. 5, 12: For it is a shame even to speak of those things which are done of them in secret.

Matt. 14, 6: But when Herod's birthday was kept, the daughter of Herodias danced before them, and pleased Herod.

Eph. 5, 18: And be not drunk with wine, wherein is excess; but be filled with the Spirit.

Rom. 13, 13. 14: Let us walk honestly, as in the day; not in rioting and drunkenness, not in chambering and wantonness, not in strife and envying. But put ye on the Lord Jesus Christ, and make not provision for the flesh, to fulfill the lusts thereof.

12.

Eph. 5, 3. 4: But fornication, and all uncleanness, or covetousness, let it not be once named among you, as becometh saints; neither filthiness, nor foolish talking, nor jesting, which are not convenient, but rather giving of thanks.

6

Phil. 4, 8: Finally, brethren, whatsoever things are true, whatsoever things are honest, whatsoever things are just, whatsoever
things are pure, whatsoever things are lovely, whatsoever things are
of good report; if there be any virtue, and if there be any praise,
think on these things.

13.

Matt. 5, 28: But I say unto you, That whosoever looketh on a
woman *to lust after her* hath committed adultery with her already in
his heart.

Matt. 15, 19: For out of the *heart* proceed evil thoughts,
murders, *adulteries, fornications,* thefts, false witness, blasphemies.

Col. 3, 5. 6: Mortify therefore your members which are upon
the earth: fornication, uncleanness, *inordinate affection, evil concupiscence,* and covetousness, which is idolatry: for which things' sake
the wrath of God cometh on the children of disobedience.

SEVENTH COMMANDMENT.

§ 83. The Law condemns every one who by theft, fraud,
usury, or aleatory devices obtains, or seeks to obtain, what is,
or should be, another's property,[1] all covetousness,[2] prodi-
gality,[3] idleness,[4] and him by whose fault his neighbor suf-
fers loss or want.[5]

1.

Exod. 20, 15: Thou shalt not steal.

Lev. 19, 11: Ye shall not steal, neither deal falsely.

1 Cor. 6, 10: Nor thieves, nor covetous, . . . nor extortioners,
shall inherit the kingdom of God.

Prov. 29, 24: Whoso is partner with a thief hateth his own soul:
he heareth cursing, and bewrayeth it not.

1 Thess. 4, 6: That no man go beyond and defraud his brother
in any matter, because that the Lord is the avenger of all such, as
we also have forewarned you and testified.

Lev. 19, 35. 36: Ye shall do no unrighteousness in judgment, in
meteyard, in weight, or in measure. Just balances, just weights,
a just ephah, and a just hin, shall ye have.

Deut. 27, 17: Cursed be he that removeth his neighbor's land-
mark. And all the people shall say, Amen.

Ps. 37, 21: The wicked borroweth, and payeth not again; but
the righteous showeth mercy, and giveth.

Prov. 28, 24: Whoso robbeth his father or his mother, and saith,
It is no transgression, the same is the companion of a destroyer.

Ps. 15, 5: He that putteth not out his money to usury, nor taketh
reward against the innocent. He that doeth these things shall never
be moved.

Hab. 2, 6: Woe to him that increaseth that which is not his!
how long? and to him that ladeth himself with thick clay!

Jer. 22, 13: Woe unto him that buildeth his house by unrighteousness, and his chambers by wrong; that useth his neighbor's service without wages, and giveth him not for his work.

James 5, 4: Behold, the hire of the laborers who have reaped down your fields, which is of you kept back by fraud, crieth; and the cries of them which have reaped are entered into the ears of the Lord of Sabaoth.

Deut. 24, 14: Thou shalt not oppress an hired servant that is poor and needy, whether he be of thy brethren, or of thy strangers that are in thy land within thy gates.

2.

Luke 12, 15: And He said unto them, Take heed, and beware of covetousness!

1 Tim. 6, 9: But they that *will* be rich fall into temptation and a snare, and into many foolish and hurtful lusts, which drown men in destruction and perdition.

Rom. 1, 29: Being filled with all unrighteousness, fornication, wickedness, *covetousness,* maliciousness; full of *envy.*

Ps. 10, 3: For the wicked boasteth of his heart's desire, and blesseth the covetous, whom the Lord abhorreth.

3.

Prov. 18, 9: He also that is slothful in his work is brother to him that is a great waster.

Luke 15, 13. 18: And not many days after the younger son gathered all together, and took his journey into a far country, and there *wasted his substance with riotous living.* (18) I will arise and go to my father, and will say unto him, Father, I have *sinned* against heaven, and before thee.

4.

2 Thess. 3, 10—12: For even when we were with you, this we commanded you, that if any would not work, neither should he eat. For we hear that there are some which walk among you disorderly, working not at all, but are busybodies. Now them that are such we command and exhort by our Lord Jesus Christ, that with quietness they work, and eat their own bread.

Eph. 4, 28: Let him that stole steal no more, but rather let him labor, working with his hands the thing which is good, that he may have to give to him that needeth.

5.

Exod. 23, 4. 5: If thou meet thine enemy's ox or his ass going astray, thou shalt surely bring it back to him again. If thou see the ass of him that hateth thee lying under his burden, and wouldest forbear to help him, thou shalt surely help with him.

Matt. 5, 42: Give to him that asketh thee, and from him that would borrow of thee turn not thou away.

Lev. 19, 36: Just balances, just weights, a just ephah, and a just hin, shall ye have: I am the Lord, your God.

Hebr. 13, 16: But to do good and to communicate forget not; for with such sacrifices God is well pleased.

EIGHTH COMMANDMENT.

§ 84. The Law condemns every one who violates the truth by maliciously thinking[1] or uttering[2] what he does not know to be true or knows to be untrue, or pretending to be, to do, or to intend what in fact he is not, or does not do or intend;[3] by willfully breaking lawful promises,[4] deceitfully withholding or concealing the truth,[5] or revealing what should remain concealed;[6] by slandering a fellow-man,[7] or neglecting duly to protect or defend his good name.[8]

1.

Zech. 8, 17: And let none of you imagine evil in your hearts against his neighbor.

Matt. 9, 4: And Jesus knowing their thoughts said, Wherefore think ye evil in your hearts?

1 Cor. 13, 7: Charity beareth all things, believeth all things, hopeth all things, endureth all things.

2.

Exod. 23, 1: Thou shalt not raise a false report. Put not thine hand with the wicked to be an unrighteous witness.

Prov. 12, 22: Lying lips are abomination to the Lord; but they that deal truly are His delight.

Prov. 19, 5: A false witness shall not be unpunished, and he that speaketh lies shall not escape.

Eph. 4, 25: Wherefore putting away lying, speak every man truth with his neighbor; for we are members one of another.

3.

Prov. 29, 5: A man that flattereth his neighbor spreadeth a net for his feet.

Ps. 5, 6. 9: Thou shalt destroy them that speak leasing: the Lord will abhor the bloody and *deceitful* man. (9) For there is no faithfulness in their mouth; their inward part is very wickedness; their throat is an open sepulcher; they flatter with their tongue.

Matt. 23, 14: Woe unto you, scribes and Pharisees, *hypocrites!* for ye devour widows' houses, and for a pretense make long prayer; therefore ye shall receive the greater damnation.

Matt. 24, 51: And shall cut him asunder, and appoint him his portion with the *hypocrites:* there shall be weeping and gnashing of teeth.

Acts 5, 2. 3: And kept back part of the price, his wife also being privy to it, and brought a certain part, and laid it at the apostles' feet. But Peter said, Ananias, why hath Satan filled thine heart to lie to the Holy Ghost, and to keep back part of the price of the land?

4.

Eccl. 5, 4: Pay that which thou hast vowed.

5.

Acts 5, 2. 3. See above sub **3.**

Prov. 31, 8. 9: Open thy mouth for the dumb in the cause of all such as are appointed to destruction. Open thy mouth, judge righteously, and plead the cause of the poor and needy.

6.

Prov. 11, 13: A talebearer revealeth secrets: but he that is of a faithful spirit concealeth the matter.

Prov. 20, 19: He that goeth about as a talebearer revealeth secrets; therefore meddle not with him that flattereth with his lips.

7.

James 4, 11: Speak not evil one of another, brethren! He that speaketh evil of his brother, and judgeth his brother, speaketh evil of the law, and judgeth the law; but if thou judge the law, thou art not a doer of the law, but a judge.

Ps. 50, 19—22: Thou givest thy mouth to evil, and thy tongue frameth deceit. Thou sittest and speakest against thy brother; thou slanderest thine own mother's son. These things hast thou done, and I kept silence; thou thoughtest that I was altogether such an one as thyself: but I will reprove thee, and set them in order before thine eyes. Now, consider this, ye that forget God, lest I tear you in pieces, and there be none to deliver.

8.

Prov. 31, 8. 9. See above sub **5.**

1 Pet. 4, 8: And above all things have fervent charity among yourselves; for charity shall cover the multitude of sins.

NINTH AND TENTH COMMANDMENTS.

§ 85. The Law condemns all men even because of the evil inclinations and moral impurities of their hearts.

Exod. 20, 17: Thou shalt not *covet* thy neighbor's house. Thou shalt not covet thy neighbor's wife, nor his man-servant, nor his maid-servant, nor his ox, nor his ass, nor anything that is thy neighbor's.

Deut. 5, 21: Neither shalt thou *desire* thy neighbor's wife, neither shalt thou *covet* thy neighbor's house, his field, or his man-servant, or his maid-servant, his ox, or his ass, or anything that is thy neighbor's.

Rom. 7, 14. 18: For we know that the Law is spiritual; but I am carnal, sold under sin. (18) For I know that in me (that is, in my flesh,) dwelleth no good thing.

Rom. 8, 7: Because the *carnal mind* is enmity against God; for it is not subject to the Law of God, neither indeed can be.

Rom. 13, 9: For this, Thou shalt not commit adultery, Thou shalt not kill, Thou shalt not steal, Thou shalt not bear false witness, *Thou shalt not covet;* and if there be any other commandment, it is briefly comprehended in this saying, namely, Thou shalt love thy neighbor as thyself.

James 1, 14. 15: But every man is tempted when he is drawn away of *his own lust,* and enticed. Then, when lust hath conceived, it bringeth forth sin: and sin, when it is finished, bringeth forth death.

Is. 64, 6: But we are all as an unclean thing, and all our righteousnesses are as filthy rags.

Ps. 143, 2: And enter not into judgment with Thy servant; for in Thy sight shall no man living be justified.

Rom. 3, 23: For all have sinned, and come short of the glory of God.

Eph. 2, 3: Among whom also we all had our conversation in times past in the lusts of our flesh, fulfilling the desires of the flesh and of the mind; and were by nature the children of wrath, even as others.

Job 14, 4: Who can bring a clean thing out of an unclean? Not one.

Gen. 8, 21: For the imagination of man's heart is evil from his youth.

NATURAL LAW AND CONSCIENCE.

§ 86. The natural moral law, which is binding upon all men[1] and was originally inscribed in the human heart,[2] was by the fall of our first ancestors obscured,[3] but not entirely effaced,[4] and, being transmitted from generation to generation as an innate inheritance,[5] though in various degrees obliterated under the influence of sin,[6] is still sufficient to convince man of his sinfulness,[7] especially as the human conscience, though also impaired and more or less perverted and benumbed by sin,[8] is still active in the human heart,[9] bearing witness to the Law and its stringency,[10] to man's responsibility for his acts,[11] and to the sinner's just condemnation according to the judgment[12] of an omniscient and almighty God.[13]

1.

Rom. 3, 19: Now we know that what things soever the *Law* saith it saith to *them who are under the Law,* that *every mouth* may be stopped, and *all the world* may become *guilty before God.*

Eph. 5, 5. 6: For this ye know, that no whoremonger, nor unclean person, nor covetous man, who is an idolater, hath any inheritance in the kingdom of Christ and of God. Let no man deceive you with vain words; for because of these things cometh the wrath of God upon *the children of disobedience.*

Col. 3, 5. 6: Mortify therefore your members which are upon the earth: fornication, uncleanness, inordinate affection, evil concupiscence, and covetousness, which is idolatry: for which things' sake the wrath of God cometh upon the *children of disobedience.*

2.

Gen. 1, 27. 31: So God *created man in His own image,* in the image of God created He him; male and female created He them. (31) And God saw everything that He had made, and, behold, it was *very good.*

Rom. 2, 15: Which show the work of the Law *written in their hearts.*

3.

· Gen. 3, 12. 13: And the man said, The *woman* whom *Thou gavest* to be with me, she *gave me* of the tree, and I did eat. And the Lord God said unto the woman, What is this that thou hast done? And the woman said, The *serpent beguiled me,* and I did eat.

4.

Gen. 3, 7. 10. 11: And the eyes of them both were opened, and *they knew* that they were naked; and they sewed fig-leaves together, and made themselves aprons. (10. 11) And he said, I heard Thy voice in the garden, and *I was afraid,* because I was naked; and I hid myself. And He said, *Who told thee* that thou wast naked?

Rom. 2, 14. 15: The Gentiles, which have not the Law, do *by nature* the things contained in the Law; these, having not the Law, are a law unto themselves: which *show* the work of the Law *written in their hearts.*

5.

Gen. 4, 3. 4. 7: And in process of time it came to pass that Cain brought of the fruit of the ground an *offering unto the Lord.* And Abel, he *also brought* of the firstlings of his flock and of the fat thereof. And the Lord had respect unto Abel and to *his offering.* (7) If thou doest well, shalt thou not be accepted? And if thou doest not well, *sin* lieth at the door. And unto thee shall be his desire, and thou shalt rule over him.

Gen. 5, 3: And Adam lived an hundred and thirty years, and begat a son *in his own likeness,* after *his image;* and called his name Seth.

Rom. 2, 14. 15. See above sub **4.**

6.

Gen. 4, 9: And the Lord said unto Cain, Where is Abel, thy brother? And he said, *I know not.* Am I my brother's keeper?

Rom. 1, 21: Because that, when they knew God, they glorified Him not as God, neither were thankful, but *became vain in their imaginations,* and their *foolish heart was darkened.*

Eph. 2, 3: Among whom also we all had our conversation in times past in the lusts of our flesh, fulfilling the desires of the flesh and of the mind; and were by nature the children of wrath, even as others.

Eph. 4, 17. 18. 22: This I say therefore, and testify in the Lord, that ye henceforth walk not as other Gentiles walk, in the *vanity of their mind,* having the *understanding darkened,* being alienated from the life of God through the *ignorance* that is in them, because of the *blindness of their heart.* (22) That ye put off concerning the former conversation the old man, which is *corrupt* according to the *deceitful lusts.*

Eph. 5, 8—13: For ye were sometimes *darkness,* but now are ye light in the Lord: walk as children of light: (for the fruit of the Spirit is in all goodness and righteousness and truth;) proving what is acceptable unto the Lord. And have no fellowship with the unfruitful *works of darkness,* but rather reprove them. For it is a shame even to speak of those things which are done of them in secret. But all things that are reproved are made manifest by the light; for whatsoever doth make manifest is light.

Gal. 4, 8: Howbeit then, when ye knew not God, ye did service unto them which by nature are no gods.

7.

Rom. 3, 19. 20: Now we know that what things soever the *Law* saith it saith to them who are under the Law, that every *mouth may be stopped,* and all the world may become *guilty* before God. Therefore by the deeds of the Law there shall no flesh be justified in His sight; for *by the Law is the knowledge of sin.*

8.

John 16, 2: They shall put you out of the synagogues; yea, the time cometh, that whosoever *killeth you* will *think that he doeth God service.*

Acts 22, 3. 4: I am verily a man which am a Jew, born in Tarsus, a city in Cilicia, yet brought up in this city at the feet of Gamaliel, and taught according to the perfect manner of the Law of the fathers, and was *zealous toward God,* as ye all are this day. And *I persecuted* this way unto the death, binding and delivering into prisons both men and women.

Acts 26, 9: I verily thought with myself that I *ought to do* many things contrary to the name of Jesus of Nazareth.

Rom. 10, 2: For I bear them record that they have a *zeal of God,* but *not according to knowledge.*

9.

Rom. 2, 15: Which *show* the work of the Law written in their hearts, their *conscience also bearing witness,* and their thoughts the mean while accusing or else excusing one another.

10.

Hebr. 10, 2: For then would they not have ceased to be offered? because that the worshipers, once purged, should have had no more *conscience of sins.*

Rom. 13, 5: Wherefore ye must *needs* be subject, not only for wrath, but also *for conscience' sake.*

Rom. 2, 15. See above sub **9.**

11.

Gen. 3, 11—13: And He said, *Who told thee* that thou wast naked? Hast *thou eaten* of the tree whereof *I commanded* thee that *thou shouldest not eat?* And the man said, The *woman* whom *Thou* gavest to be with me, *she* gave me of the tree, and *I did eat.* And the Lord God said unto the woman, What is this that *thou hast done?* And the woman said, The *serpent* beguiled me, and *I did eat.*

Rom. 2, 15: Their *conscience* also bearing witness, and their thoughts the mean while *accusing* or else *excusing* one another.

12.

Gen. 4, 13. 14: And Cain said unto the Lord, *My punishment* is greater than I can bear. Behold, Thou hast driven me out this day from the face of the earth; and from Thy face shall I be hid; and *I shall be a fugitive* and a *vagabond in the earth;* and it shall come to pass that every one that findeth me shall *slay me.*

Rom. 2, 14—16: For when the Gentiles, which have not the Law, do by nature the things contained in the Law, these, having not the Law, are a *law* unto themselves: which show the work of the *Law* written in their hearts, their conscience also bearing *witness,* and their thoughts the mean while *accusing* or else *excusing* one another. In the day when God shall *judge* the secrets of men by Jesus Christ according to my Gospel.

13.

Rom. 2, 14—16. See above sub **12.**

Gen. 3, 8—10: And they heard the voice of the Lord God walking in the garden in the cool of the day. And Adam and his wife *hid themselves* from the presence of the Lord God .amongst the trees of the garden. And the Lord God called unto Adam, and said unto him, Where art thou? And he said, I heard Thy voice in the garden, and I was *afraid,* because I was naked; and I hid myself.

UNIVERSAL CONDEMNATION.

§ 87. The natural law, also the Sinaitic Decalogue,[1] as far as it concerns all mankind and is but a codification of the original moral law,[2] is condemnatory of the natural ' state and the conduct of every man,[3] notwithstanding the remnant of free will by which man in his depraved state is in a measure capable of a certain outward conformity with some of the Law's demands, *viz.,* of performing the *materiale* of some of the works prescribed, and of omitting some outward acts prohibited by the Law;[4] for the justification obtained by the application of a part only of the moral rule[5] is so far from being a real justification,[6] that it is rather but another proof of the depth of human depravity, which by the false application of a moral rule pronounces him righteous whom a proper application of that rule must utterly condemn.[7]

1.

Deut. 4, 13: And He declared unto you His covenant, which He commanded you to perform, even ten commandments; and He wrote them upon two tables of stone.

Exod. 34, 28: And He wrote upon the tables the words of the covenant, the ten commandments.

Exod. 20. Deut. 5. Matt. 5, 17—48; 22, 37—40. Rom., 13, 9.

2.

Rom. 2, 14. 15: For when the Gentiles, which have not *the Law,* do *by nature* the things contained *in the Law,* these having not *the Law,* are *a law* unto themselves: which show the work of the *Law* written *in 'their hearts.*

Rom. 5, 20: Moreover, the *Law entered,* that the offense might abound. But where sin abounded, grace did much more abound.

Rom. 7, 7: What shall we say, then? Is the Law sin? God forbid! Nay, I had not known sin but by *the Law;* for I had not known lust, except *the Law* had said, *Thou shalt not covet.*

Matt. 5, 17. 21. 22: Think not that I am come to destroy *the Law,* or the prophets: I am not come to destroy, but to fulfill. (21. 22) Ye have heard that it was said by them of old time, Thou shalt not kill; and whosoever shall kill shall be in danger of the judgment. But I say unto you, That whosoever is angry with his brother without a cause shall be in danger of the judgment; and whosoever shall say to his brother, Raca, shall be in danger of the council; but whosoever shall say, Thou fool, shall be in danger of hell fire.

Matt. 5, 27. 28: Ye have heard that it was said by them of old time, Thou shalt not commit adultery. But I say unto you, That whosoever looketh on a woman to lust after her hath committed adultery with her already in his heart.

3.

Cf. §§ 75. 76. 85.

4.

Cf. Rom. 2, 14. See above sub 2.

Luke 18, 11: The Pharisee stood and prayed thus with himself, God, I thank Thee that I am not as other men are, extortioners, unjust, adulterers, or even as this publican.

Matt. 19, 18—20: He saith unto him, Which? Jesus said, Thou shalt do no murder, Thou shalt not commit adultery, Thou shalt not steal, Thou shalt not bear false witness, Honor thy father and thy mother: and, Thou shalt love thy neighbor as thyself. The young man saith unto Him, All these things have I kept from my youth up: what lack I yet?

5.

Rom. 3, 23: For all have sinned, and come short of the glory of God.

Matt. 5, 21. 22. 27. 28. See above sub 2.

James 2, 10: For whosoever shall keep the whole Law, and yet offend in one point, he is guilty of all.

Luke 18, 11: The Pharisee stood and prayed thus with himself, *God, I thank Thee* that I am not as other men are, extortioners, unjust, adulterers, or even as this publican.

6.

1 Cor. 4, 4: For I know nothing by myself; yet am I not hereby justified: but he that judgeth me is the Lord.

7.

Luke 18, 14: I tell you, this man went down to his house justified rather than the other; for every one that exalteth himself shall be abased, and he that humbleth himself shall be exalted.

Luke 18, 11. See above sub 5.

Matt. 5, 20. 26: For I say unto you, That except your righteousness shall *exceed* the *righteousness* of the scribes and *Pharisees,* ye shall *in no case* enter into the kingdom of heaven. (26) Verily, I say unto thee, Thou shalt *by no means* come out thence, till thou hast paid the uttermost farthing.

MATERIALE OF GOOD AND EVIL ACTS.

§ 88. The performance of the *materiale* only of works prescribed by the divine Law is no more the performance of good works[1] than God can be truly said to work evil[2] as such, when, while He has no part in the *formale* of the evil acts of men, He concurs in such acts as to their *materiale,*[3] without which divine concurrence all acts of created beings would be impossible.[4]

1.

Cf. § 87.

2.

Ps. 145, 17: The Lord is *righteous* in *all* His ways, and holy in *all* His works.

Ps. 5, 5: The foolish shall not stand in Thy sight: Thou hatest *all* workers of iniquity.

James 1, 17: Every *good gift* and every *perfect gift* is from above, and cometh down from the Father of lights, with whom is *no variableness,* neither *shadow of turning.*

3.

Is. 45, 7: I form the light, and create darkness: I make peace, *and create evil:* I the Lord *do all these things.*

Amos 3, 6: Shall there be *evil* in a city, and the *Lord hath not done it?*

Lament. 3, 35—38: To turn aside the right of a man before the face of the Most High, to subvert a man in his cause, *the Lord approveth not.* Who is he that saith, and it cometh to pass, when *the Lord commandeth it not?* Out of the mouth of the Most High *proceedeth not evil* and good.

4.

Acts 17, 28: For in Him we live, and move, and have our being.

Prov. 16, 9: A man's heart deviseth his way, but *the Lord directeth his steps.*

Deut. 32, 39: See now that I, even I, am He, and there is no god with me: I kill, and I make alive; I wound, and I heal: neither is there any that can deliver out of my hand.

Job 34, 13—15: Who hath given Him a charge over the earth? or who hath disposed the whole world? If He set His heart upon man, if He gather unto Himself his spirit and his breath, all flesh shall perish together, and man shall turn again unto dust.

DIVINE GOVERNMENT OF EVIL.

§ 89. The evil acts of men are, furthermore, under divine control, inasmuch as God in His providence prevents the conception or the execution of many evil designs,[1] confines within certain bounds others, whose conception and execution He permits,[2] and directs them to such ends and determines them to such purposes as His wisdom, goodness, and justice have ordained.[3]

1.

Gen. 20, 6: And God said unto him in a dream, Yea, I know that thou didst this in the integrity of thy heart; for *I also withheld thee from sinning* against me: therefore *suffered I thee not to touch her.*

Gen. 31, 24. 29: And *God* came to Laban the Syrian in a dream by night, and said unto him, *Take heed that thou speak not* to Jacob either good or *bad!* (29) It is *in the power of my hand* to do you *hurt:* but the *God* of your father *spake unto me* yesternight, saying, *Take thou heed* that thou speak not to Jacob either good or bad.

Ps. 33, 10: The Lord bringeth the counsel of the heathen *to naught:* He *maketh* the devices of the people *of none effect.*

Is. 37, 36: Then the angel of the Lord went forth, and smote in the camp of the Assyrians a hundred and fourscore and five thousand: and when they arose early in the morning, behold, they were all dead corpses.

1 Kings 13, 4: And it came to pass, when king Jeroboam heard the saying of the man of God which had cried against the altar in Bethel, that he put forth his hand from the altar, saying, Lay hold on him! And *his hand,* which he put forth against him, *dried up,* so that he *could not pull it in* again to him.

Gen. 19, 11: And they smote the men that were at the door of the house with blindness, both small and great, so that they wearied themselves to find the door.

Exod. 14, 28: And the waters returned, and covered the chariots, and the horsemen, and all the host of Pharaoh that came into the sea after them; there remained not so much as one of them.

Numb. 22, 12: And God said unto Balaam, Thou shalt not go with them; *thou shalt not curse the people,* for they are blessed.

2.

1 Cor. 10, 13: There hath no temptation taken you but such as is common to man. But God is faithful, who *will not suffer* you to be tempted above that ye are able, but will with the temptation also *make a way to escape,* that ye may be able to bear it.

John 7, 30: Then they sought to take Him; but no man laid hands on Him, *because His hour was not yet come.*

3.

Acts 4, 27. 28: For of a truth against Thy holy Child Jesus, whom Thou hast anointed, both *Herod* and *Pontius Pilate,* with the *Gentiles* and the *people of Israel,* were gathered together, for *to do whatsoever Thy hand* and *Thy counsel determined before to be done.*

Gen. 45, 4. 5: And Joseph said unto his brethren, Come near to me, I pray you! And they came near. And he said, I am Joseph, your brother, whom *ye sold* into Egypt. Now therefore be not grieved, nor angry with yourselves, that ye sold me hither, for *God did send me* before you *to preserve life.*

Gen. 50, 20: But as for you, *ye thought evil* against me; but *God meant it unto good* to *bring to pass,* as it is this day, to *save much people alive.*

Rom. 8, 28: And we know that all things *work together for good* to them that love God, to them who are the called *according to His purpose.*

MEANS OF GOVERNMENT.

§ 90. Among the means by which God curbs the evil inclinations or propensities of men in their state of natural depravity, and directs them to His wise, good, and just purposes, we find the moral law, the divine institutions of matrimony and civil government, the laws of nature, and temporal death.

MORAL LAW A CURB OR BAR.

§ 91. The moral law serves as a curb or bar to the inclinations of men in two ways: first, inasmuch as it is a norm for the various functions of the human conscience,[1] and secondly, as the *materiale* of a part of its precepts forms the basis of, and enters into, civil legislation.[2]

1.

Cf. § 86.

2.

Deut. 17—27. (Chapters containing the Law.) Also the codes of all nations.

MATRIMONY.

§ 92. The divine institution of matrimony, which is the status of union for life[1] of one man and one woman,[2] established and sustained by their mutual consent,[3] for legitimate sexual intercourse,[4] the procreation of children,[5] and mutual aid and assistance,[6] serves as a curb not only to the licentiousness of sexual desires,[7] but also to various other depraved inclinations by affording incentives to habits of industry and economy, sobriety, stability, and good fellowship among men.[8]

1.

Rom. 7, 2: For the woman which hath an husband *is bound* by the law to her husband *so long as he liveth;* but if the husband be *dead,* she is *loosed* from the law of her husband.

1 Cor. 7, 39: The wife is *bound* by the law *as long as her husband liveth;* but if her husband be *dead,* she is *at liberty* to be married to whom she will; only in the Lord.

Gen. 2, 24: Therefore shall a man leave his father and his mother, and shall *cleave* unto his wife; and they shall be one flesh.

Matt. 19, 6: Wherefore they are no more twain, but one flesh. What therefore God hath joined together *let not man put asunder.*

2.

Gen. 2, 24: Therefore shall *a man* leave his father and his mother, and shall cleave unto *his wife;* and *they* shall be one flesh.

Matt. 19, 4—6: And He answered and said unto them, Have ye not read that He which made them at the beginning made them male and female, and said, For this cause shall *a man* leave father and mother, and shall cleave to *his wife;* and they *twain* shall be one flesh? Wherefore they are no more *twain,* but one flesh.

Rom. 7, 2: For the *woman* which hath *an husband* is bound by the law *to her husband* so long as *he* liveth; but if *the husband* be dead, *she* is loosed from the law of *her husband.*

1 Cor. 7, 39: *The wife* is bound by the law as long as *her husband* liveth; but if *her husband* be dead, *she* is at liberty to be married to whom she will; only in the Lord.

3.

Gen. 2, 22—24: And the rib, which the Lord God had taken from man, made He a woman, and *brought her unto the man.* And *Adam* said, *This is now bone of my bones, and flesh of my flesh:* she shall be called Woman, because she was taken out of Man. Therefore shall a man leave his father and his mother, and *shall cleave unto his wife;* and they shall be one flesh.

Gen. 24, 58: And they called Rebekah, and said unto her, Wilt thou go with this man? And she said, I will go.

1 Cor. 7, 12. 13: If any brother hath a wife that believeth not, and she *be pleased to dwell with him,* let him not put her away. And the woman which hath an husband that believeth not, and if he *be pleased to dwell with her,* let her not leave him.

1 Cor. 7, 5: Defraud ye not one the other, except it be with consent for a time.

4.

Gen. 2, 24: Therefore shall a man leave his father and his mother, and shall cleave unto his wife; and *they shall be one flesh.*

Matt. 19, 5. 6: And they twain *shall be one flesh.* Wherefore they are no more twain, but *one flesh.*

Eph. 5, 31: For this cause shall a man leave his father and mother, and shall be joined unto his wife, and they two shall be one flesh.

5.

Gen. 1, 28: God *blessed* them, and God said unto them, *Be fruitful, and multiply,* and replenish the earth, and subdue it.

6.

Gen. 2, 18. 20: And the Lord God said, It is not good that the man should be alone; I will make him an *help* meet for him. (20) But for Adam there was not found an *help* meet for him.

Eph. 5, 28. 29: So ought men to love their wives *as their own bodies.* He that loveth his wife loveth himself. For no man ever

yet hated his own flesh, but *nourisheth* and cherisheth it, even as
the Lord the Church.

Eph. 5, 33: Let every one of you in particular so love his wife
even as himself; and the wife see that she reverence her husband.

7.

1 Cor. 7, 2—5: Nevertheless, to avoid fornication, let every man
have his own wife, and let every woman have her own husband. Let
the husband render unto the wife due benevolence, and likewise also
the wife unto the husband. The wife hath not power of her own body,
but the husband; and likewise also the husband hath not power of
his own body, but the wife. Defraud ye not one the other, except it
be with consent for a time, that ye may give yourselves to fasting
and prayer; and come together again, that Satan tempt you not for
your incontinency.

8.

1 Tim. 5, 8: But if any *provide* not for his own, and specially
for those *of his own house,* he hath denied the faith, and is worse
than an infidel.

Ps. 127, 4. 5: As arrows are in the hand of a mighty man, so
are children of the youth. Happy is the man that hath his quiver
full of them: they shall not be ashamed, but they shall speak with
the enemies in the gate.

Ps. 128, 2. 3: For thou shalt *eat the labor of thine hands.* Happy
shalt thou be, and *it shall be well* with thee. Thy *wife* shall be as a
fruitful vine by the sides of thine house; thy *children* like *olive
plants* round about thy table.

CIVIL GOVERNMENT.

§ 93. The divine institution of civil government[1] serves
as a bar to the evil propensities of men, forasmuch as civil
governments are endowed with legislative, judicial, and ex-
ecutive authority to enact, maintain, administer, and execute
civil laws for the protection[2] of the life, health, honor, property, civil status, lawful pursuits, and other legitimate in-
terests of individuals, the existence, possessions, peace, order,
and other civil rights of lawful societies and communities,
and the peace, prosperity, and security of municipalities and
states.

1.

Prov. 8, 15: *By me* kings reign, and princes decree justice.

Dan. 2, 21: And He changeth the times and the seasons; He
removeth kings, and *setteth up kings;* He giveth wisdom unto the
wise, and knowledge to them that know understanding.

Rom. 13, 1: Let every soul be subject unto the higher powers. For there is *no power but of God;* the *powers that be* are *ordained of God.*

John 19, 11: Jesus answered, Thou couldest have no power at all against me, except *it were given thee* from above; therefore he that delivered me unto thee hath the greater sin.

1 Pet. 2, 13. 14: Submit yourselves to every ordinance of man *for the Lord's sake:* whether it be to the king, as supreme; or unto governors, as unto them that are sent by him.

Rom. 13, 4: For he is the *minister of God* to thee for good. But if thou do that which is evil, be afraid; for he beareth not the sword in vain: for *he is the minister of God,* a revenger to execute wrath upon him that doeth evil.

2.

1 Tim. 2, 2: That we may lead a quiet and peaceable life in all godliness and honesty.

Rom. 13, 3. 4. 6: For rulers are not a terror to good works, but to the evil. Wilt thou, then, not be afraid of the power? Do that which is good, and thou shalt have praise of the same; for he is the minister of God to thee for good. But if thou do that which is evil, be afraid; for he beareth not the sword in vain: for he is the minister of God, a revenger to execute wrath upon him that doeth evil. (6) For for this cause pay ye tribute also; for they are God's ministers, attending continually upon this very thing.

Matt. 22, 21: Render unto Caesar the things which are Caesar's, and unto God the things that are God's.

LAWS OF NATURE.

§ 94. The laws of nature are under divine providence a curb and bar to the perverse will of man or to the execution of his evil purposes, forasmuch as man, though he may in a measure govern or modify natural objects or control natural forces, can never change or control the laws of nature,[1] but can make nature subservient to his purposes only in accordance to the physical laws laid down by the Creator.[2]

1.

Job 38. Gen. 1 and 2.

2.

Ps. 104, 24: O Lord, how manifold are Thy works! In wisdom hast Thou made them all: the earth is full of Thy riches.

Matt. 5, 36: Neither shalt thou swear by thy head, because thou canst not make one hair white or black.

Job 34, 13—15: Who hath given Him a charge over the earth? or who hath disposed the whole world? If He set His heart upon man, if He gather unto Himself his spirit and his breath, all flesh shall perish together, and man shall turn again unto dust.

TEMPORAL DEATH.

§ 95. Temporal death, the termination of temporal life by the separation of body and soul,[1] though not a law of nature,[2] is, in consequence of sin,[3] in the course of nature since the fall of man,[4] and, coming on either by the dispensing providence of God at the moment fixed by His decree,[5] or under His permissive providence at a period determined by, or consequent to, the acts of men,[6] terminates the evil activity on earth of those whose temporal life it brings to its close.

1.

Luke 12, 20: But God said unto him, Thou fool, this night *thy soul shall be required of thee.*

2 Tim. 4, 6: For I am now ready to be offered, and the time of *my departure* is at hand.

Phil. 1, 23: For I am in a strait betwixt two, having a desire *to depart,* and to be with Christ, which is far better.

2 Cor. 5, 1. 4. 8: For we know that if our earthly house of *this tabernacle were dissolved,* we have a building of God, an house not made with hands, eternal in the heavens. (4) For we that are in this tabernacle do groan, being burdened: not for that we would be *unclothed,* but clothed upon, that mortality might be swallowed up of life. (8) We are confident, I say, and willing rather to be *absent from the body,* and to be present with the Lord.

2.

Rom. 5, 12: Wherefore, as by one man sin entered into the world, *and death by sin;* and so death passed upon all men, for that all have sinned.

3.

Gen. 2, 17: For in the day that thou eatest thereof thou shalt surely die.

4.

Eccl. 12, 7: Then shall the dust return to the earth as it was; and the spirit shall return unto God who gave it.

2 Sam. 14, 14: For *we must needs die,* and are as water spilt on the ground, which cannot be gathered up again; neither doth God respect any person.

Ps. 90, 10: The days of our years are threescore years and ten; and if by reason of strength they be fourscore years, yet is their strength labor and sorrow; for it is soon cut off, and we fly away.

5.

Luke 2, 26: And it was revealed unto him by the Holy Ghost that he *should not see death before* he had seen the Lord's Christ.

Numb. 20, 25. 26: Take Aaron and Eleazar, his son, and bring them up unto Mount Hor; and strip Aaron of his garments, and put them upon Eleazar, his son: and Aaron shall be gathered unto his people, and shall die there.

Deut. 32, 48—50: And the Lord spake unto Moses that selfsame day, saying, Get thee up into this mountain Abarim, unto Mount Nebo, which is in the land of Moab, that is over against Jericho, and behold the land of Canaan which I give unto the children of Israel for a possession, and die in the mount whither thou goest up, and be gathered unto thy people, as Aaron, thy brother, died in Mount Hor, and was gathered unto his people.

6.

1 Sam. 31, 4—6: Then said Saul unto his armor-bearer, Draw thy sword, and thrust me through therewith, lest these uncircumcised come and thrust me through, and abuse me. But his armor-bearer would not; for he was sore afraid. Therefore Saul took a sword, and fell upon it. And when his armor-bearer saw that Saul was dead, he fell likewise upon his sword, and died with him. So Saul died, and his three sons, and his armor-bearer, and all his men, that same day together.

Matt. 27, 5: And he cast down the pieces of silver in the temple, and departed, and went and hanged himself.

2 Sam. 17, 23: And when Ahithophel saw that his counsel was not followed, he saddled his ass, and arose, and gat him home to his house, to his city, and put his household in order, and hanged himself, and died, and was buried in the sepulcher of his father.

See also ESCHATOLOGY.

CHRISTOLOGY.

DEFINITION.

§ 96. Christology is the doctrine of Holy Scripture concerning the Person and the Office and Work of Christ, the Redeemer and Savior of mankind.

The Person of Christ.

NATURES OF CHRIST.

§ 97. Jesus Christ is the Son of God, very God, begotten of the Father from eternity,[1] and also true man,[2] conceived by the Holy Ghost[3] and born of the Virgin Mary,[4] in the fullness of time.

1 a.

Jer. 23, 6: And this is His name whereby He shall be called, *The Lord, Our Righteousness.*

Luke 2, 11: Unto you is born this day in the city of David a Savior, which is Christ *the Lord.*

John 20, 28: And Thomas answered and said unto Him, *My Lord and my God!*

Rom. 9, 5: Whose are the fathers, and of whom as concerning the flesh Christ came, who is *over all, God* blessed forever. Amen.

1 John 5, 20: This (Jesus Christ) is the *true God* and eternal life.

John 14, 9: Jesus saith unto him, Have I been so long time with you, and yet hast thou not known me, Philip? He that hath seen *me* hath seen *the Father.*

b.

Rom. 8, 32: God spared not *His own Son.*

John 1, 18: No man hath seen God at any time; the *only-begotten Son,* which is in the bosom of the Father, He hath declared Him.

Hebr. 1, 5: For unto which of the angels said He at any time, Thou art *my Son,* this day *have I begotten Thee?* And again, I will be to Him a Father, and He shall be to me *a Son?*

John 3, 16: For God so loved the world, that He gave *His only-begotten Son.*

c.

Prov. 8, 22. 23: The Lord possessed me in the beginning of His way, before His works of old. I was set up *from everlasting,* from the beginning, or ever the earth was.

Is. 9, 6: For unto us a Child is born, unto us a Son is given: and the government shall be upon His shoulder; and His name shall be called Wonderful, Counselor, The Mighty God, *The Everlasting Father,* The Prince of Peace.

John 1, 1. 2: *In the beginning* was the Word, and the Word was with God, and the Word was God. The same *was in the beginning* with God.

Hebr. 13, 8: Jesus Christ the same yesterday, and to-day, and forever.

John 8, 58: Before Abraham *was,* I *am.*

Ps. 102, 26. 27: They shall perish, but *Thou shalt endure;* yea, all of them shall wax old like a garment; as a vesture shalt Thou change them, and they shall be changed. But *Thou art the same,* and Thy years shall have *no end.*

Hebr. 1, 10—12: And, Thou, Lord, in the beginning hast laid the foundation of the earth; and the heavens are the works of Thine hands. They shall perish, *but Thou remainest;* and they all shall wax old as doth a garment, and as a vesture shalt Thou fold them up, and they shall be changed; but *Thou art the same,* and *Thy years shall not fail.*

d.

Matt. 18, 20: *Where* two or three are gathered together in my name, *there am I* in the midst of them.

Matt. 28, 20: And, lo, *I am with you alway,* even unto the end of the world.

e.

Matt. 28, 18: *All power* is given unto me in heaven and in earth.

f.

John 2, 25: For He *knew* what was in man.

John 21, 17: (Simon said,) Lord, Thou *knowest* all things.

Col. 2, 3: In whom are hid *all the treasures of wisdom and knowledge.*

g.

John 1, 3: *All things were made by Him;* and without Him was not anything made that was made.

Col. 1, 16: For by Him were *all things created,* that are in heaven, and that are in earth, visible and invisible, whether they be thrones, or dominions, or principalities, or powers: *all things were created by Him* and for Him.

Hebr. 1, 1—3: God, who at sundry times and in divers manners spake in time past unto the fathers by the prophets, hath in these last days spoken unto us by His Son, whom He hath appointed heir of all things, *by whom also He made the worlds;* who, being the brightness of His glory, and the express image of His person, and *upholding all things* by the word of *His power,* etc.

h.

Luke 7, 14: Young man, *I* say unto thee, Arise!

i.

Luke 18, 31—33. (Foretelling future events.)

Matt. 21, 2. 3: Go into the village over against you, and straight-way ye shall find an ass tied, and a colt with her, etc.

k.

Matt. 9, 2. 6: And, behold, they brought to Him a man sick of the palsy, lying on a bed. And Jesus, seeing their faith, said unto the sick of the palsy, Son, be of good cheer; *thy sins be forgiven thee.* (6) But that ye may know that the *Son of Man hath power on earth to forgive sins,* (then said He to the sick of the palsy,) Arise, take up thy bed, and go unto thine house.

l.

Hebr. 1, 6: And again, when He bringeth in the First-Begotten into the world, He saith, And let all the angels of God *worship Him!*

John 5, 23: That all men should *honor the Son, even as they honor the Father.* He that *honoreth* not the *Son* honoreth not the Father which hath sent Him.

Phil. 2, 10: That at the name of Jesus every knee should bow, of things in heaven, and things in earth, and things under the earth.

1 Cor. 1, 2: Call upon the name of Jesus Christ, our Lord.

2 a.

1 Tim. 2, 5. 6: For there is one God, and one Mediator between God and men, the MAN *Christ Jesus,* who gave Himself a ransom for all, to be testified in due time.

Luke 23, 47: Now when the centurion saw what was done, he glorified God, saying, Certainly this was a righteous *man.*

b.

Matt. 1, 1—17. (Genealogy of Christ from Abraham to Joseph.)

Luke 1 and 2. (Christ's conception and birth.)

Rom. 9, 5: Of whom as *concerning the flesh Christ came,* who is over all, God blessed forever. Amen.

Gal. 4, 4: But when the fullness of the time was come, God sent forth His Son, *made of a woman,* made under the Law.

Hebr. 2, 14: Forasmuch as the children are partakers of *flesh and blood,* He also *Himself likewise took part of the same.*

Luke 21, 27: And then shall they see the *Son of Man* coming in a cloud with power and great glory.

c.

Matt. 26, 38: My *soul* is exceeding sorrowful, even unto death.

John 10, 15: As the Father knoweth me, even so know I the Father: and I lay down *my life* for the sheep.

Luke 10, 21: In that hour Jesus rejoiced in *spirit.*

Luke 23, 46: Father, in Thy hands I commend *my spirit:* and having said thus, He gave up *the ghost.*

Matt. 26, 12. 26: For in that she hath poured this ointment on *my body,* she did it for my burial. (26) And as they were eating, Jesus took bread, and blessed it, and brake it, and gave it to the disciples, and said, Take, eat; this is my body.

Luke 24, 39: Behold my hands and my feet, that it is I myself, etc.

John 19, 33—36. (Christ's death on the cross.)

d.

Hebr. 2, 14. 18: Forasmuch as the children are partakers of flesh and blood, He also Himself likewise took part of the same. (18) For in that He Himself *hath suffered, being tempted,* He is able to succor them that are tempted.

Luke 24, 43: And He took it, and *did eat* before them.

Luke 22, 18: For I say unto you, I will not *drink* of the fruit of the vine, until the kingdom of God shall come.

Acts 10, 41: Who did *eat and drink* with Him after He rose from the dead.

Matt. 4. 2: And when He had *fasted* forty days and forty nights, He was afterward an *hungred.*

Matt. 4, 11. 12: Then the devil leaveth Him, and, behold, angels came and ministered unto Him. Now when Jesus had heard that John was cast into prison, *He departed into Galilee.*

John 19, 28: After this, Jesus, knowing that all things were now accomplished, that the Scripture might be fulfilled, saith, *I thirst.*

John 4, 6: Now Jacob's well was there. Jesus therefore, *being wearied* with His journey, sat thus on the well.

John 19, 34. 37: But one of the soldiers with a spear pierced *His side,* and forthwith came there out *blood and water.* (37) And again another scripture saith, They shall look on Him *whom they pierced.*

3.

Matt. 1, 18. 20: Now the *birth* of Jesus Christ was on this wise: When as *His mother Mary* was espoused to Joseph, before they came together, she was *found with child of the Holy Ghost.* (20) For that which is *conceived* in her is *of the Holy Ghost.*

Luke 1, 35: And the angel answered and said unto her, The Holy Ghost shall come upon thee, and the power of the Highest shall overshadow thee: therefore also that holy thing which *shall be born of thee* shall be called the Son of God.

4.

Luke 2, 7: And she *brought forth her firstborn son,* and wrapped Him in swaddling clothes, and laid Him in a manger, because there was no room for them in the inn.

Matt. 1, 25: And knew her not till she had *brought forth her firstborn son:* and he called His name Jesus.

Gal. 4, 4: But when the fullness of the time was come, God sent forth His Son, *made of a woman,* made under the Law.

PERSONAL UNION.

§ 98. The divine nature and the human nature of Christ were, from the moment of His conception,[1] and are forever,[2] inseparably united in one complete theanthropic person.[3]

1.

John 1, 14: And the *Word* was made *flesh*, and dwelt among us, and we beheld *His glory*, the glory as of the *Only-Begotten of the Father*, full of grace and truth.

Luke 1, 43: And whence is this to me, that the *mother* of my *Lord* should come to me?

Hebr. 2, 14: Forasmuch as the children are partakers of flesh and blood, He also Himself likewise took part of the same.

2.

1 Pet. 3, 22: Who is gone into heaven, and is on the right hand of God, angels and authorities and powers being made subject unto Him.

3.

Matt. 16, 13. 16: When Jesus came into the coasts of Caesarea Philippi, He asked His disciples, saying, Whom do men say that I, the *Son of Man,* am? (16) And Simon Peter answered and said, *Thou art the Christ, the Son of the living God.*

Rom. 1, 3. 4: Concerning *His Son* Jesus Christ, *our Lord,* which was *made of the seed of David* according to the *flesh;* and declared to be the *Son of God* with power, according to the spirit of holiness, by the resurrection from the dead.

Rom. 9, 5: Of whom *as concerning the flesh* Christ came, who is *over all, God* blessed forever. Amen.

1 John 5, 20: And we know that the *Son of God* is *come,* and hath given us an understanding, that we may know Him that is true, and we are in Him that is true, even in His Son *Jesus Christ. This* is the *true God,* and eternal life.

DUALITY OF NATURES.

§ 99. Of the two natures personally united in Christ, the one, the divine nature, is and ever was truly and essentially divine,[1] and the other, the human nature, is and from its conception was essentially human,[2] consisting of a human body[3] and a human rational soul,[4] with its own human intelligence and will,[5] there being in the one person a union and not a mixture of natures.[6]

1.

John 1, 1: *In the beginning was the Word . . .* and the Word was *God.*

John 17, 5: And now, O Father, glorify Thou me with Thine own self with the *glory which I had* with Thee *before the world was.*

John 8, 58: Jesus said unto them, Verily, verily, I say unto you, Before Abraham was, *I am.*

2.

1 Tim. 2, 5: There is one God, and one Mediator . . . *the man* Christ Jesus.

Luke 9, 56: For the *Son of Man* is not come to destroy men's lives, but to save them.

Rom. 9, 5: Of whom as *concerning the flesh* Christ came.

3.

Luke 24, 39: Behold my *hands* and my *feet,* etc.

Matt. 26, 12: For in that she hath poured this ointment on *my body,* she did it for my burial.

John 2, 21: But He spake of the temple of *His body.*

Matt. 21, 18: As He returned into the city, He *hungered.*

4.

Matt. 26, 38: My *soul* is exceeding sorrowful, even unto death.

Luke 23, 46: Father, into Thy hands I commend *my spirit:* and having said thus, He gave up *the ghost.*

5.

Luke 2, 52: And Jesus *increased* in *wisdom* and stature, and in favor with God and man.

Luke 22, 42: Father, if Thou be willing, remove this cup from me: nevertheless not *my will,* but *Thine,* be done.

6.

Matt. 16, 13. 16: Whom do men say that I, the *Son of Man,* am? (16) And Simon Peter answered and said, *Thou* art the Christ, the *Son of the living God.*

UNITY OF PERSON.

§ 100. Though two complete and distinct natures are united in Christ,[1] there is in Him no union of two persons,[2] since His human nature at no time subsisted by itself,[3] but only in personal union, not with the Father,[4] nor with the Holy Ghost,[5] but with God the Son, the second Person in the Trinity.[6]

1.

Cf. § 99.

2.

Luke 1, 35: The Holy Ghost shall come upon thee, and the power of the Highest shall overshadow thee: therefore also *that holy thing* which shall be *born of thee* shall be called the *Son of God.*

1 Tim. 2, 5: There is one God, and *one Mediator* . . . the man Christ Jesus.

3.

John 1, 14: And the Word *was made* flesh.

Luke 1, 35. See above sub **2.**

4.

John 17, 5: And now, *O Father,* glorify Thou *me* with *Thine own self* with the glory which I had *with Thee* before the world was.

1 John 1, 7: But if we walk in the light, as He is in the light, we have fellowship one with another, and the blood of *Jesus Christ, His Son,* cleanseth us from all sin.

John 5, 21. 27: As the *Father* raiseth up the dead, and quickeneth them, even so the *Son* quickeneth whom He will. (27) And hath given Him authority to execute judgment also, because He is the *Son of Man.*

5.

Matt. 12, 28: But if *I* cast out devils *by* the *Spirit of God.* . . .

John 15, 26: But when the Comforter is come, whom *I* will send unto you *from the Father,* even *the Spirit of truth,* which proceedeth *from the Father,* He shall testify *of me.*

6.

Texts sub **4** and **5.**

COMMUNION OF NATURES.

§ 101. Though the two natures personally united in Christ are and remain essentially distinct,[1] each retaining its own essential properties or attributes, its own intelligence and will, so that His divinity is not His humanity nor a part of the same, nor His humanity His divinity: yet there is in Christ a *communion* of natures, so that the divine nature is the nature of the Son of Man,[2] and the human nature the nature of the Son of God,[3] the *concretum* of the one being predicable of the *concretum* of the other,[4] and the one being where the other is.[5]

1.

Cf. §§ 99. 100.

2.

Jer. 23, 5. 6: Behold, the days come, saith the Lord, that I will raise unto *David* a righteous *Branch,* and a King shall reign and prosper, and shall execute judgment and justice in the earth. In His days Judah shall be saved, and Israel shall dwell safely: and this is HIS *name* whereby HE *shall be called,* The LORD, Our Righteousness.

Col. 2, 9: For in *Him* dwelleth *all* the *fullness* of the *Godhead* bodily.

3.

Hebr. 2, 14: Forasmuch, then, as the children are partakers of *flesh and blood,* HE also Himself likewise *took part of the same,* that through death He might destroy him that had the power of death, that is, the devil.

John 1, 14: And the *Word* was *made flesh,* and dwelt among us, and we beheld *His glory,* the glory as *of the Only-Begotten of the Father,* full of grace and truth.

Gal. 4, 4: God sent forth His Son, made of a woman.

Rom. 1, 3: Concerning *His Son* Jesus Christ, our Lord, which was *made of the seed of David* according to *the flesh.*

4.

Matt. 16, 13. 16: Whom do men say that *I, the Son of Man,* am? (16) And Simon Peter answered and said, *Thou art* the Christ, *the Son of the living God.*

Jer. 23, 5. 6. See above sub 2.

1 Cor. 15, 47: The first man is of the earth, earthy; the *second man is the Lord from heaven.*

5.

Col. 2, 9: For in Him dwelleth *all the fullness of the Godhead bodily.*

Luke 2, 11: For unto you is *born* this day *in the city of David* a Savior, which is Christ *the Lord.*

COMMUNICATION OF ATTRIBUTES.

§ 102. Though in the person of Christ each nature retains its essential attributes,[1] yet each nature also communicates its attributes to the other in the personal union, so that the divine nature participates in attributes of the human nature,[2] and the human nature in those of the divine nature.[3]

1.

Cf. § 99.

1 Pet. 3, 18: For *Christ* also hath once *suffered* for sins, the Just for the unjust, that He might bring us to God, being *put to death in the flesh,* but quickened by the Spirit.

1 Pet. 4, 1: Forasmuch, then, as Christ hath *suffered* for us *in the flesh,* arm yourselves likewise with the same mind.

Rom. 1, 3: Concerning His Son Jesus Christ, *our Lord,* which was *made of the seed of David* according to *the flesh.*

2.

Rom. 9, 5: Of whom as concerning the flesh Christ came.

Acts 20, 28: To feed the Church of *God,* which He hath purchased with *His own blood.*

· 1 Cor. 2, 8: Which none of the princes of this world knew; for had they known it, they would not have *crucified* the *Lord of glory.*

Acts 3, 15: And *killed* the *Prince of Life,* whom God hath *raised* from the dead, whereof we are witnesses.

Gal. 2, 20: I am crucified with Christ: nevertheless I live; yet not I, but Christ liveth in me: and the life which I now live in the flesh I live by the faith of the *Son of God,* who loved me, and *gave Himself* for me.

1 John 1, 7: And the *blood* of Jesus Christ, *His Son,* cleanseth· us from all sin.

3.

Matt. 28, 18: *All power* is *given unto me* in heaven and in earth.

John 1, 14: And the *Word* was made *flesh,* and *dwelt* among us, and we beheld *His glory,* the *glory as of the Only-Begotten* of the Father, full of grace and truth.

GENUS IDIOMATICUM.

§ 103. Thus attributes of. either nature are ascribed to the entire person of Christ,[1] divine attributes are predicated of the *concretum* of His human nature,[2] and human attributes are ascribed to the *concretum* of His divine nature.[3] — *Genus idiomaticum.*

1.

John 21, 17: Lord, Thou *knowest all things.*

Hebr. 13, 8: *Jesus Christ* the same *yesterday, and to-day, and forever.*

Matt. 1, 23: Behold, a virgin shall be with child, and shall *bring forth a son,* and they shall call *His* name Emmanuel, which being interpreted is, *God* with us.

Luke 2, 4—11. (Narrative of the nativity.)

Rom. 9, 5: Of whom as concerning the FLESH *Christ* came, who is over all, GOD *blessed forever.* Amen.

2.

John 3, 13: And no man hath ascended up to heaven, but He that *came down from heaven,* even the *Son of Man* which *is in heaven.*

Matt. 9, 6: But that ye may know that the *Son of Man hath power* on earth *to forgive sins,* (then saith He to the sick of the palsy,) Arise, take up thy bed, and go unto thine house.

Jer. 23, 5. 6: Behold, the days come, saith the Lord, that I will raise *unto David a righteous Branch,* and a King shall reign and prosper, and shall execute judgment and justice in the earth. In His days Judah shall be saved, and Israel shall dwell safely: and this is *His* name whereby *He* shall be *called, The Lord,* Our Righteousness.

Jer. 33, 16: In those days shall Judah be saved, and Jerusalem

shall dwell safely: and this is the name whereby He shall be called,
The Lord, Our Righteousness.

Matt. 22, 42. 43: What think ye of Christ? Whose son is He?
They say unto Him, *The son of David.* He saith unto them, How,
then, doth David in spirit *call Him Lord?*

John 6, 62: What and if ye shall see the *Son of Man* ascend up
where He was before?

3.

Rom. 8, 32: He that spared not *His own Son,* but *delivered Him
up* for us all, how shall He not with Him also freely give us all things?

Gal. 4, 4: God sent forth *His Son, made of a woman,* made *under
the Law.*

Col. 1, 13. 14: Who hath delivered us from the power of darkness,
and hath translated us into the kingdom of *His dear Son:* in whom
we have redemption through *His blood,* even the forgiveness of sins.

John 1, 14: The *Word* was *made flesh,* and *dwelt among us,* and
we beheld His glory, the glory as of *the Only-Begotten of the Father,*
full of grace and truth.

Rom. 1, 3: Concerning *His Son* Jesus Christ, our Lord, which
was *made of the seed of David* according to the *flesh.*

1 Cor. 2, 8: Had they known it, they would not have *crucified
the Lord of glory.*

Acts 3, 15: And *killed* the *Prince of Life,* whom God hath *raised
from the dead.*

GENUS MAJESTATICUM.

§ 104. Again, though the human nature in the person
of Christ remains truly human, yet all the divine properties and perfections and the honor and glory thereto pertaining[1] are as truly communicated to His human nature,
so that the perfections which the divine nature has as essential attributes, the human nature has as communicated
attributes, such as omnipresence,[2] omniscience,[3] omnipotence.[4]
— *Genus auchematicum sive majestaticum.*

1.

Cf. § 26, 8.

2.

Matt. 18, 20: Where two or three are gathered together in my
name, *there am I* in the midst of them.

Matt. 28, 20: Lo, I am with you alway, even unto the end of the
world.

Eph. 1, 23: Which is His body, the fullness of Him *that filleth
all in all.*

John 3, 13: And no man hath ascended up to heaven but He that
came down from heaven, even the *Son of Man* which *is in heaven.*

3.

·John 21, 17: And he said unto Him, Lord, *Thou knowest all things;* Thou knowest that I love Thee.

John 2, 24. 25: But Jesus did not commit Himself unto them, because *He knew all men,* and needed not that any should testify of man; for *He knew what was in man.*

Col. 2, 3: In whom are hid *all the treasures of wisdom and knowledge.*

4.

John 17, 2: As Thou hast given Him *power over all flesh,* that *He should give eternal life* to as many as Thou hast given Him.

Phil. 3, 21: *Who shall change our vile body,* that it may be fashioned like unto His glorious body, according to the working whereby *He is able even to subdue all things unto Himself.*

Matt. 28, 18: *All power* is *given unto me* in heaven and in earth.

GENUS APOTELESMATICUM.

§ 105. The personal union of the two natures in Christ, the assumption of the human nature by the divine nature in one person, has taken place for the purpose of the salvation of mankind,[1] and in the execution of the works pertaining to His threefold office the entire person has performed and performs what either nature has performed or performs,[2] both natures concurring in such works,[3] each performing in communion with the other that which is proper to itself.[4] — *Genus apotelesmaticum.*

1.

John 3, 16: God so loved the world that He *gave His only-begotten Son,* that whosoever believeth in Him *should not perish,* but *have everlasting life.*

Gal. 4, 4. 5: But when the fullness of the time was come, God *sent forth His Son, made of a woman, made under the Law, to redeem them* that were under the Law, *that we might receive the adoption of sons.*

1 John 3, 8: *For this purpose* the Son of God was manifested, *that He might destroy the works of the devil.*

1 John 4, 10: Herein is love, not that we loved God, but that He loved us, *and sent His Son to be the propitiation for our sins.*

2.

1 Cor. 15, 3: For I delivered unto you first of all that which I also received, how that *Christ died* for our sins according to the Scriptures.

Gal. 1, 4: *Who gave Himself for our sins,* that He might deliver us from this present evil world, according to the will of God and our Father.

.Eph. 5, 2: And walk in love, as *Christ* also hath loved us, *and hath given Himself for us* an offering and a sacrifice to God for a sweet-smelling savor.

3.

1 John 1, 7: The *blood* of *Jesus Christ, His Son,* cleanseth us from all sin.

Acts 20, 28: To feed the Church of *God,* which *He* hath *purchased with His own blood.*

Gen. 3, 15: And I will put enmity between thee and the woman, and between thy seed and *her Seed; it* shall bruise thy head, and *thou shalt bruise His heel.*

Gen. 22, 18: And in thy seed shall all the nations of the earth be blessed.

1 Tim. 2, 5. 6: There is one God, and *one Mediator* between God and men, *the man Christ Jesus, who gave Himself* a ransom for all, to be testified in due time.

Hebr. 2, 14. 15: Forasmuch, then, as the children are partakers of flesh and blood, *He* also Himself likewise took part of the same, that *through death He might destroy* him that had the power of death, that is, the devil, and deliver them who through fear of death were all their lifetime subject to bondage.

Rom. 5, 10. 11: For if, when we were enemies, we were reconciled to God by *the death of His Son,* much more, being reconciled, we shall be *saved by His life.* And not only so, but we also joy in God through *our Lord Jesus Christ,* by whom we have now received *the atonement.*

Gal. 4, 4. 5: But when the fullness of the time was come, God sent forth *His Son, made of a woman, made under the Law,* to redeem them that were under the Law, that we might receive the adoption of sons.

1 John 3, 8: For this purpose the *Son of God* was manifested, that *He might destroy* the works of the devil.

Luke 2, 30—32: For mine eyes have seen Thy salvation, which Thou hast prepared before the face of all people: a light to lighten the Gentiles, and the glory of Thy people Israel.

Rom. 8, 32: He that spared not *His own Son,* but *delivered Him up* for us all, how shall He not with Him also freely give us all things?

4.

1 Tim. 2, 5. 6: There is one God, and one Mediator between God and men, the *man Christ Jesus, who gave Himself a ransom* for all, to be testified in due time.

Matt. 20, 28: Even as the *Son of Man* came not to be ministered unto, but to minister, and *to give His life a ransom* for many.

Rom. 8, 3. 4: For what the Law could not do, in that it was weak through the flesh, God sending *His own Son* in the likeness of sinful flesh, and for sin, condemned sin *in the flesh,* that the righteousness of the Law might be fulfilled in us, who walk not after the flesh, but after the Spirit.

IMPECCABILITY OF CHRIST.

§ 106. While the human nature of Christ was and is at all times truly human, it was at all times free from every taint of original[1] or actual[2] sin and absolutely impeccable,[3] and therefore at no time in itself obnoxious to death or any penalty of sin.[4]

1.

Luke 1, 35: Therefore also that *holy thing* which shall be *born* of thee shall be called the Son of God.

1 John 3, 5: And in Him is no sin.

2.

John 8, 46: Which of you convinceth me of *sin?* And if I say the truth, why do ye not believe me?

2 Cor. 5, 21: For He hath made Him to be sin for us who *knew no sin,* that we might be made the righteousness of God in Him.

Hebr. 4, 15: But was in all points tempted like as we are, yet *without sin.*

Hebr. 7, 26. 27: For such an high priest became us who is *holy, harmless, undefiled, separate from sinners,* and made higher than the heavens; who needeth *not* daily, as those high priests, to offer up sacrifice, first for his own *sins,* and then for the people's; for this He did once, when He offered up Himself.

3.

Hebr. 4, 15: But was *in all points* tempted like as we are, yet *without sin.*

Hebr. 6, 18: That by two immutable things, in which it was *impossible* for God to lie, we might have a strong consolation.

1 John 3, 5: In Him is no sin.

4.

John 10, 18: No man taketh it from me, but I *lay it down of myself.* I have *power to lay it down,* and I have power *to take it again.*

Hos. 13, 14: I will ransom them from the power of the grave; I will redeem them from death. O *death, I will be thy plagues;* O *grave, I will be thy destruction:* repentance shall be hid from mine eyes.

Rom. 6, 10: For in that He died, He died unto sin once: but in that He liveth, He liveth unto God.

STATES OF CHRIST.

§ 107. Though the human nature of Christ was at all times essentially the same, Christ was not at all times in the same state, but to a certain period of time in a state of humiliation, and from a certain time in a state of exaltation, according to His human nature.

STATE OF HUMILIATION.

§ 108. The state of humiliation[1] was that state in which Christ, according to His human nature,[2] personally united with His divine nature, voluntarily,[3] and in a measure which was requisite for the performance of the work of redemption,[4] abstained from the full and constant[5] use of the divine perfections communicated to His human nature.[6]

1.

Phil. 2, 8: And being found in fashion as a man, He *humbled Himself,* and became obedient unto death, even the death of the cross.

Hebr. 5, 7: Who in the *days of His flesh,* when He had offered up prayers and supplications with strong crying and tears unto Him that was able to save Him from death, and was heard in that He feared.

2 Cor. 5, 16: Wherefore henceforth know we no man after the flesh; yea, though we have known Christ *after the flesh,* yet now henceforth know we Him *no more.*

2.

Hebr. 2, 6. 9: What is *man* that Thou art mindful of him? or the *son of man,* that Thou visitest him? (9) But we see *Jesus,* who was *made a little lower* than the angels for the suffering of death, crowned with glory and honor, that He by the grace of God should taste death for every man.

1 Pet. 3, 18: For Christ also hath once suffered for sins, the Just for the unjust, that He might bring us to God, being *put to death in the flesh,* but quickened by the Spirit.

Luke 2, 52: And *Jesus increased* in wisdom and stature, and in favor with God and man.

Mal. 3, 6: For I am the Lord, I change not; therefore ye sons of Jacob are not consumed.

3.

Phil. 2, 7. 8: But *made Himself* of no reputation, and *took upon Him* the form of a servant, and was made in the likeness of men: and being found in fashion as a man, He *humbled Himself,* and became obedient unto death, even the death of the cross.

8

2 Cor. 8, 9: Ye know the grace of our Lord Jesus Christ, that, though He was rich, yet for your sakes He became poor.

John 10, 18: *No man taketh it from me,* but *I lay it down of myself.* I have power to lay it down, and I have power to take it again.

Hebr. 12, 2: Looking unto *Jesus,* the Author and Finisher of our faith, who *for the* JOY *that was set before Him endured the* CROSS, *despising the shame.*

4.

Matt. 20, 28: Even as the Son of Man came not to be ministered unto, but *to minister, and to give His life a ransom for many.*

2 Cor. 8, 9: For ye know the grace of our Lord Jesus Christ, that, though He was rich, yet for your sakes *He became poor, that ye through His poverty might be rich.*

5.

John 1, 14: And the Word was made flesh, and dwelt among us, (and *we beheld His glory,* the glory as of the Only-Begotten of the Father,) full of grace and truth.

John 2, 11: This beginning of *miracles* did Jesus in Cana of Galilee, and *manifested forth His glory.*

John 11, 40: Said I not unto thee, that, if thou wouldest believe, thou shouldest *see the glory of God?*

John 18, 6: As soon, then, as He had said unto them, I am he, they went backward, and fell to the ground.

6.

John 17, 5: And now, O Father, *glorify Thou me* with Thine own self with the *glory which I had with Thee before the world was.*

2 Cor. 8, 9: For ye know the grace of our Lord Jesus Christ, that, *though He was rich,* yet for your sakes He became poor, that ye through His poverty might be rich.

Luke 23, 35: He saved others; let Him save Himself, if He be Christ, the chosen of God.

Mark 13, 32: But of that day and that hour *knoweth* no man, no, not the angels which are in heaven, *neither the Son,* but the Father.

Mark 1, 12. 13: And immediately the Spirit driveth Him into the wilderness. And He was there in the wilderness forty days, tempted of Satan; and was with the wild beasts; and the angels ministered unto Him.

Luke 2, 51. 52: And He *went down* with them, and came to Nazareth, and *was subject unto them.* But His mother kept all these sayings in her heart. And Jesus *increased in wisdom* and stature, and in favor with God and man.

Phil. 2, 5—8: Let this mind be in you, which was also in Christ Jesus: who, being in the form of God, *thought it not robbery* to be *equal* with God, but *made Himself of no reputation,* and took upon Him the *form of a servant,* and was made in the *likeness of men;* and being found in *fashion as a man,* He *humbled Himself,* and *became obedient* unto death, even the death of the cross.

STAGES OF HUMILIATION.

§ 109. The stages of Christ's humiliation were His conception, birth, suffering, death, and burial.

CONCEPTION OF CHRIST.

§ 110. The conception of Christ, by the Holy Ghost,[1] in the Virgin Mary,[2] whereby the Son of God[3] assumed a human nature,[4] was the beginning of His humiliation, not[5] inasmuch as it was the assumption of a human nature by the Son of God, but in so far as the manner in which the incarnation took place was by conception in the womb of a sinful woman,[6] from whom the Son of God took His human nature,[7] but without a stain of sin,[8] that He might atone for, and cover, our innate sinfulness.[9]

1.

Luke 1, 35. 38: *The Holy Ghost shall come upon thee,* and the power of the Highest shall overshadow thee: *therefore* also that *holy thing which shall be born of thee* shall be called the Son of God. (38) And Mary said, Behold the handmaid of the Lord; *be it unto me according to thy word.* And the angel departed from her.

2.

Is. 7, 14: Behold, a *virgin shall conceive,* and bear a son, and shall call His name Immanuel.

Matt. 1, 23: Behold, a *virgin shall be with child,* and shall bring forth a son, and they shall call His name Emmanuel, which being interpreted is, God with us.

Luke 1, 31. 42: And, behold, thou shalt *conceive in thy womb,* and bring forth a son, and shalt call His name Jesus. (42) Blessed art thou among women, and blessed is the *fruit of thy womb!*

3.

Luke 1, 35: That holy thing *which shall be born of thee* shall be called the *Son of God.*

Is. 7, 14: And shall call His name *Immanuel.*

Matt. 1, 23: And they shall call His name *Emmanuel,* which being interpreted is, *God with us.*

Gal. 4, 4: But when the fullness of the time was come, God sent forth *His Son, made of a woman,* made under the Law.

4.

Gen. 3, 15: And I will put enmity between thee and the woman, and between thy seed and *her Seed;* it shall bruise thy head, and thou shalt bruise His heel.

Hebr. 2, 14: As the children are partakers of *flesh and blood,* He also Himself *likewise took part of the same.*

Luke 1, 43: And whence is this to me, that the *mother of my Lord* should come to me?

Rom. 1, 3: Concerning *His Son* Jesus Christ, our Lord, which was *made of the seed of David* according to *the flesh.*

5.

Phil. 2, 11: And that every tongue should confess that *Jesus Christ is Lord,* to the glory of God the Father.

John 1, 14: And the *Word was made flesh,* and dwelt among us, (and we *beheld His glory,* the glory as of the Only-Begotten of the Father,) full of grace and truth.

6.

Luke 2, 48. 49: Son, why hast Thou thus dealt with us? Behold, Thy father and I have sought Thee sorrowing. And He said unto them, *How is it that ye sought me? Wist ye not* that I must be about my Father's business?

John 2, 4: Jesus saith unto her, Woman, what have I to do with thee?

7.

2 Sam. 7, 12: I will set up *thy seed* after thee, which shall proceed out of thy bowels, and I will establish His kingdom.

Acts 2, 30: Therefore being a prophet, and knowing that God had sworn with an oath to him, that of the *fruit of his loins,* according to the flesh, he would raise up Christ to sit on his throne, etc.

Rom. 1, 3: Concerning His Son Jesus Christ, our Lord, which was made *of the seed of David* according to the flesh.

Hebr. 2, 14. 15: Forasmuch as the children are partakers of *flesh and blood,* He also Himself *likewise took part of the same,* that through death He might destroy him that had the power of death, that is, the devil, and deliver them who through fear of death were all their lifetime subject to bondage.

8.

Luke 1, 35: Therefore also that *holy thing* which shall be born of thee shall be called the Son of God.

Hebr. 4, 15: For we have not an high priest which cannot be touched with the feeling of our infirmities, but was in all points tempted like as we are, yet *without sin.*

9.

Hebr. 2, 11. 17. 18: For both He that sanctifieth and they who are sanctified are all of one; for which cause He is not ashamed to call them brethren. (17. 18) Wherefore in all things it behooved Him to be made like unto His brethren, that He might be a merciful and faithful high priest in things pertaining to God, to make reconciliation for the sins of the people. For in that He Himself hath suffered, being tempted, He is able to succor them that are tempted.

BIRTH OF CHRIST.

§ 111. The birth of Christ, the God-man,[1] was a truly natural birth in great poverty,[2] Christ, true God and man,[3] being thereby born at the time[4] and place[5] predicted by the prophets, the son of a virgin,[6] made under the Law,[7] in the form of a servant,[8] and in the likeness of men,[9] that men might be made children of God.[10]

1.

Luke 2, 5. 6: To be taxed with Mary, his espoused wife, being great with child. And so it was, that, while they were there, *the days were accomplished* that *she should be delivered.*

Luke 1, 31: And, behold, thou shalt conceive in thy womb, and *bring forth* a son, and shalt call His name Jesus.

Is. 7, 14: Behold, a virgin shall conceive, and *bear a son,* and shall call His name *Immanuel.* Cf. Matt. 1, 22—25.

Is. 9, 6: For unto us *a Child is born,* unto us a Son is given: and the government shall be upon His shoulder: and His name shall be called Wonderful, Counselor, *The Mighty God, The Everlasting Father,* The Prince of Peace.

2.

Luke 2, 7: And she brought forth her firstborn son, and wrapped him in *swaddling clothes,* and laid him *in a manger,* because there was *no room for them in the inn.*

2 Cor. 8, 9: For ye know the grace of our Lord Jesus Christ, that, though He was rich, yet for your sakes *He became poor,* that ye through His poverty might be rich.

3.

Gal. 4, 4: But when the fullness of the time was come, *God* sent forth His Son, *made of a woman,* made under the Law.

Is. 7, 14: Behold, a virgin shall conceive, and *bear a son,* and shall call His name *Immanuel.*

Luke 1, 35: The Holy Ghost shall come upon thee, and the power of the Highest shall overshadow thee; therefore also that holy thing *which shall be born of thee* shall be called *the Son of God.*

Luke 1, 43: And whence is this to me, that the *mother* of *my Lord* should come to me?

4.

Gen. 49, 10: The *scepter shall not depart from Judah,* nor a lawgiver from between his feet, until *Shiloh come;* and unto Him shall the gathering of the people be.

Dan. 9, 24: *Seventy weeks* are determined upon thy people and upon thy holy city, to finish the transgression, and to make an end of sins, and to make reconciliation of iniquity, and to bring in everlasting righteousness, and to seal up the vision and prophecy, and to anoint the Most Holy.

Matt. 2, 1: Now when Jesus was born in Bethlehem of Judaea *in the days of Herod the king,* etc.

Luke 2, 1. 2: And it came to pass in those days, that there went out a decree from *Caesar Augustus,* that all the world should be taxed. (And this taxing *was first made* when *Cyrenius was governor of Syria.*)

5.

Micah 5, 2: Thou, *Bethlehem Ephratah,* though thou be little among the thousands of Judah, yet out of thee shall He come forth unto me that is to be Ruler in Israel.

Matt. 2, 1: Now when Jesus was *born in Bethlehem of Judaea* in the days of Herod the king, etc.

Matt. 2, 4—6: And when he had gathered all the chief priests and scribes of the people together, he demanded of them 'where Christ should be born. And they said unto him, In *Bethlehem of Judaea;* for thus it is written by the prophet, And thou *Bethlehem,* in the land of Juda, art not the least among the princes of Juda: for out of thee shall come a Governor that shall rule my people Israel.

Luke 2, 4. 6: And Joseph also went up from Galilee, out of the city of Nazareth, *into Judaea,* unto the city of David, which is called *Bethlehem.* (6) And so it was, that, while they were *there,* the days were accomplished that she *should be delivered.*

6.

Matt. 1, 25: And knew her not till she had brought forth her *firstborn* son: and he called His name Jesus.

Luke 1, 27. 34: And the *virgin's* name was Mary. (34) Then said Mary unto the angel, How shall this be, seeing *I know not a man?*

7.

Gal. 4, 4: But when the fullness of the time was come, God sent forth His Son, made of a woman, *made under the Law.*

Luke 2, 21: And when eight days were accomplished for the *circumcising* of the Child, His name was called Jesus, which was so named of the angel before He was conceived in the womb.

8.

Phil. 2, 7: But made Himself of no reputation, and took upon Him the *form of a servant,* and was made in the likeness of men.

Luke 2, 7. 12. 16: And she brought forth her firstborn son, and wrapped him in *swaddling clothes,* and laid him in a *manger;* because there was no room for them in the inn. (12) Ye shall find the babe wrapped in *swaddling clothes,* lying *in a manger.* (16) And they came with haste, and found Mary, and Joseph, and the babe lying *in a manger.*

9.

Phil. 2, 7: But made Himself of no reputation, and took upon Him the form of a servant, and was made *in the likeness of men.*

10.

Gal. 4, 4. 5: But when the fullness of the time was come, God sent forth His Son, made of a woman, made under the Law, to redeem them that were under the Law, *that we might receive the adoption of sons.*

John 3, 16: For God so loved the world, that He gave His only-begotten Son, etc.

Is. 9, 6—9: For unto us a Child is born, unto us a Son is given: and the government shall be upon His shoulder: and His name shall be called Wonderful, Counselor, The Mighty God, The Everlasting Father, The Prince of Peace. Of the increase of His government and peace there shall be no end, upon the throne of David, and upon His kingdom, to order it, and to establish it with judgment and with justice from henceforth even forever. The zeal of the Lord of hosts will perform this. The Lord sent a word into Jacob, and it hath lighted upon Israel. And all the people shall know, even Ephraim and the inhabitant of Samaria.

SUFFERING OF CHRIST.

§ 112. The suffering of Christ, the God-man,[1] was real suffering[2] of body[3] and soul,[4] in obedience to the Father's will,[5] that He might make atonement for our disobedience[6] and earn for us eternal bliss.[7]

1.

Rom. 8, 32: He that spared not *His own Son,* but *delivered Him up* for us all, how shall He not with Him also freely give us all things?

Acts 3, 15: And *killed* the *Prince of Life,* whom God hath raised from the dead.

Acts 20, 28: Take heed therefore unto yourselves, and to all the flock, over the which the Holy Ghost hath made you overseers, to feed the Church of *God,* which He hath *purchased with His own blood.*

1 Cor. 2, 8: Which none of the princes of this world knew; for had they known it, they would not have *crucified* the *Lord of glory.*

1 Pet. 4, 1: Forasmuch, then, as *Christ* hath *suffered* for us in the flesh, arm yourselves likewise with the same mind; for he that hath *suffered in the flesh* hath ceased from sin.

1 Pet. 3, 18: For *Christ* also hath once *suffered* for sins, the Just for the unjust, that He might bring us to God, being put to death in the flesh, but quickened by the Spirit.

2.

Ps. 31, 10—12: For my life is spent with grief, and my years with sighing: my strength faileth because of mine iniquity, and my bones are consumed. I was a reproach among all mine enemies, but especially among my neighbors, and a fear to mine acquaintance: they that did see me without fled from me. I am forgotten as a dead man out of mind: I am like a broken vessel.

Ps. 40, 13: Be pleased, O Lord, to deliver me! O Lord, make haste to help me!

Ps. 69, 2—4: I sink in deep mire where there is no standing: I am come into deep waters, where the floods overflow me. I am weary of my crying: my throat is dried: mine eyes fail while I wait for my God. They that hate me without a cause are more than the hairs of mine head: they that would destroy me, being mine enemies wrongfully, are mighty: then I restored that which I took not away.

Matt. 26, 38: My soul is exceeding sorrowful, even unto death: tarry ye here, and watch with me.

Acts 2, 24: Whom God hath raised up, having loosed the *pains* of death, because it was not possible that He should be holden of it.

Luke 24, 26: Ought not Christ to have suffered these things, and to enter into His glory?

Luke 22, 42—44: Father, if Thou be willing, remove this cup from me: nevertheless, not my will, but Thine, be done. And there appeared an angel unto Him from heaven, *strengthening* Him. And being in an *agony,* He prayed more earnestly: and His *sweat* was as it were great drops of blood falling down to the ground.

Is. 53, 8: He was taken from prison and from judgment: and who shall declare His generation? For He was cut off out of the land of the living: for the transgression of my people was He stricken.

3.

John 18, 22: One of the officers which stood by *struck* Jesus with the palm of his hand, saying, Answerest Thou the high priest so?

Matt. 26, 67. 68: Then did they *spit* in His face, and *buffeted* Him; and others *smote* Him with the palms of their hands, saying, Prophesy unto us, Thou Christ, Who is he that smote Thee?

Luke 22, 63: And the men that held Jesus mocked Him, and *smote* Him.

John 19, 2. 3: And the soldiers platted a *crown of thorns,* and put it *on His head;* and they put on Him a purple robe, and said, Hail, King of the Jews! and they *smote* Him with their hands.

4.

Matt. 26, 38: My *soul* is exceeding sorrowful, even unto death.

5.

John 14, 31: As the Father gave me *commandment,* even so I do.

John 18, 11: Put up thy sword into the sheath: the cup which *my Father hath given me,* shall I not drink it?

Luke 22, 42: Father, if Thou be willing, remove this cup from me: nevertheless, *not my will, but Thine,* be done.

Matt. 26, 39. 42: O my Father, if it be possible, let this cup pass from me: nevertheless, *not as I will,* but *as Thou wilt.* (42) He went away again the second time, and prayed, saying, O my Father, if this cup may not pass away from me, except I drink it, *Thy will be done.*

Phil. 2, 8: And being found in fashion as a man, He humbled Himself, and became *obedient unto death,* even the death of the cross.

6.

Is. 53, 4: Surely, He hath borne *our* griefs, and carried our sorrows: yet we did esteem Him stricken, smitten of God, and afflicted.

Gal. 3, 13: Christ hath redeemed us from the curse of the Law, being made a *curse for us;* for it is written, Cursed is every one that hangeth on a tree!

7.

Hebr. 2, 10: For it became Him, for whom are all things, and by whom are all things, in *bringing many sons unto glory,* to make the Captain of their salvation perfect through sufferings.

Hebr. 5, 9: And being made perfect, He became the *author of eternal salvation unto all* them that obey Him.

Gal. 4, 5: To redeem them that were under the Law, *that we might receive the adoption of sons.*

DEATH OF CHRIST.

§ 113. The death of Christ, the God-man,[1] an ignominious death on the cross,[2] was not a termination of His natural life in the course of nature,[3] but a violent,[4] though on His part voluntary,[5] separation of body and soul,[6] without, however, any cessation or suspension of the personal union of God and man in Christ, His body and soul remaining personally united with the divine nature of the Son of God.[7]

1.

Rom. 5, 10: For if, when we were enemies, we were reconciled to God by the *death of His Son,* much more, being reconciled, we shall be saved by His life.

Acts 20, 28: Take heed therefore unto yourselves, and to all the flock, over the which the Holy Ghost hath made you overseers, to feed the Church of *God,* which He hath purchased with *His own blood.*

2.

Matt. 27, 33—35: And when they were come unto a place called Golgotha, that is to say, a place of a skull, they gave Him vinegar to drink mingled with gall: and when He had tasted thereof, He would not drink. And they crucified Him, and parted His garments, casting lots, that it might be fulfilled which was spoken by the prophet, They parted my garments among them, and upon my vesture did they cast lots.

Mark 15, 20. 21: And when they had mocked Him, they took off the purple from Him, and put His own clothes on Him, and led Him out to crucify Him. And they compel one Simon a Cyrenian, who passed by, coming out of the country, the father of Alexander and Rufus, to bear His cross.

Luke 23, 33: And when they were come to the place which is called Calvary, there they crucified Him, and the malefactors, one on the right hand, and the other on the left.

John 19, 17—19: And He bearing His cross went forth into a place called the place of a skull, which is called in the Hebrew Golgotha, where they crucified Him, and two other with Him, on either side one, and Jesus in the midst. And Pilate wrote a title, and put it on the cross. And the writing was, Jesus of Nazareth, the King of the Jews.

Phil. 2, 8: And being found in fashion as a man, He humbled Himself, and became obedient unto death, even the death of the cross.

Luke 22, 37: For I say unto you that this that is written must yet be accomplished in me, And He was reckoned among the transgressors; for the things concerning me have an end.

3.

Is. 53, 12: Therefore will I divide Him a portion with the great, and He shall divide the spoil with the strong, because *He hath poured out* His soul unto death: and He was numbered with the transgressors; and He bare the sin of many, and made intercession for the transgressors.

John 10, 18: No man taketh it from me, but I lay it down of myself. I have power to lay it down, and I have power to take it again.

4.

Luke 18, 33: And they shall scourge Him, and *put Him to death:* and the third day He shall rise again.

Acts 3, 15: And *killed* the Prince of Life, whom God hath raised from the dead.

Is. 53, 8. 9: He was taken from prison and from judgment: and who shall declare His generation? For He was *cut off* out of the land of the living: for the transgression of my people was He stricken. And He made His grave with the wicked, and with the rich in His death, because He had done no violence, neither was any deceit in His mouth.

5.

John 10, 18: No man taketh it from me, but I lay it down of myself. I have power to lay it down, and I have power to take it again. This commandment have I received of my Father.

Matt. 20, 28: Even as the Son of Man came not to be ministered unto, but to minister, and to *give* His life a ransom for many.

6.

Luke 23, 46: And when Jesus had cried with a loud voice, He said, Father, into Thy hands *I commend my spirit:* and having said thus, He *gave up the ghost.*

7.

Col. 2, 9: For in Him dwelleth all the fullness of the Godhead bodily.

Acts 2, 26. 31: Therefore did my heart rejoice, and my tongue was glad; moreover, also my flesh shall rest in hope. (31) He, seeing this before, spake of the resurrection of Christ, that His soul was not left in hell, neither His flesh did see corruption.

BURIAL OF CHRIST.

§ 114. The burial of Christ, His body being laid in Joseph's sepulcher,[1] while His soul was in paradise,[2] was a manifest confirmation of His death and its continuation to the third day,[3] during which time, however, corruption did not touch His body.[4]

1.

Matt. 27, 58—60: He went to Pilate, and begged the body of Jesus. Then Pilate commanded the body to be delivered. And when Joseph had taken the body, he wrapped it in a clean linen cloth, and laid it in his own new tomb, which he had hewn out in the rock. And he rolled a great stone to the door of the sepulcher, and departed.

Luke 23, 55: And the women also, which came with Him from Galilee, followed after, and beheld the sepulcher, and how His body was laid.

John 19, 38. 41. 42: (38. Joseph asks for the body.) (41. 42) Now in the place where He was crucified there was a garden; and in the garden a new sepulcher, wherein was never man yet laid. There laid they Jesus therefore because of the Jews' preparation day; for the sepulcher was nigh at hand.

1 Cor. 15, 4: And that He was buried, and that He rose again the third day, according to the Scriptures.

2.

Luke 23, 43: Verily, I say unto thee, To-day shalt thou be *with me in paradise.*

3.

Matt. 27, 64—66: Command therefore that the sepulcher be *made sure* until the third day, lest His disciples come by night, and steal Him away, and say unto the people, He is risen from the dead: so the last error shall be worse than the first. Pilate said unto them, Ye have a watch: go your way; *make it as sure as ye can.* So they went, and *made the sepulcher sure,* sealing the stone, and setting a watch.

4.

Ps. 16, 10: For Thou wilt not leave my soul in hell; neither wilt Thou suffer Thine Holy One to see corruption.

Acts 2, 27 ff.: (Ps. 16, 10 quoted and expounded.)

STATE OF EXALTATION.

§ 115. The state of exaltation[1] is that state in which Christ, according to His human nature, laying aside the infirmities of the flesh,[2] resumed the full and constant use and manifestation of the divine attributes communicated to His human nature personally united with His divine nature.[3]

1.

Acts 5, 31: Him hath God *exalted* with His right hand to be a Prince and a Savior, for to give repentance to Israel, and forgiveness of sins.

Phil. 2, 9: Wherefore God also hath highly *exalted* Him, and given Him a name which is above every name.

Ps. 110, 7: He shall drink of the brook in the way: therefore shall He *lift up the head.*

John 17, 24: Father, I will that they also, whom Thou hast given me, be with me where I am, that they may behold *my glory* which Thou hast *given me;* for Thou lovedst me before the foundation of the world.

Ps. 8, 6. 7: Thou madest Him to have dominion over the works of Thy hands. Thou hast *put all things under* His feet: all sheep and oxen, yea, and the beasts of the field.

Hebr. 2, 7—9: Thou madest Him a little lower than the angels; Thou crownedst Him with glory and honor, and didst set Him over the works of Thy hands: Thou hast put all things in subjection under His feet. For in that He put all in subjection under Him, He left nothing that is not put under Him. But now we see not yet all things put under Him. But we see Jesus, who was made a little lower than the angels for the suffering of death, crowned with glory and honor, that He by the grace of God should taste death for every man.

Eph. 4, 10: He that descended is the same also that ascended up far above all heavens, that He might fill all things.

2.

Rom. 6, 9: Knowing that Christ, being raised from the dead, dieth no more; death hath no more dominion over Him.

3.

Phil. 2, 9: Wherefore God also hath highly exalted Him, and *given Him a name which is above every name.*

Eph. 1, 20: Which He wrought in Christ, when He raised Him from the dead, and *set Him at His own right hand* in the heavenly places.

John 17, 5: And now, O Father, *glorify Thou me* with Thine own self with the glory which I had with Thee before the world was.

Eph. 4, 10: He that descended is the same also that ascended up *far above all heavens,* that He might fill all things.

John 1Q, 17. 18: Therefore doth my Father love me, because I lay down my life, *that I might take it again.* No man taketh it from me, but I lay it down of myself. I have power to lay it down, and I have power to take it again. This commandment have I received of my Father.

John 2, 19: Jesus answered and said unto them, Destroy this temple, and in three days *I will raise it up.*

STAGES OF EXALTATION.

§ 116. The stages of Christ's exaltation are His descent into hell, His resurrection, His ascension into heaven, His sitting at the right hand of God, His coming to judge the quick and the dead.

DESCENT INTO HELL.

§ 117. Christ's descent into hell was that act by which the God-man,[1] Christ glorified,[2] according to His human nature[3] after its quickening in the tomb,[4] appeared in the prison of condemned spirits,[5] a herald of their judgment and His victory.[6]

1.

1 Pet. 3, 18: For *Christ* also hath once suffered for sins, the Just for the unjust, that He might bring us to God, being put to death in the flesh, but quickened by the Spirit.

·2.

Phil. 2, 9—11: Wherefore God also hath *highly exalted Him,* and given Him a name which is above every name, that at the name of Jesus every knee should bow, of things in heaven, and things in earth, and *things under the earth;* and that every tongue should confess that Jesus Christ is Lord, to the glory of God the Father.

1 Pet. 3, 18: For Christ also hath once suffered for sins, the Just for the unjust, that He might bring us to God, being put to death in the flesh, but *quickened* by *the Spirit*. Cf. 1 Pet. 1, 3—9; 2, 11. 12; 3, 9. 16; 4, 12—14. 19; 5, 3. 5. 6. 10 — texts showing that in the kingdom of Christ the way to glory is through suffering, and that glory will follow the cross.

1 Pet. 3, 19: *By which* also He went and preached unto the spirits in prison. Cf. v. 21. 22.

3.

1 Pet. 3, 18. 19: For Christ also hath once *suffered* for sins, the Just for the unjust, that He might bring us to God, being *put to death in the flesh,* but *quickened* by the Spirit; by which also *He went* and preached unto the spirits in prison.

4.

1 Pet. 3, 18. 19. See above.

5.

1 Pet. 3, 19. 20: By which also He *went* and preached unto the *spirits in prison,* which sometime were *disobedient,* when once the longsuffering of God waited in the days of Noah, while the ark was a-preparing, wherein few, that is, eight souls, were saved by water.

2 Pet. 2, 4: For if God spared not *the angels that sinned,* but cast them *down to hell,* and delivered them *into chains* of darkness, to be reserved *unto judgment,* etc.

Luke 16, 22. 23: And it came to pass that the beggar died, and was carried by the angels into Abraham's bosom. The rich man also died, and was buried; and *in hell* he lift up his eyes, being in torments, and seeth Abraham afar off, and Lazarus in his bosom.

6.

1 Pet. 3, 19. 20: By which also He went and *preached unto the spirits in prison,* which sometime *were disobedient, when once the longsuffering of God waited* in the days of Noah, while the ark was a-preparing, wherein few, that is, eight souls, were saved by water.

Rev. 1, 18: I am He that liveth, and was dead; and, behold, I am alive for evermore, Amen; and have the keys of hell and death.

CHRIST'S RESURRECTION.

§ 118. Christ's resurrection, by which the God-man,[1] according to His human nature,[2] with the same body which was laid in the grave,[3] but in a glorified state,[4] came forth from the sepulcher on the third day of His burial, was a public and glorious manifestation of the divine Sonship of Christ,[5] and also the divine acknowledgment of the completeness and sufficiency of our redemption,[6] a proclamation of His victory over sin and death,[7] a confirmation of the truth of His doctrine,[8] and the firstfruit of the resurrection of all believers,[9] as God thus publicly led from the bonds of death the Substitute of mankind and the Head of His Church,[10] and Christ thereby fulfilled His promise that He would rise on the third day,[11] and thus imprinted upon His work and doctrine a further seal of divine authority.[12]

1.

Rom. 1, 3. 4: Concerning His Son *Jesus Christ,* our Lord, which was made *of the seed of David according to the flesh,* and declared to be *the Son of God* with power, according to the spirit of holiness, *by the resurrection from the dead.*

Rom. 6, 4. 9: Therefore we are buried with Him by baptism into death, that, like as *Christ* was *raised up* from the dead by the glory of the Father, even so we also should walk in newness of life. (9) Knowing that *Christ,* being *raised from the dead,* dieth no more; death hath no more dominion over Him.

Rom. 8, 11: But if the Spirit of Him that *raised up Jesus* from the dead dwell in you, He that raised up *Christ* from the dead shall also quicken your mortal bodies by *His Spirit* that dwelleth in you.

Acts 2, 24: Whom God hath *raised up,* having loosed the pains of death, because it was *not possible* that He should be holden of it.

2.

Mark 16, 6: And he saith unto them, Be not affrighted! Ye seek *Jesus of Nazareth,* which was crucified: *He is risen;* He is not here. Behold the place where they laid Him.

Matt. 17, 23: And they shall *kill Him,* and the third day *He shall be raised again.*

Rom. 8, 34: Who is he that condemneth? It is *Christ that died,* yea, rather, *that is risen again,* who is even at the right hand of God, *who also maketh intercession* for us.

2 Cor. 5, 15: And that *He died* for all, that they which live should not henceforth live unto themselves, but unto Him *which died for them, and rose again.*

Matt. 28, 5. 6: And the angels answered and said unto the women, Fear not ye; for I know that ye seek *Jesus, which was crucified.* He is not here; for *He is risen,* as He said. Come, see the place *where the Lord lay.*

3.

John 20, 20. 25. 27: And when He had so said, He showed unto them *His hands and His side.* Then were the disciples glad when *they saw the Lord,* etc.

Luke 24, 39. 40: Behold *my hands and my feet,* that *it is I myself:* handle me, and see; for a spirit hath not flesh and bones, as ye see me have. And when He had thus spoken, He *showed them His hands and His feet.*

Matt. 28, 6: He is not here; for *He is risen,* as He said. Come, .see the *place where the Lord lay.*

4.

Luke 24, 26. 31: Ought not Christ to have suffered these things, and to *enter into His glory?* (31) And their eyes were opened, and they knew Him; *and He vanished out of their sight.*

5.

Rom. 1, 4: And *declared to be the Son of God* with power, according to the Spirit of holiness, *by the resurrection from the dead.*

6.

Mark 16, 6: And He saith unto them, Be not affrighted! Ye seek *Jesus of Nazareth, which was crucified:* He is risen; He is not here. Behold the place where they laid Him.

Rom. 4, 25: Who was *delivered for our offenses,* and was *raised again for our justification.*

Rom. 8, 34: Who is he that condemneth? It is *Christ that died,* yea, rather, *that is risen again,* who is even at the right hand of God, who also maketh intercession for us.

7.

Col. 2, 15: And having *spoiled principalities and powers,* He *made a show of them openly, triumphing* over them in it.

Rev. 1, 17. 18: And when I saw Him, I fell at His feet as dead. And He laid His right hand upon me, saying unto me, Fear not; I am the first and the last: *I am He that liveth, and was dead;* and, behold, I am *alive for evermore,* Amen; and have *the keys of hell and of death.*

Rom. 6, 9: Knowing that *Christ, being raised* from the dead, *dieth no more; death hath no more dominion over Him.*

8.

1 Cor. 15, 14—18: And if Christ be *not risen,* then *is our preaching vain,* and *your faith is also vain.* Yea, and we are found *false witnesses* of God, because we have testified of God that He raised up Christ, whom He raised not up, if so be that the dead rise not. For if the dead rise not, then is not Christ raised: *and if Christ be not raised, your faith is vain;* ye are yet in your sins. Then they also which are fallen asleep in Christ are perished.

Matt. 28, 6: He is not here; for He is risen, *as He said.*

Luke 24, 44: And He said unto them, *These are the words which I spake unto you* while I was yet with you, that *all things must be fulfilled* which were written in the law of Moses, and in the prophets, and in the psalms, concerning me.

9.

1 Cor. 15, 20: But now is Christ risen from the dead, and become *the firstfruits of them that slept.*

1 Thess. 4, 14: For if we believe that *Jesus* died and *rose again,* even so *them also which sleep in Jesus will God bring with Him.*

John 11, 25. 26: Jesus said unto her, *I am the Resurrection, and the Life:* he that believeth in me, though he were dead, *yet shall he live;* and whosoever liveth and *believeth in me shall never die.*

1 Pet. 1, 3: Blessed be the God and Father of our Lord Jesus Christ, which according to His abundant mercy hath begotten us again unto *a lively hope by the resurrection of Jesus Christ from the dead.*

John 14, 19: Yet a little while, and the world seeth me no more; but ye see me: *because I live, ye shall live also.*

10.

Hebr. 13, 20: The God of peace that *brought again from the dead our Lord Jesus, that great Shepherd of the sheep,* through the blood of the everlasting covenant, etc.

Eph. 1, 20—23: Which He wrought in *Christ,* when He *raised Him from the dead,* and set Him at His own right hand in the heavenly places, far above all principality, and power, and might, and dominion, and every name that is named, not only in this world, but also in that which is to come: and hath put all things under His feet, and gave Him to be *the Head over all things to the Church,* which is *His body,* the *fullness of Him that filleth all in all.*

Eph. 4, 15: But speaking the truth in love, may grow up into *Him* in all things, *which is the Head,* even *Christ.*

11.

John 2, 19. 21: Jesus answered and said unto them, Destroy *this temple,* and *in three days I will raise it up.* (21) But He spake of *the temple of His body.*

Matt. 17, 22. 23: And while they abode *in Galilee,* Jesus *said unto them,* The Son of Man shall be betrayed into the hands of men: and they shall kill Him, and *the third day He shall be raised again.*

Matt. 20, 19: And shall deliver Him to the Gentiles to mock, and to scourge, and to crucify Him: and *the third day He shall rise again.*

Luke 24, 6. 7: He is not here, but is risen: *remember how He spake unto you when He was yet in Galilee,* saying, The Son of Man must be delivered into the hands of sinful men, and be crucified, *and the third day rise again.*

12.

1 Cor. 15, 14—18: And if Christ be not risen, then is our preaching vain, and your faith is also vain. Yea, and we are found false witnesses of God, because we have testified of God that He raised up Christ whom He raised not up, if so be that the dead rise not. For

if the dead rise not, then is not Christ raised: and if Christ be not raised, your faith is vain; ye are yet in your sins. Then they also which are fallen asleep in Christ are perished.

John 2, 18. 19: Then answered the Jews and said unto Him, *What sign* showest Thou unto us, seeing *that Thou doest these things?* Jesus answered and said unto them, Destroy *this temple,* and *in three* days *I will raise it up.*

CHRIST'S ASCENSION INTO HEAVEN.

§ 119. Christ's ascension into heaven was the glorious termination of His visible conversation with His Church on earth[1] and the visible[2] entrance of the God-man,[3] according to His human nature,[4] into His heavenly kingdom,[5] in which, while He is ever and everywhere present with His Church on earth,[6] He is being worshiped and adored in His glory by the heavenly host.[7]

1.

Luke 24, 51: And it came to pass, while He blessed them, He was *parted from them,* and *carried up into heaven.*

Acts 1, 11: Ye men of Galilee, why stand ye gazing *up into heaven?* This same Jesus which is *taken up from you into heaven* shall so *come* in like manner as ye have seen Him *go into heaven.*

2.

Acts 1, 9—11: And when He had spoken these things, while they *beheld* He was *taken up;* and a cloud received Him *out of their sight.* And while they *looked* steadfastly toward heaven *as He went up,* behold, two men stood by them in white apparel which also said, Ye men of Galilee, why stand ye gazing up into heaven? This same Jesus which is taken up from you into heaven shall so come in like manner as ye have *seen Him go into heaven.*

3.

Mark 16, 19: So, then, after *the Lord* had spoken unto them, *He was received up into heaven,* and sat on *the right hand of God.*

Ps. 47, 5: *God* is gone up with a shout, *the Lord* with the sound of a trumpet.

John 3, 13: And no *man* hath *ascended up to heaven,* but He that *came down* from heaven, even *the Son of Man* which *is in heaven.*

4.

John 3, 13: And no *man* hath ascended up to heaven, but He that came down from heaven, even *the Son of Man* which is in heaven.

Acts 1, 11: This *same Jesus* which is *taken up from you* into heaven shall so come in like manner as ye have seen Him go into heaven.

5.

Mark 16, 19: So, then, after the Lord had spoken unto them, He was received up into *heaven,* and *sat on the right hand of God.*

Eph. 4, 10: He that descended is the same also that *ascended* up far above all heavens, *that He might fill all things.*

John 17, 24: Father, I will that they also whom Thou hast given me be with me *where I am,* that they may *behold my glory* which Thou hast given me.

2 Tim. 4, 18: And *the Lord* shall deliver me from every evil work, and will preserve me unto *His heavenly kingdom:* to whom be *glory for ever and ever.* Amen.

6.

Matt. 18, 20: For where *two or three* are *gathered* together *in my name,* there *am I in the midst of them.*

Matt. 28, 20: Lo, I *am with you alway,* even *unto the end of the world.*

7.

Matt. 25, 31: When the Son of Man shall come in His glory, and *all the holy angels with Him,* then shall He sit upon the throne of His glory.

Rev. 5, 6: And I beheld, and, lo, in *the midst of the throne* and of the four beasts, and *in the midst of the elders,* stood *a Lamb as it had been slain.*

CHRIST'S SITTING AT THE RIGHT HAND OF GOD.

§ 120. Christ's sitting at the right hand of God the Father Almighty[1] is the full and constant participation, according to His human nature,[2] in the exercise of the universal dominion, rule, and government over heaven and earth and all creatures,[3] and especially over His Church on earth,[4] which power and sovereign majesty the Son of God had possessed and exercised before the incarnation[5] and communicated to His human nature in the incarnation,[6] but from the full and continual use of which, according to His human nature, He had voluntarily abstained in His state of humiliation.[7]

1.

Mark 16, 19: So, then, after the Lord had spoken unto them, He was received up into heaven, and *sat on the right hand of God.*

Acts 3, 20. 21: And He shall send *Jesus Christ,* which before was preached unto you: whom the *heaven must receive* until the times of restitution of all things, which God hath spoken by the mouth of all His holy prophets since the world began.

Eph. 1, 20: Which He wrought in *Christ,* when He raised Him from the dead, *and set Him at His own right hand* in the heavenly places.

Hebr. 1, 3. 13: Who . . . *sat down on the right hand of the Majesty on high.* (13) But to which of the angels said He at any time, *Sit on my right hand,* until I make thine enemies thy footstool?

Ps. 110, 1: The Lord said unto my Lord, *Sit Thou at my right hand,* until I make Thine enemies Thy footstool.

2.

Phil. 2, 9—11: Wherefore God also hath highly *exalted Him,* and *given Him* a name which is above every name, that at the name of *Jesus* every knee should bow, of things in heaven, and things in earth, and things under the earth, and that every tongue should confess that *Jesus* Christ is Lord, to the glory of God the Father.

1 Pet. 3, 22: Who is *gone* into heaven, and is on the right hand of God, angels and authorities and powers being *made subject* unto Him.

Eph. 1, 20—23: Which He wrought in Christ, when He *raised Him from the dead,* and *set Him* at His own right hand in the heavenly places, far above all principality, and power, and might, and dominion, and every name that is named, not only in this world, but also in that which is to come: and hath *put* all things under His feet, and *gave* Him to be the Head over all things to the Church, which is His body, the fullness of Him that filleth all in all.

Hebr. 12, 2: Who for the joy that was set before Him *endured the cross,* despising the shame, and is *set down* at the right hand of the throne of God.

Luke 22, 69: Hereafter shall the *Son of Man* sit on the right hand of the power of God.

3.

Phil. 2, 9—11: Wherefore God also hath highly *exalted Him,* and given Him a name which is *above every name,* that at the name of Jesus *every knee should bow,* of things in heaven, and things in earth, and things under the earth, and that every tongue should confess that Jesus Christ *is Lord,* to the glory of God the Father.

Eph. 1, 20—23: Which He wrought in Christ, when He raised Him from the dead, and set Him at His own right hand in the heavenly places, far *above all principality, and power, and might, and dominion,* and every name that is named, not only *in this world,* but also *in that which is to come:* and hath put *all things under His feet,* and gave Him to be the *Head over all things* to the Church, which is His body, the fullness of Him that filleth all in all.

1 Pet. 3, 22: Who is gone into heaven, and is on the right hand of God, *angels and authorities and powers being made subject unto Him.*

Hebr. 2, 8: Thou hast put *all things in subjection* under His feet. For in that He put *all in subjection under Him,* He left *nothing that is not put under Him.*

4.

Eph. 5, 23: For the husband is the head of the wife, even as Christ is the *Head of the Church:* and He is the Savior of the body.

Acts 2, 33: Therefore, being by the right hand of God *exalted,* and having received of the Father the promise of the Holy Ghost, He hath *shed forth this which ye now see and hear.*

Acts 5, 30. 31: The God of our fathers raised up Jesus, whom ye slew and hanged on a tree. Him hath God exalted with His right hand to be *a Prince and a Savior,* for *to give repentance to Israel* and forgiveness of sins.

5.

Hebr. 1, 8: But unto the Son He saith, Thy throne, O God, is for ever and ever: a scepter of righteousness is the scepter of Thy kingdom.

Ps. 45, 7. 8: Thou lovest righteousness, and hatest wickedness: therefore *God,* Thy God, hath *anointed* Thee with the oil of gladness *above Thy fellows.* All Thy garments smell of myrrh, and aloes, and cassia, out of the ivory palaces, whereby they have made Thee glad.

John 17, 5: And now, O Father, *glorify Thou me* with Thine own self with *the glory which I had with Thee before the world was.*

6.

Col. 2, 9: For in Him dwelleth all the fullness of the Godhead *bodily.*

Phil. 2, 6. 7: Who, being *in the form of God,* thought it *not robbery to be equal with God,* but made Himself of no reputation, and took upon Him the form of a servant, and was *made in the likeness of men.*

7.

Phil. 2, 5—9: Let this mind be in you which was also in Christ Jesus, who, being in the form of God, thought it not robbery to be equal with God, but *made Himself of no reputation, and took upon Him the form of a servant,* and was made in the likeness of men: and being found in fashion as a man, *He humbled Himself,* and became *obedient unto death,* even the death of the cross. Wherefore God also hath highly exalted Him, and given Him a name which is above every name.

CHRIST'S COMING TO JUDGMENT.

§ 121. Christ's coming to judge the quick and the dead will be the visible culmination of His exaltation, inasmuch as it will then be made manifest unto men and angels, good and evil, that all power is given to Him in heaven and in earth,[1] that He is, according to His human nature also, above all principality and power,[2] when the Son of Man,[3] who was unjustly sentenced before the tribunal of a human court,[4] will pronounce the final sentence of all generations,[5] consign all His enemies to their eternal doom,[6] and lead His Church Triumphant to the full enjoyment of eternal bliss.[7]

1.

Matt. 28, 18: And Jesus came and spake unto them, saying, All power is given unto me in heaven and in earth.

Matt. 25, 31. 32: When the Son of Man shall come in His glory, and all the holy angels with Him, then shall He sit upon the throne of His glory: and before Him shall be gathered all nations: and He shall separate them one from another, as a shepherd divideth his sheep from the goats.

2.

Eph. 1, 20—22: Which He wrought in Christ, when He *raised Him from the dead, and set Him* at his own right hand in the heavenly places, *far above all principality, and power, and might, and dominion, and every name that is named, not only in this world,* but also in *that which is to come:* and hath put *all things under His feet,* and gave Him to be *the Head over all things* to the Church.

3.

Matt. 25, 31: When the *Son of Man* shall come in His glory, and all the holy angels with Him, then shall He sit upon the throne of His glory.

Luke 21, 27. 36: And then shall they see *the Son of Man* coming in a cloud with power and great glory. (36) Watch ye therefore, and pray always, that ye may be accounted worthy to escape all these things that shall come to pass, and to stand before *the Son of Man.*

4.

Luke 23, 22—25: And he said unto them the third time, Why, what evil hath He done? I have found no cause of death in Him: I will therefore chastise Him, and let Him go. And they were instant with loud voices, requiring that He might be crucified. And the voices of them and of the chief priests prevailed. And Pilate gave sentence that it should be as they required. And he released unto them him that for sedition and murder was cast into prison, whom they had desired; but he delivered Jesus to their will.

5.

Matt. 25, 32—34: And before Him shall be gathered *all nations:* and He shall *separate them* one from another, as a shepherd divideth his sheep from the goats: and He shall set the sheep on *His right* hand, but the goats on *the left.* Then shall the King say unto them on His right hand, *Come, ye blessed of my Father, inherit the king-dom* prepared for you from the foundation of the world!

6.

Matt. 25, 41. 46: Then shall He say also unto them on the left hand, *Depart from me, ye cursed, into everlasting fire,* prepared for the devil and his angels! (46) And these shall go away *into everlasting punishment,* but the righteous into life eternal.

7.

Matt. 25, 34. 46: Then shall the King say unto them on His right hand, *Come, ye blessed of my Father, inherit the kingdom* prepared for you from the foundation of the world! (46) And these shall go away into everlasting punishment, but *the righteous into life eternal.*

1 Thess. 4, 14. 17: For if we believe that Jesus died and rose again, even so them also which sleep in Jesus *will God bring with Him.* (17) Then we which are alive and remain shall be caught up together with them in the clouds, *to meet the Lord in the air: and so shall we ever be with the Lord.*

The Office of Christ.

§ 122. The office of Christ is threefold, sacerdotal, prophetic, and royal.

CHRIST THE PRIEST.

§ 123. Christ, the God-man,[1] was and is our High Priest,[2] and our only[3] Priest, inasmuch as He in the work of redemption mediated between God and man,[4] performing by His active obedience[5] in man's stead[6] that which God demanded of man, and which man did not and could not in his fallen state perform, a complete fulfillment of all the precepts of the Law,[5] and suffering in His passive obedience[7] as man's substitute[8] that which according to the Law and God's righteous judgment man must have suffered here and hereafter, torments[9] and ignominy,[10] death[11] and damnation,[12] thus by His vicarious sacrifice[13] rendering full satisfaction to divine justice,[14] making complete atonement and expiation for all the sins[15] of all mankind,[16] reconciling the world with God,[17] propitiating God in our behalf,[18] redeeming all men from the bondage,[19] the curse,[20] and the penalty[21] of the Law, from sin,[22] death,[23] and the power of the devil,[24] and earning, purchasing, and procuring for all sinners perfect righteousness,[25] life,[26] and eternal bliss;[27] and He still mediates between God and man by appearing for us before God in heaven,[28] pleading our cause as our Advocate,[29] and securing in God's judgment the full acquittal of all who believe in Him.[30]

1.

2 Cor. 5, 19: To-wit, that *God* was in Christ, *reconciling the world* unto Himself, not imputing their trespasses unto them; and hath committed unto us the word of reconciliation.

Acts 20, 28: Take heed therefore unto yourselves, and to all the flock, over the which the Holy Ghost hath made you overseers, to feed the Church of *God,* which *He hath purchased* with His own blood.

1 John 1, 7: But if we walk in the light, as He is in the light, we have fellowship one with another; and *the blood of Jesus* Christ, *His Son,* cleanseth us from all sin.

Hebr. 4, 14: Seeing, then, that we have a great *High Priest,* that is *passed into the heavens, Jesus,* the *Son of God,* let us hold fast our profession.

Hebr. 5, 8: Though He were a son, yet learned He obedience by the things which He suffered.

1 Tim. 2, 5: For there is one God, and one *Mediator* between God and men, *the man* Christ *Jesus.*

Matt. 20, 28: Even as *the Son of Man* came not to be ministered unto, but to minister, and *to give His life a ransom for many.*

2.

Hebr. 5, 6: As He saith also in another place, Thou art a *Priest* forever, after the order of Melchisedec.

Hebr. 7, 24. 26: But this man, because He continueth ever, hath an unchangeable *priesthood.* (26) For such an *High Priest* became us, who is holy, harmless, undefiled, separate from sinners, and made higher than the heavens.

Ps. 110, 4: The Lord hath sworn, and will not repent, Thou art a *Priest* forever, after the order of Melchisedec.

3.

Cf. § 124.

4.

1 Tim. 2, 5. 6: There is one God, and one *Mediator between God and men,* the man Christ Jesus, who gave Himself a ransom for all, to be testified in due time.

Hebr. 9, 14. 15: How much more shall the blood of Christ, who through the eternal Spirit *offered Himself* without spot to God, purge your conscience from dead works to serve the living God? And for this cause He is *the Mediator* of the new testament, that by means of death, for the redemption of the transgressions that were under the first testament, they which are called might receive the promise of eternal inheritance.

5.

Hebr. 10, 7: Then said I, Lo, I come, (in the volume of the book it is written of me,) *to do Thy will,* O God.

Matt. 5, 17: Think not that I am come to destroy the Law, or the prophets: I am not come to destroy, but *to fulfill.*

Luke 2, 51: And He went down with them, and came to Nazareth, and *was subject unto them.*

Rom. 5, 19: So by *the obedience of One* shall many be made righteous.

Gal. 4, 4. 5: But when the fullness of the time was come, God sent forth His Son, made of a woman, *made under the Law,* to redeem them that were under the Law, that we might receive the adoption of sons.

John 13, 1: Now before the feast of the passover, when Jesus knew that His hour was come that He should depart out of this world unto the Father, *having loved His own* which were in the world, *He loved them* unto the end.

John 14, 31: But that the world may know that *I love the Father;* and as the Father gave me *commandment,* even *so I do.*

6.

Rom. 5, 19: So by the *obedience* of One shall many be made *righteous.*

Gal. 4, 4. 5: But when the fullness of the time was come, God sent forth His Son, made of a woman, *made under the Law,* to redeem them that were under the Law, that we might receive the adoption of sons.

See also texts sub **5.**

7.

Phil. 2, 8: And being found in fashion as a man, He humbled Himself, and became *obedient unto death, even the death of the cross.*

John 14, 31: But that the world may know that I love the Father, and as the Father gave me commandment, even so I do.

8.

Is. 53, 4—7: Surely, He hath borne OUR *griefs,* and carried OUR *sorrows:* yet we did esteem Him stricken, smitten of God, and afflicted. But he was wounded *for* OUR *transgressions,* He was bruised *for* OUR *iniquities:* the chastisement of *our peace* was upon Him, and with His stripes we are healed. All we like sheep have gone astray; we have turned every one to his own way; and the Lord hath laid *on Him* the iniquity of *us all.* He was oppressed, and He was afflicted, yet He opened not His mouth: He is brought as a lamb to the slaughter, and as a sheep before her shearers is dumb, so He openeth not His mouth.

1 Tim. 2, 6: Who gave Himself a *ransom for all,* to be testified in due time.

2 Cor. 5, 21: For He hath made Him to be sin *for us* who knew no sin, that we might be made the righteousness of God in Him.

Gal. 3, 13: Christ hath redeemed us from the curse of the Law, being made *a curse for us;* for it is written, Cursed is every one that hangeth on a tree.

9.

Luke 18, 33: And they shall *scourge* Him, and put Him to death: and the third day He shall rise again.

Is. 53, 5. 6: But He was *wounded* for our transgressions, He was *bruised* for our iniquities: the *chastisement* of our peace was upon Him; and with His *stripes* we are healed. All we like sheep have gone astray; we have turned every one to his own way; and the Lord hath laid on Him the iniquity of us all.

10.

Luke 18, 32: For He shall be delivered unto the Gentiles, and shall be *mocked,* and *spitefully entreated,* and *spitted* on.

Luke 23, 35—39: And the people stood beholding. And the rulers also with them *derided Him,* saying, *He saved others; let Him save ·Himself,* if He be Christ, the chosen of God! And the soldiers also *mocked* Him, coming to Him, and offering Him vinegar, and saying, *If Thou be the King of the Jews, save Thyself!* And a superscription also was written over Him in letters of Greek, and Latin, and Hebrew, *THIS IS THE KING OF THE JEWS.* And one of the male-factors which were hanged *railed on Him,* saying, If Thou be Christ, save Thyself and us!

Matt. 27, 27—30: Then the soldiers of the governor took Jesus into the common hall, and gathered unto Him the whole band of soldiers. And they stripped Him, and put on Him a *scarlet robe.* And when they had platted a *crown of thorns,* they put it upon His head, and a *reed* in His right hand: and they *bowed the knee* before Him, and mocked Him, saying, *Hail, King of the Jews!* And they *spit* upon Him, and took the reed, and smote Him on the head.

11.

Hebr. 2, 9: But we see Jesus, who was made a little lower than the angels for the *suffering of death,* crowned with glory and honor, that He by the grace of God should *taste death for every man.*

Rom. 5, 6—8: For when we were yet without strength, ·in due time *Christ died for the ungodly.* For scarcely for a righteous man will one die: yet peradventure for a good man some would even dare to die. But God commendeth His love toward us, in that, while we were yet sinners, *Christ died for us.*

1 John 3, 16: Hereby perceive we the love of God, because He *laid down His life for us:* and we ought to lay down our lives for the brethren.

Is. 53, 12: Because He hath *poured out His soul unto death.* . . .

12.

Matt. 27, 46: And about the ninth hour Jesus cried with a loud voice, saying, Eli, Eli, lama sabachthani? that is to say, *My God, my God, why hast Thou forsaken me?*

13.

Tit. 2, 14: Who *gave Himself* FOR US, that He might redeem us from all iniquity, and purify unto Himself a peculiar people, zealous of good works.

John 6, 51: I am the living bread which came down from heaven. If any man eat of this bread, he shall live forever: and the bread that I will give is my flesh, which *I will give for the life of the world.*

John 1, 29: Behold the *Lamb of God* which taketh away the sin of the world.

Is. 53, 5—7: But He was *wounded for our transgressions,* He was *bruised for our iniquities:* the *chastisement of our peace* was upon Him; and with His stripes we are healed. All we like sheep have gone astray; we have turned every one to his own way; and the Lord hath *laid on Him the iniquity of us all.* He was oppressed, and He was afflicted, yet He opened not His mouth: He is brought as *a lamb to the slaughter,* and as a sheep before her shearers is dumb, so He openeth not His mouth.

Hebr. 9, 14: How much more shall the blood of Christ, who through the eternal Spirit *offered Himself* without spot to God, purge *your conscience* from dead works to serve the living God?

Hebr. 7, 27: Who needeth not daily, as those high priests, to offer up sacrifice, first for His own sins, and then *for the people's:* for this He did once when He *offered up Himself.*

Eph. 5, 2: And walk in love, as Christ also hath loved us, and hath *given Himself for us an offering* and *a sacrifice to God* for a sweet-smelling savor.

Hebr. 5, 7: Who in the days of His flesh, when He had offered up prayers and supplications with strong crying and tears unto Him that was able to save Him from death, and was heard in that He feared.

14.

Rom. 3, 25: Whom GOD *hath set forth to be a propitiation* through faith in His blood, *to declare His righteousness* for the remission of sins that are past, through the forbearance of God.

15.

1 John 2, 2: And He is the propitiation for *our sins,* and not for ours only, but also *for the sins of the whole world.*

1 John 1, 7: But if we walk in the light, as He is in the light, we have fellowship one with another, and the blood of Jesus Christ, His Son, *cleanseth us from all sin.*

Tit. 2, 14: Who gave Himself for us, that He might redeem us *from all iniquity,* and purify unto Himself a peculiar people, zealous of good works.

16.

2 Cor. 5, 14. 15. 19: For the love of Christ constraineth us; because we thus judge, that if One died *for all,* then were all dead: and that *He died for all,* that they which live should not henceforth live unto themselves, but unto Him which died for them, and rose again. (19) To-wit, that God was in Christ, reconciling *the world* unto Himself, not imputing *their* trespasses unto them; and hath committed unto us the word of reconciliation.

John 1, 29: Behold the Lamb of God which taketh away the sin of *the world.*

1 John 2, 2: He is the propitiation for our sins: and not for ours only, but also for the sins of *the whole world.*

Col. 1, 20: And, having made peace through the blood of His cross, by Him to reconcile all things unto Himself; by Him, I say, whether they be things in earth or things in heaven.

Gal. 4, 5: To redeem *them that were under the Law,* that we might receive the adoption of sons.

Hebr. 2, 9: But we see Jesus, who was made a little lower than the angels for the suffering of death, crowned with glory and honor, that He by the grace of God should taste death *for every man.*

1 Tim. 2, 6: Who gave Himself a ransom *for all,* to be testified in due time.

Rom. 8, 32: He that spared not His own Son, but delivered Him up *for us all,* how shall He not with Him also freely give us all things?

1 Cor. 8, 11: And through thy knowledge shall the weak brother *perish, for whom Christ died?*

2 Pet. 2, 1: But there were false prophets also among the people, even as there shall be false teachers among you, who privily shall bring in damnable heresies, even denying *the Lord that bought them,* and bring upon themselves *swift destruction.*

17.

2 Cor. 5, 18. 19: And all things are of God, who hath *reconciled us to Himself* by Jesus Christ, and hath given to us the ministry of reconciliation; to-wit, that God was in Christ, *reconciling the world unto Himself,* not imputing their trespasses unto them; and hath committed unto us the word of reconciliation.

Rom. 5, 10: For if, when we were *enemies, we were reconciled to God* by the death of His Son, much more, being reconciled, we shall be saved by His life.

Eph. 2, 16: And that He might *reconcile both unto God* in one body by the cross, having slain the enmity thereby.

Col. 1, 20: And, having made peace through the blood of His cross, by Him to *reconcile all things unto Himself;* by Him, I say, whether they be things in earth or things in heaven.

18.

Col. 1, 20: And, having *made peace* through the blood of His cross, by Him to reconcile all things unto Himself; by Him, I say, whether they be things in earth or things in heaven.

1 Thess. 1, 10: And to wait for His Son from heaven, whom He raised from the dead, even Jesus, which *delivered us from the wrath* to come.

Rom. 8, 32: He that spared not His own Son, but *delivered Him up for us all,* how shall He not with Him also *freely give us all things?*

1 John 2, 2: And He is the *propitiation for our sins,* and not for ours only, but also for the sins of the whole world.

Rom. 3, 25: Whom God hath set forth to be a *propitiation* through faith in His blood, to declare His righteousness for the remission of sins that are past, through the forbearance of God.

19.

Gal. 4, 5—7: To *redeem* them *that were under the Law,* that we might receive the *adoption of sons.* And because ye are *sons,* God hath sent forth the Spirit of His Son into your hearts, crying, Abba, Father! Wherefore thou art *no more a servant,* but a son; and if a son, then an heir of God through Christ.

Gal. 5, 1: Stand fast therefore in the *liberty* wherewith *Christ hath made us free,* and be not entangled again with the *yoke of bondage.*

20.

Gal. 3, 13: Christ hath *redeemed us from the curse of the Law,* being made a *curse for us;* for it is written, Cursed is every one that hangeth on a tree.

21.

Is. 53, 5: But He was wounded for our transgressions, He was bruised for our iniquities: the chastisement of our peace was upon Him; and with His stripes we are healed.

22.

Hebr. 1, 3: Who, being the brightness of His glory and the express image of His person, and upholding all things by the word of His power, when He had by Himself *purged our sins,* sat down on the right hand of the Majesty on high.

Hebr. 9, 28: So Christ was once offered to *bear the sins* of many; and unto them that look for Him shall He appear the second time without sin unto salvation.

1 John 1, 7: But if we walk in the light, as He is in the light, we have fellowship one with another, and the *blood* of Jesus Christ, His Son, *cleanseth us from all sin.*

1 Pet. 1, 18. 19: Forasmuch as ye know that ye were not *redeemed* with corruptible things, as silver and gold, *from your vain*

conversation received by tradition from your fathers, but with the precious blood of Christ, as of a lamb *without blemish and without spot.*

Rev. 1, 5: And from Jesus Christ, who is the faithful Witness, and the First-Begotten of the dead, and the Prince of the kings of the earth. Unto Him that loved us, and washed us *from our sins* in His own blood, etc.

23.

Hebr. 2, 9. 15: But we see Jesus, who was made a little lower than the angels for the suffering of death, crowned with glory and honor, that He by the grace of God should *taste death for every man.* (15) And *deliver* them who through *fear of death* were all their lifetime subject to bondage.

Hos. 13, 14: I will ransom them *from the power of the grave;* I will *redeem them from death. O death,* I will be *thy plagues; O grave,* I will be *thy destruction.* Repentance shall be hid from mine eyes.

2 Cor. 5, 15: And that He died for all, that they which live *should* not henceforth *live* unto themselves, but *unto Him which died for them,* and rose again.

24.

Hebr. 2, 14. 15: That through death He might *destroy him* that had the power of death, that is, *the devil, and deliver* them who through fear of death were all their lifetime subject to bondage.

25.

Rom. 5, 19: For as by one man's disobedience many were made sinners, so by the obedience of One *shall many be made righteous.*

Rom. 3, 25: Whom God hath set forth to be a propitiation through faith in His blood, to declare *His righteousness for the remission of sins* that are past, through the forbearance of God.

1 Cor. 1, 30: But of Him are ye in Christ Jesus, who of God is made unto us wisdom, and *righteousness,* and sanctification, and redemption.

Jer. 23, 6: In His days Judah shall be saved, and Israel shall dwell safely: and this is His name whereby He shall be called, *The Lord, Our Righteousness.*

2 Cor. 5, 21: For He hath made Him to be sin for us who knew no sin, that *we might be made the righteousness of God in Him.*

26.

1 John 4, 8: He that loveth not knoweth not God; for God is love.

27.

John 3, 14—16: And as Moses lifted up the serpent in the wilderness, even so must the Son of Man be lifted up, that whosoever believeth in Him should not perish, but *have eternal life.* For God so loved the world that He gave His only-begotten Son, that whosoever believeth in Him should not perish, but *have everlasting life.*

28.

Rom. 8, 34: Who is he that condemneth? It is *Christ* that died, yea, rather, that is risen again, who is even at the right hand of God, who *also maketh intercession for us.*

Hebr. 9, 24: For Christ is not entered into the holy places made with hands, which are the figures of the true, but into heaven itself, *now to appear in the presence of God for us.*

29.

1 John 2, 1. 2: My little children, these things write I unto you, that ye sin not. And if any man sin, *we have an advocate* with the Father, *Jesus Christ,* the Righteous: and He is the propitiation for our sins, and not for ours only, but also for the sins of the whole world.

Hebr. 7, 25: Wherefore He is able also to save them to the uttermost that come unto God by Him, seeing He ever liveth *to make intercession for them.*

John 17, 9. 20: *I pray for them:* I pray not for the world, but for them which Thou hast given me; for they are Thine. (20) *Neither pray I for these alone,* but *for them* also *which shall believe on me* through their word.

30.

Rom. 8, 33. 34: Who shall *lay anything to the charge* of God's elect? It is God that *justifieth. Who is he that condemneth?* It is Christ that died, yea, rather, that is risen again, who is even at the right hand of God, who also maketh intercession for us.

John 17, 15. 24: I pray not that Thou shouldest take them out of the world, but that Thou shouldest keep them from the evil. (24) Father, I will that they also whom Thou hast given me be with me where I am, that they may behold my glory which Thou hast given me; for Thou lovedst me before the foundation of the world.

CHRIST OUR ONLY HIGH PRIEST.

§ 124. That Christ, and He alone, was qualified to be the Redeemer and Savior of mankind appears when we consider that:

a) Being God and man in one inseparable person,[1] He was not personally under, but above the Law which was to be fulfilled, nor for His own sake bound to obey the Law's commandments;

b) Being man,[2] without being of necessity under the Law,[3] He could become man's substitute, as, in His humiliation, He was made under the Law;

c) Being free from every taint of sin,[4] He could render perfect obedience to the Law;

d) Though to His human nature divine attributes were communicated, it was by His humiliation rendered possible that He should undergo the penalties imposed upon man for sin;[5]

e) Being free from original sin and having committed no kind of actual sin,[6] He could make vicarious atonement by bearing the punishment of others;

f) Since He who fulfilled the Law and suffered the penalty for sin was the eternal, infinite God,[7] His active and passive obedience was of infinite and everlasting value, sufficient to purchase righteousness and eternal salvation[8] not for one man only, but for all the world, whose substitute He was;

g) He being the only person thus qualified, there cannot be salvation in any other, nor can any other name under heaven be given among men whereby we must be saved.[9]

a.

Cf. § 98.

b.

Matt. 12, 8: For the Son of Man is Lord even of the Sabbath day. Cf. §§ 97. 99.

c.

Cf. § 106.

d.

Cf. § 108.

e.

Cf. § 106.

f.

Cf. § 97.

Hebr. 10, 12. 14: But this Man, after He had offered one sacrifice for sins forever, sat down on the right hand of God. (14) For by one offering He hath *perfected forever them that are* sanctified.

g.

Acts 4, 12: Neither is there salvation in any other; for there is none other name under heaven given among men whereby we must be saved.

1 Tim. 2, 5. 6: For there is one God, and one Mediator between God and men, the man Christ Jesus, who gave Himself a ransom for all, to be testified in due time.

CHRIST THE PROPHET.

§ 125. Christ is the promised Prophet[1] to mankind, inasmuch as, being Himself the Wisdom[2] and the Truth[3] and having in Him all the treasures of wisdom and knowledge,[4] He in the days of His visible conversation on earth proclaimed unto man the will and counsel of God and the only true way of salvation,[5] predicted future events,[6] confirmed, by manifold miracles wrought in His own power, the divine authority of His doctrine,[7] imbued with the Holy Ghost and commissioned as His infallible witnesses and messengers His holy apostles,[8] charged all Christians to preach the Gospel unto every creature,[9] gave the power of the keys and the sacraments to His Church on earth,[10] instituted the holy ministry,[11] and still performs His prophetic office wherever in His name and by His order, publicly or in private, His truth and doctrine is preached and applied and His ordinances are administered.[12]

1.

Deut. 18, 18: *I will raise them up a Prophet* from among their brethren, like unto thee, and will put my words in His mouth; and He shall speak unto them all that I shall command Him.

John 6, 14: Then those men, when they had seen the miracle that Jesus did, said, This is of a truth *that Prophet that should come* into the world.

Matt. 17, 5: This is my beloved Son, in whom I am well pleased; *hear ye Him!*

Eph. 2, 17: And came and *preached* peace to you which were afar off, and to them that were nigh.

Acts 3, 22: For Moses truly said unto the fathers, A Prophet shall the Lord, your God, raise up unto you of your brethren, like unto me; Him shall ye hear in all things whatsoever He shall say unto you.

2.

Prov. 8, 12. 22. 31: I, Wisdom, dwell with prudence, and find out knowledge of witty inventions. (22) The Lord possessed me in the beginning of His way, before His works of old. (31) Rejoicing in the habitable part of His earth; and my delights were with the sons of men.

3.

John 14, 6: I am the Way, *the Truth,* and the Life; no man cometh unto the Father but by me.

10

Matt. 11, 27: All things are delivered unto me of my Father: and no man knoweth the Son but the Father; *neither knoweth any man the Father save the Son,* and he to whomsoever *the Son will reveal Him.*

4.

Is. 11, 1. 2: And there shall come forth a rod out of the stem of Jesse, and a Branch shall grow out of his roots: and the Spirit of the Lord shall rest upon Him, the *Spirit of wisdom and understanding,* the Spirit of counsel and might, the Spirit *of knowledge* and of the fear of the Lord.

Col. 2, 3: In whom are hid all the treasures of wisdom and knowledge.

1 Cor. 1, 30: But of Him are ye in Christ Jesus, who of God is made *unto us wisdom,* and righteousness, and sanctification, and redemption.

5.

Is. 61, 1: The Spirit of the Lord God is upon me, because the Lord hath anointed me to preach good tidings unto the meek; He hath sent me to bind up the broken-hearted, *to proclaim liberty to the captives, and the opening of the prison to them that are bound.*

Luke 4, 18: The Spirit of the Lord is upon me, because He hath anointed me to preach the Gospel to the poor; He hath sent me to heal the broken-hearted, *to preach deliverance* to the captives, and recovering of sight to the blind, to set at liberty them that are bruised.

Mark 1, 14: Now after that John was put in prison, Jesus came into Galilee, *preaching the Gospel* of the kingdom of God.

Matt. 5, 20. 22: For *I say unto you,* That except your righteousness shall exceed the righteousness of the scribes and Pharisees, ye shall in no case enter into the kingdom of heaven. (22) But *I say unto you,* That whosoever is angry with his brother without a cause shall be in danger of the judgment.

Matt. 9, 35: And Jesus went about all the cities and villages, *teaching in their synagogues,* and *preaching the Gospel* of the kingdom, and healing every sickness and every disease among the people.

John 1, 18: No man hath seen God at any time; the only-begotten Son, which is in the bosom of the Father, *He hath declared Him.*

6.

Luke 18, 31—33: Then He took unto Him the twelve, and said unto them, Behold, we go up to Jerusalem, and all things that are written by the prophets concerning the Son of Man shall be accomplished. For He shall be delivered unto the Gentiles, and shall be mocked, and spitefully entreated, and spitted on: and they shall scourge Him, and put Him to death: and the third day He shall rise again.

Matt. 21, 2. 3: Saying unto them, Go into the village over against you, and straightway ye shall find an ass tied, and a colt with her:

loose them, and bring them unto me. And if any man say aught unto you, ye shall say, The Lord hath need of them; and straightway he will send them.

Luke 21, 5—35. (Christ foretells the destruction of the temple and of Jerusalem, and speaks of the signs which shall come before the last day.)

7.

Luke 7, 14: And He came and touched the bier: and they that bare him stood still. And he said, Young man, *I say unto* thee, Arise!

John 2, 11: This beginning of *miracles* did Jesus in Cana of Galilee, and *manifested forth His glory; and His disciples believed on Him.*

John 10, 25. 38: Jesus answered them, *I told you,* and ye believed not; the *works that I do* in my Father's name, they *bear witness* of me. (38) But if I do, though ye believe not me, believe the works: that ye may know, and believe, that the Father is in me, and I in Him.

John 6, 36: But I said unto you, That ye also have *seen me,* and *believe* not.

John 3, 2: (Nicodemus said,) Rabbi, we know that Thou art a *teacher come from God; for* no man can do these *miracles* that Thou doest, except God be with him.

Acts 2, 22: Ye men of Israel, hear these words: Jesus of Nazareth, a man *approved* of God among you *by miracles* and wonders and signs, which God did by Him in the midst of you, as ye yourselves also know.

8.

Acts 1, 8: But ye shall receive power, after that the Holy Ghost is come upon you: and *ye shall be witnesses unto me* both in Jerusalem, and in all Judaea, and in Samaria, and *unto the uttermost part of the earth.*

John 15, 27: And ye also shall bear witness, because ye have been with me from the beginning.

Luke 24, 48. 49: And ye are witnesses of these things. And, behold, I send the promise of my Father upon you; but tarry ye in the city of Jerusalem, until ye be endued with power from on high.

9.

Matt. 28, 18—20: And Jesus came and spake unto them, saying, All power is given unto me in heaven and in earth. Go ye therefore, and teach all nations, baptizing them in the name of the Father, and of the Son, and of the Holy Ghost, *teaching them* to observe all things whatsoever I have commanded you. And, lo, I am with you alway, even unto the end of the world.

10.

John 20, 21—23: As my Father hath sent me, even so send I you. And when He had said this, He breathed on them, and saith unto them, Receive ye the Holy Ghost: whosesoever sins ye remit, they are remitted unto them; and whosesoever sins ye retain, they are retained.

Matt. 18, 18—20: Verily, I say unto you, Whatsoever ye shall bind on earth shall be bound in heaven, and whatsoever ye shall loose on earth shall be loosed in heaven. Again I say unto you, That if two of you shall agree on earth as touching anything that they shall ask, it shall be done for them of my Father which is in heaven. For where two or three are gathered together in my name, there am I in the midst of them.

11.

2 Cor. 5, 18. 20: And all things are of God, who hath reconciled us to Himself by Jesus Christ, and *hath given to us the ministry of reconciliation.* (20) Now, then, *we are ambassadors for Christ,* as though *God did beseech you by us:* we pray you in Christ's stead, Be ye reconciled to God! See also the texts sub 12.

12.

Luke 10, 16: He that heareth you *heareth me;* and he that despiseth you despiseth me; and he that despiseth me despiseth Him that sent me.

Luke 24, 47: And that repentance and remission of sins should *be preached in His name* among all nations, beginning at Jerusalem.

2 Cor. 5, 20: Now, then, we are ambassadors for Christ, as though God did beseech you by us: *we pray you in Christ's stead,* Be ye reconciled to God!

Eph. 4, 11: And *He gave* some, *apostles;* and some, *prophets;* and some, *evangelists;* and some, *pastors and teachers.*

1 Cor. 3, 9: For we are laborers together with God: ye are *God's* husbandry, ye are *God's* building.

1 Cor. 4, 1: Let a man so account of us, as of *the ministers of Christ,* and stewards of the mysteries of God.

CHRIST THE KING.

§ 126. Christ is King in a threefold kingdom, the kingdom of power, the kingdom of grace, and the kingdom of glory.

John 18, 37: Pilate therefore said unto Him, Art Thou a King, then? Jesus answered, *Thou sayest that I am a King.* To this end was I born, and for this cause came I into the world, that I should bear witness unto the truth. Every one that is of the truth heareth my voice.

Rev. 19, 16: And He hath on His vesture and on His thigh a name written, *King of kings,* and Lord of lords.

CHRIST'S KINGDOM OF POWER.

§ 127. In His kingdom of power Christ the God-man with His omnipotence governs the universe, controlling and directing all creatures according to His wise, good, and just purposes.

Matt. 28, 18: All power is given unto me in heaven and in earth.

Phil. 2, 10. 11: That at the name of Jesus every knee should bow, of things in heaven, and things in earth, and things under the earth, and that every tongue should confess that Jesus Christ is Lord, to the glory of God the Father.

Eph. 1, 21. 22: Far above all principality, and power, and might, and dominion, and every name that is named, not only in this world, but also in that which is to come: and hath put all things under His feet, and gave Him to be the Head over all things to the Church.

Ps. 8, 6. 7: Thou madest Him to have dominion over the works of Thy hands; Thou hast put all things under His feet: all sheep and oxen, yea, and the beasts of the field.

Dan. 7, 14: And there was given Him dominion, and glory, and a kingdom, that all people, nations, and languages, should serve Him. His dominion is an everlasting dominion, which shall not pass away, and His kingdom that which shall not be destroyed.

Hebr. 2, 7. 8: Thou madest Him a little lower than the angels; Thou crownedst Him with glory and honor, and didst set Him over the works of Thy hands: Thou hast put all things in subjection under His feet. For in that He put all in subjection under Him, He left nothing that is not put under Him. But now we see not yet all things put under Him.

1 Pet. 3, 22: Who is gone into heaven, and is on the right hand of God, angels and authorities and powers being made subject unto Him.

See also Ps. 2.

CHRIST'S KINGDOM OF GRACE.

§ 128. In His spiritual kingdom of grace Christ, the only Head of His Church,[1] rules His spiritual subjects jointly and severally by His Word,[2] which alone in the Church is the law of the realm demanding unconditional obedience,[3] and the divine instruction never to be violated in the execution of His royal will and the administration of His ordinances by the Church and the ministers of the Church and of Christ,[4] who graciously and abundantly provides for and powerfully protects and defends this kingdom and all His subjects within the same.[5]

1.

Eph. 1, 22. 23: And hath put all things under His feet, and gave Him to be *the Head over all* things *to the Church,* which is His body, the fullness of Him that filleth all in all.

Eph. 5, 23. 24: For the husband is the head of the wife, even as *Christ is the Head of the Church:* and He is the Savior of the body. Therefore as *the Church is subject unto Christ,* so let the wives be to their own husbands in everything.

2.

John 18, 36: Jesus answered, *My kingdom is not of this world:* if my kingdom were of this world, then would my servants fight, that I should not be delivered to the Jews: but *now is my kingdom not from hence.*

2 Cor. 10, 4. 5: For the *weapons* of our warfare are *not carnal,* but mighty through God to the pulling down of strongholds, casting down imaginations, and every high thing that exalteth itself against the *knowledge of God,* and *bringing into captivity every thought* to the *obedience of Christ.*

Jer. 23, 5. 6: Behold, the days come, saith the Lord, that I will raise unto David a righteous Branch, and *a King* shall reign and prosper, and shall execute judgment and justice in the earth. In His days *Judah shall be saved,* and Israel shall dwell safely: and this is His name whereby He shall be called, *The Lord, Our Righteousness.*

John 18, 37: Pilate therefore said unto Him, Art Thou a King, then? Jesus answered, Thou sayest that *I am a King. To this end* was I born, and for this cause came I into the world, *that I should bear witness unto the truth.* Every one that is of the truth *heareth my voice.*

John 10, 16: And other sheep I have, which are not of this fold: *them also I must bring,* and they shall hear *my voice;* and there shall be *one fold, and one shepherd.*

John 8, 31. 32: Then said Jesus to those Jews which believed on Him, If ye continue *in my Word,* then are ye *my disciples indeed;* and ye shall know the *truth,* and the truth shall make you free.

3.

Luke 10, 16: He that heareth you heareth me; *and he that despiseth you despiseth me;* and he that despiseth me despiseth Him that sent me.

John 10, 27: My sheep hear *my voice,* and I know them, *and they follow me.*

2 Thess. 3, 6. 14: Now we *command* you, brethren, *in the name of our Lord Jesus Christ,* that ye withdraw yourselves from every brother that walketh disorderly, and not after the tradition which he received of us. (14) And *if any man obey not* our *word* by this epistle, note that man, and *have no company with him,* that he might be ashamed.

Rom. 16, 17: Now I beseech you, brethren, *mark them* which cause divisions, and offenses *contrary to the doctrine* which ye have learned, *and avoid them.*

2 Cor. 10, 4. 5: For the weapons of our warfare are *not carnal,* but mighty through God to the pulling down of strongholds, *casting down imaginations,* and every high thing *that exalteth itself against the knowledge of God,* and bringing into *captivity* every thought to the obedience of Christ.

4.

Matt. 28, 18—20: And Jesus came and spake unto them, saying, *All power* is given unto me in heaven and in earth. *Go ye therefore,* and teach all nations, *baptizing* them in the name of the Father, and ·of the Son, and of the Holy Ghost, *teaching them* to observe *all things* whatsoever I have *commanded you.* And, lo, I am with you alway, even unto the end of the world.

Luke 22, 19: And He took bread, and gave thanks, and brake it, and gave unto them, saying, This is my body which is given for you: *this do* in remembrance of me.

1 Cor. 11, 24. 25: And when He had given thanks, He brake it, and said, Take, eat: this is my body, which is broken for you: *this do* in remembrance of me. After the same manner also He took the cup, when He had supped, saying, This cup is the new testament in my blood: *this do ye,* as oft as ye drink it, in remembrance of me.

Tit. 1, 5—9: For this cause left I thee in Crete, that thou shouldest set in order the things that are wanting, and ordain elders in every city, as I had appointed thee: *if any be* blameless, the husband of one wife, having faithful children not accused of riot or unruly. For a bishop *must be* blameless, as the steward of God; not self-willed, not soon angry, not given to wine, no striker, not given to filthy lucre, but a lover of hospitality, a lover of good men, sober, just, holy, temperate, holding fast the faithful word *as he hath been taught,* that he may be able by sound doctrine both to exhort and to convince the gainsayers. — See also 1 Tim. 5, 7—20.

Matt. 18, 15—17: Moreover, if thy brother shall trespass against thee, *go and tell him* his fault between thee and him alone. If he shall hear thee, thou hast gained thy brother. But if he will not hear thee, then *take with thee one or two more,* that in the mouth of two or three witnesses every word may be established. And if he shall neglect to hear them, *tell it unto the church:* but if he neglect to hear the church, *let him be unto thee* as an heathen man and a publican.

1 Cor. 5, 13: But them that are without God judgeth. Therefore *put away* from among yourselves that wicked person.

5.

John 17, 6. 14. 16: I have manifested Thy name unto the men which Thou *gavest me* out of the world: Thine they were, and Thou *gavest them me;* and they have kept Thy Word. (14) I have given them Thy Word; and the world hath hated them, because they are not of the world, even as I am not of the world. (16) They are not of the world, even as I am not of the world.

Eph. 1, 19. 20: And what is the exceeding greatness of *His power to us-ward who believe,* according to the working of His mighty power, which *He wrought in Christ,* when He raised Him from the dead, and set Him at His own right hand in the heavenly places.

Matt. 16, 18: And I say also unto thee, That thou art Peter, and upon this rock I will build my Church; *and the gates of hell shall not prevail against it.*

John 17, 11. 12: And now I am no more in the world, but these are in the world, and I come to Thee. Holy Father, *keep* through Thine own name *those whom Thou hast given me,* that they may be one, as we are. While I was with them in the world, *I kept them in Thy name.* Those that Thou gavest me *I have kept,* and *none of them is lost,* but the son of perdition, that the Scripture might be fulfilled.

John 10, 28. 29: And *I give* unto them eternal life; and *they shall never perish, neither shall any man pluck them out of my hand.* My Father, which gave them me, is greater than all; and *no man is able to pluck them out of my Father's hand.*

Is. 40, 11: He shall feed His flock like a shepherd: He shall gather the lambs with His arm, and carry them in His bosom, and shall gently lead those that are with young.

Ezek. 34, 16: I will seek that which was lost, and bring again that which was driven away, and will bind up that which was broken, and will strengthen that which was sick: but I will destroy the fat and the strong; I will feed them with judgment.

Ps. 23: The Lord is my Shepherd, etc.

CHRIST'S KINGDOM OF GLORY.

§ 129. In His kingdom of glory Christ the God-man will forever reign[1] over angels and archangels[2] and the glorified elect,[3] the Church Triumphant, when we shall serve Him hereafter in perfect obedience, praise and adore Him, our Savior and our King.[4]

1.

Luke 22, 29: I appoint unto you a kingdom, as my Father hath appointed unto me.

Luke 1, 33: And He shall *reign* over the house of Jacob *forever;* and of His kingdom there shall be *no end.*

Is. 9, 7: Of the increase of His government and peace *there shall be no end,* upon the throne of David, and upon His kingdom, to order it, and to establish it with judgment and with justice from *henceforth even forever.*

Luke 23, 42. 43: And he said unto Jesus, Lord, remember me when Thou comest into Thy kingdom. And Jesus said unto him, Verily, I say unto thee, To-day shalt thou be with me in paradise.

2.

Matt. 25, 31: When the Son of Man shall come in His glory, and *all the holy angels* with Him, *then* shall He sit upon the *throne of His glory.* — See also Rev. 5, 5—13.

3.

Col. 3, 4: When Christ, who is our life, shall appear, then shall ye also appear *with Him in glory.*

Phil. 3, 20. 21: For our conversation is in heaven, from whence also we look for the Savior, the Lord Jesus Christ, who shall change our vile body, that it may be fashioned *like unto His glorious body,* according to the working whereby He is able even to subdue all things unto Himself.

Rom. 8, 30: Moreover, whom He did predestinate, them He also called: and whom He called, them He also justified: and whom He justified, *them He also glorified.*

1 Thess. 2, 12: That you would walk worthy of God, who hath called *you* unto *His kingdom and glory.*

1 Thess. 4, 17: Then we which are alive and remain shall be caught up together with them in the clouds, to meet the Lord in the air: and so shall *we ever be with the Lord.*

Luke 12, 32: Fear not, little flock; for it is your Father's good pleasure to *give you the kingdom.*

Luke 22, 18: For I say unto you, I will not drink of the fruit of the vine until *the kingdom of God shall come.*

Matt. 25, 34: Then shall the King say unto them on His right hand, Come, ye blessed of my Father, *inherit the kingdom* prepared for you from the foundation of the world.

4.

John 12, 26: If any man serve me, let him follow me; and where I am, there shall also my servant be. If any man serve me, him will my Father honor.

John 17, 24: Father, I will that they also whom Thou hast given me be with me where I am, that they may behold my glory which Thou hast given me; for Thou lovedst me before the foundation of the world.

2 Tim. 4, 8: Henceforth there is laid up for me a crown of righteousness, which the Lord, the righteous Judge, shall give me at that day: and not to me only, but unto all them also that love His appearing.

Rev. 19, 6. 7: And I heard as it were the voice of a great multitude, and as the voice of many waters, and as the voice of mighty thunderings, saying, Alleluja! for the Lord God Omnipotent reigneth. Let us be glad and rejoice, and give honor to Him; for the marriage of the Lamb is come, and His wife hath made herself ready.

Hebr. 12, 22—24: But ye are come unto Mount Sion, and unto the city of the living God, the heavenly Jerusalem, and to an innumerable company of angels, to the general assembly and church of the firstborn, which are written in heaven, and to God, the Judge of all, and to the spirits of just men made perfect, and to Jesus, the Mediator of the new covenant, and to the blood of sprinkling that speaketh better things than that of Abel.

Tit. 2, 13: Looking for that blessed hope and the glorious appearing of the great God and our Savior Jesus Christ.

2 Pet. 1, 11: For so an entrance shall be ministered unto you abundantly into the everlasting kingdom of our Lord and Savior Jesus Christ.

Rev. 22, 3. 4: And there shall be no more curse: but the throne of God and of the Lamb shall be in it; and His servants shall serve Him: and they shall see His face; and His name shall be in their foreheads.

SOTERIOLOGY.

DEFINITION.

§ 130. Soteriology is the doctrine of Holy Scripture concerning the application of the merits of Christ to the individual sinner,[1] whereby the sinner is led to the actual possession and enjoyment of the blessings which Christ has procured for all mankind.[2]

1.

2 Cor. 5, 19. 20: God was in Christ, reconciling the world unto Himself, not imputing their trespasses unto them; and hath committed unto us the word of reconciliation. Now, then, we are ambassadors for Christ, as though God did beseech you by us: we pray you in Christ's stead, *Be ye reconciled* to God!

1 Cor. 1, 4—6: I thank my God always on your behalf for the grace of God which is *given you* by Jesus Christ, that in everything *ye are enriched* by Him, in all utterance, and in all knowledge, even as the *testimony of Christ was confirmed in you.*

2.

John 1, 16: And *of His fullness* have *all we received,* and grace for grace.

1 Cor. 1, 7: So that ye come behind in no *gift,* waiting for the coming of our Lord Jesus Christ.

Eph. 1, 7. 8. 11: In whom *we have* redemption through His blood, the forgiveness of sins, according to the riches of His grace, wherein He hath abounded toward us in all wisdom and prudence; (11) in whom also *we have obtained* an inheritance.

PROMPTING CAUSE.

§ 131. The application of the merits and benefits of Christ to the individual sinner is the work of God alone,[1] who is moved thereto by the same universal grace[2] which moved Him to procure and work the redemption of mankind.[3]

1.

Eph. 2, 5. 8: Even when we were dead in sins, *hath quickened* us together with Christ (by grace ye are saved). (8) For by grace are ye saved through faith; and that not of yourselves: it is *the gift of God.*

1 Cor. 12, 3: *No man* can say that Jesus is the Lord *but by the Holy Ghost.*

2.

Eph. 1, 7: In whom we have redemption through His blood, the forgiveness of sins, *according to the riches of His grace.*

Eph. 2, 4—6: But God, who is *rich in mercy, for His great love* wherewith He loved us, even *when we were dead in sins,* hath quickened us together with Christ, (by grace ye are saved;) and hath raised us up together, and made us sit together in heavenly places in Christ Jesus. (V. 8 sub 1.)

1 Tim. 2, 4: Who will have *all men* to be saved, and to come unto the knowledge of the truth.

2 Tim. 1, 9: Who hath saved us, and called us with an holy calling, not according to our works, but *according to His own purpose and grace,* which was given us in Christ Jesus before the world began.

Col. 1, 23: If ye continue in the faith grounded and settled, and be not moved away from *the hope of the Gospel,* which ye have heard, and *which was preached to every creature which is under heaven,* whereof I, Paul, am made a minister.

Matt. 11, 28: Come unto me, *all ye* that labor and are heavy laden, and I will give you rest.

Ezek. 18, 31. 32: Cast away from you all your transgressions whereby ye have transgressed, and make you a new heart and a new spirit; for why will ye die, O house of Israel? For *I have no pleasure in the death of him that dieth,* saith the Lord God: wherefore turn yourselves, and live ye!

3.

John 3, 16: For God *so loved the world* that He gave His only-begotten Son, that whosoever believeth in Him should not perish, but have everlasting life.

1 John 4, 9. 10: In this was manifested the love of God toward us, because that God sent His only-begotten Son into *the world,* that we might live through Him. Herein is love, not that we loved God,

but that He loved us, and sent His Son to be the propitiation for our sins.

2 Cor. 8, 9: For ye know the grace of our Lord Jesus Christ, that, though He was rich, yet for your sakes He became poor, that ye through His poverty might be rich.

INSTRUMENTAL CAUSE.

§ 132. The means by which the benefits of Christ are offered and appropriated to the sinner,[1] and by which not only the capability of accepting what is offered, but also such acceptance itself is wrought in Him,[2] are the means of grace, the written and the spoken word of the Gospel[3] and the holy Sacraments.[4]

1.

Gal. 3, 2. 18. 22: This only would I learn of you, *Received ye* the Spirit by the works of the Law, or *by the hearing of faith?* (18) For if the inheritance be of the Law, it is no more of promise: but *God gave* it to Abraham *by promise.* (22) But the Scripture hath concluded all under sin, that the promise by faith of Jesus Christ might be *given to them that believe.*

John 14, 27: Peace I leave with you, *my peace I give unto you:* not as the world giveth, give I unto you. *Let not your heart be troubled,* neither let it be afraid.

Acts 2, 38: Then Peter said unto them, Repent, and *be baptized,* every one of you, in the name of Jesus Christ for the remission of sins, *and ye shall receive* the gift of the Holy Ghost.

Rom. 1, 16: For I am not ashamed of the *Gospel of Christ:* for it is the *power of God unto salvation* to every one that believeth, to the Jew first, and also to the Greek.

2 Cor. 5, 19: To-wit, that God was in Christ, reconciling the world unto Himself; . . . and hath committed unto us the *word of reconciliation.*

2.

Rom. 10, 14. 17: How, then, shall they call on Him in whom they have not believed? and *how shall they believe in Him of whom they have not heard?* and how shall they hear without a preacher? (17) So, then, *faith cometh by hearing,* and hearing by the Word of God.

John 17, 20: Neither pray I for these alone, but for them also which shall *believe on me through their word.*

Acts 11, 14: Who shall tell thee *words whereby* thou and all thy house *shall be saved.*

James 1, 21: Wherefore lay apart all filthiness and superfluity of naughtiness, and receive with meekness the engrafted *Word, which is able to save* your *souls.*

Col. 1, 28: Whom *we preach,* warning every man, and teaching every man in all wisdom, that we may present every man *perfect* in Christ Jesus.

3.

2 Tim. 3, 15—17: And that from a child thou hast known the *Holy Scriptures,* which are *able to make thee wise unto salvation through faith* which is in Christ Jesus. *All Scripture* is given by inspiration of God, and is *profitable* for doctrine, for reproof, for correction, for instruction in righteousness, that the man of God may be perfect, throughly furnished unto all good works.

John 5, 39: Search the *Scriptures;* for *in them* ye think *ye have eternal life:* and they are they which testify of me.

Col. 1, 28: Whom *we preach,* warning every man, and teaching every man in all wisdom, *that we may present every man perfect in Christ Jesus.*

1 Cor. 1, 21: For after that in the wisdom of God the world by wisdom knew not God, it pleased God *by the foolishness of preaching to save them that believe.*

1 Cor. 15, 1. 2: Moreover, brethren, I declare unto you *the Gospel which I preached* unto you, which also ye have received, and wherein ye stand, *by which also ye are saved,* if ye keep in memory what I preached unto you, unless ye have believed in vain.

Eph. 1, 7—9: In whom *we have redemption* through His blood, *the forgiveness of sins,* according to the riches of His grace, wherein He hath abounded toward us in all wisdom and prudence, *having made known unto us the mystery of His will,* according to His good pleasure which He hath purposed in Himself.

4.

Eph. 5, 26: That He might *sanctify and cleanse it* with *the washing of water by the Word.*

Mark 16, 16: He that believeth and *is baptized* shall be *saved;* but he that believeth not shall be damned.

Tit. 3, 5: Not by works of righteousness which we have done, but according to His mercy *He saved us, by the washing of regeneration* and renewing of the Holy Ghost.

THE GOSPEL.

§ 133. The Gospel, in the strict sense of the term,[1] is the divine doctrine[2] by which God announces to all mankind[3] His grace and mercy in Christ Jesus,[4] earnestly offers to all that hear it[5] forgiveness of sins and the righteousness which Christ has earned by His obedience unto death (*vis collativa*), and by the power inherent in such grace efficaciously operates[6] in their hearts toward the acceptance[7] of

His gracious gifts, and perseverance in faith[8] and in holiness of life,[9] and produces such effects wherever they are not frustrated by man's obstinate resistance[10] (*vis operativa seu effectiva*).

1.

Mark 1, 15: The time is fulfilled, and the kingdom of God is at hand. Repent ye, and *believe the Gospel!*

Rom. 1, 16: For I am not ashamed of the *Gospel of Christ;* for it is the power of God unto salvation to every one that believeth, to the Jew first, and also to the Greek.

2.

Acts 14, 3: Long time therefore abode they, *speaking boldly in the Lord,* which gave testimony unto the *Word of His grace,* and granted signs and wonders to be done by their hands.

Gal. 1, 11. 12: But I certify you, brethren, that the *Gospel which was preached* of me is *not after man.* For I neither received it of man, neither was I taught it, but *by the revelation of Jesus Christ.*

Luke 10, 16: He that *heareth you heareth me;* and he that despiseth you despiseth me; and he that despiseth me despiseth Him that sent me.

1 Pet. 1, 25: But the *Word of the Lord* endureth forever. And this is the Word *which by the Gospel is preached* unto you.

1 Thess. 1, 8: For from you sounded out the *Word of the Lord* not only in Macedonia and Achaia, but also in every place your faith to God-ward is spread abroad, so that we need not to speak anything.

Acts 4, 29: And now, *Lord,* behold their threatenings, and grant unto Thy servants that with all boldness they may *speak Thy Word.*

Luke 1, 77: To *give knowledge* of salvation unto His people by the remission of their sins.

1 Cor. 2, 12. 13: That we might *know the things* that are freely given to us of God. Which things also we speak, not in the *words* which man's wisdom teacheth, but *which the Holy Ghost teacheth.*

1 Cor. 1, 5—7: In everything ye are enriched by Him in *all utterance* and in *all knowledge;* even as the *testimony of Christ* was confirmed in you, so that ye come behind in no gift.

3.

Mark 16, 15: And He said unto them, Go ye *into all the world,* and preach *the Gospel to every creature.*

Luke 24, 47: And that repentance and remission of sins should be *preached* in His name *among all nations,* beginning at Jerusalem.

Matt. 24, 14: And *this Gospel* of the kingdom shall be *preached in all the world* for a witness *unto all nations;* and then shall the end come.

Rom. 1, 5: By whom we have received grace and apostleship, *for obedience to the faith among all nations,* for His name.

Rom. 10, 17. 18: So, then, *faith cometh by hearing,* and hearing by the Word of God. But I say, *Have they not heard?* Yes, verily; their sound went *into all the earth* and their words *unto the ends of the world.*

4.

Luke 1, 76. 77: And thou, child, shalt be called *the prophet of the Highest;* for thou shalt go before the face of the Lord to prepare His ways, to give knowledge *of salvation* unto His people *by the remission of their sins.*

5.

Acts 13, 46: Then Paul and Barnabas waxed bold, and said, It was necessary that the *Word of God* should first have been spoken to you; but seeing *ye put it from you,* and *judge yourselves unworthy of everlasting life,* lo, we turn to the Gentiles.

Col. 1, 26: Even the mystery which hath been hid from ages and from generations, but now is *made manifest to His saints.*

2 Thess. 2, 10: And with all deceivableness of unrighteousness *in them that perish,* because *they received not the love of the truth, that they might be saved.*

1 Thess. 2, 13: For this cause also thank we God without ceasing, because, when *ye received* the Word of God which ye heard of us, *ye received it* not as the word of men, but as it is in truth, the Word of God, which effectually worketh also in you that believe.

6.

Rom. 15, 18: For I will not dare to speak of any of those things which *Christ hath* not *wrought by me,* to *make the Gentiles obedient, by word* and deed. Cf. 1 Thess. 2, 13, above sub **5**: "*effectually worketh.*"

Rom. 1, 16: For I am not ashamed of the Gospel of Christ; for it is the *power of God unto salvation* to every one that believeth, to the Jew first, and also to the Greek.

1 Cor. 3, 5: Who, then, is Paul, and who is Apollos, but *ministers by whom ye believed,* even as the Lord gave to every man?

1 Thess. 1, 5: For our *Gospel* came not unto you in word only, but also *in power,* and in the Holy Ghost, and in much assurance, as ye know what manner of men we were among you for your sake.

Col. 1, 5. 6: For the hope which is laid up for you in heaven, whereof ye heard before in the word of the truth of the *Gospel,* which is come unto you, as it is in all the world, and *bringeth forth fruit,* as it doth also in you, since the day ye heard of it, and knew the grace of God in truth.

Hebr. 4, 12: For the Word of God is quick, and *powerful,* and sharper than any two-edged sword, *piercing* even to the dividing asunder of soul and spirit, and of the joints and marrow, and is a discerner of the thoughts and intents of the heart.

Acts 11, 21: And the *hand of the Lord* was with them; and *a great number believed,* and turned unto the Lord.

Gal. 3, 5: He that ministereth to you the Spirit, and *worketh miracles among you,* doeth He it by the works of the Law, or *by the hearing of faith?*

James 1, 18: Of His own will *begat He us with the word of truth,* that we should be a kind of firstfruits of His *creatures.*

1 Cor. 4, 15: For though ye have ten thousand instructors in Christ, yet have ye not many fathers; for in Christ Jesus *I have begotten you through the Gospel.*

1 Pet. 1, 23: Being *born again,* not of corruptible seed, but of incorruptible, *by the Word of God,* which liveth and abideth forever.

7.

Gal. 3, 2: This only would I learn of you, *Received ye the Spirit* by the works of the Law, or *by the hearing of faith?*

John 17, 20: Neither pray I for these alone, but for them also which shall *believe on me through their word.*

Acts 26, 17. 18: Delivering thee from the people, and from the Gentiles, unto whom now I send thee, *to open their eyes,* and *to turn them from darkness to light,* and from the power of Satan unto God, that they may *receive forgiveness of sins,* and inheritance among them which are sanctified by faith that is in me.

1 Cor. 15, 2: *By which* also *ye are saved,* if ye keep in memory *what I preached unto you,* unless ye have believed in vain.

Acts 11, 14: Who shall tell thee *words whereby thou and all thy house shall be saved.*

1 Cor. 1, 21: For after that in the wisdom of God the world by wisdom knew not God, it pleased God *by the foolishness of preaching to save them* that believe.

1 Pet. 3, 21: The like figure whereunto even *Baptism doth also now save us,* (not the putting away of the filth of the flesh, but the answer of a good conscience toward God,) by the resurrection of Jesus Christ.

8.

1 John 1, 4: And these things *write we* unto you, that *your joy may be full.*

1 John 2, 24: Let that therefore abide in you *which ye have heard* from the beginning. If *that which ye have heard* from the beginning shall remain in you, *ye also shall continue in the Son and in the Father.*

9.

John 17, 17: *Sanctify them through Thy truth:* Thy Word is truth.

Rom. 12, 1: I *beseech you* therefore, brethren, *by the mercies of God,* that ye *present your bodies a living sacrifice,* holy, acceptable unto God, which is your reasonable service.

10.

Cf. §§ 138 and 141.

THE SACRAMENTS IN GENERAL.

§ 134. The sacraments are sacred acts[1] of divine institution,[2] in which, wherever they are properly administered[3] by the use of the prescribed external elements[4] in conjunction with the divine words of institution,[5] God is, in a manner peculiar to each sacrament, present with the Word and elements,[6] earnestly offers to all who partake of the sacrament[7] forgiveness of sins[8] and eternal salvation,[9] and operates toward the acceptance of these blessings, or toward greater assurance of their possession.[10]

1.

1 Cor. 11, 24. 25: *This* DO in remembrance of me. . . . *This* DO *ye,* as oft as ye drink it, in remembrance of me.

Matt. 28, 19: Go ye therefore, and teach all nations, *baptizing* them in the name of the Father, and of the Son, and of the Holy Ghost.

2.

Matt. 28, 19: *Go ye* therefore, and teach all nations, *baptizing them in the name of the Father, and of the Son, and of the Holy Ghost.*

1 Cor. 11, 23—25: For I have *received of the Lord* that which also I delivered unto you, That *the Lord Jesus* the same night in which He was betrayed *took bread;* and when He had *given thanks,* He brake it, and said, *Take, eat; this is my body,* which is broken for you: this do in remembrance of me. After the same manner also *He took the cup,* when He had supped, *saying, This cup is the new testament in my blood: this do ye, as oft as ye drink it,* in remembrance of me.

Matt. 26, 26—28: And as they were eating, Jesus took bread, and blessed it, and brake it, and gave it to the disciples, and said, Take, eat; this is my body. And He took the cup, and gave thanks, and gave it to them, saying, Drink ye all of it; for this is my blood of the new testament, which is shed for many for the remission of sins.

Mark 14, 22—24: And as they did eat, Jesus took bread, and blessed, and brake it, and gave to them, and said, Take, eat; this is my body. And He took the cup, and when He had given thanks, He gave it to them: and they all drank of it. And He said unto them, This is my blood of the new testament, which is shed for many.

Luke 22, 19. 20: And He took bread, and gave thanks, and brake it, and gave unto them, saying, This is my body which is given for you: this do in remembrance of me. Likewise also the cup after supper, saying, This cup is the new testament in my blood, which is shed for you.

11

3.

See texts sub 2.

4.

Eph. 5, 27: That He might sanctify and cleanse it with the washing of *water* by the Word.

John 3, 5. 23: Jesus answered, Verily, verily, I say unto thee, Except a man be born of *water* and of the Spirit, he cannot enter into the kingdom of God. (23) And John also was baptizing in Aenon, near to Salim, because there was much *water* there: and they came, and were baptized.

1 Cor. 10, 16: The *cup* of blessing which we bless, is it not the communion of the blood of Christ? The *bread* which we break, is it not the communion of the body of Christ?

5.

Eph. 5, 26: That He might sanctify and cleanse it with the washing of water *by the Word.*

1 Cor. 10, 16: The cup of blessing *which we bless,* is it not the communion of the blood of Christ? The bread which we break, is it not the communion of the body of Christ?

1 Cor. 11, 24. 25: And when He had given thanks, He brake it, and *said,* Take, eat; this is my body, which is broken for you: *this do* in remembrance of me. After the same manner also He took the cup, when He had supped, *saying,* This cup is the new testament in my blood: *this do ye,* as oft as ye drink it, in remembrance of me.

6.

Matt. 3, 16. 17: And *Jesus,* when He was baptized, went up straightway out of the water: and lo, the heavens were opened unto Him, and he saw the *Spirit of God* descending like a dove, and lighting upon Him: and lo, a voice from heaven, saying, *This is my beloved Son,* in whom *I* am well pleased.

John 3, 5: Jesus answered, Verily, verily, I say unto thee, Except a man be born of water and *of the Spirit,* he cannot enter into the kingdom of God.

1 Cor. 11, 29: For he that eateth and drinketh unworthily eateth and drinketh damnation to himself, not discerning *the Lord's body.*

7.

Luke 7, 30: But the *Pharisees and lawyers rejected the counsel of God* against themselves, *being not baptized* of him.

Luke 22, 19. 20: And He took bread, and gave thanks, and brake it, *and gave unto them,* saying, This is my body which is *given for you:* this do in remembrance of me. Likewise also the cup after supper, saying, This cup is the new testament in my blood, which *is shed for you.*

8.

Acts 21, 16: And now why tarriest thou? Arise, and *be baptized,* and *wash away thy sins,* calling on the name of the Lord.

Acts 2, 38: Then Peter said unto them, Repent, and *be baptized, every one of you,* in the name of Jesus Christ *for the remission of sins,* and ye shall receive the gift of the Holy Ghost.

Luke 3, 3: And he came into all the country about Jordan, preaching the *baptism* of repentance *for the remission of sins.*

Eph. 5, 26: That He might *sanctify* and *cleanse it* with the *washing of water by the Word.*

1 Pet. 3, 21: The like figure whereunto even *Baptism doth* also now *save us,* (not the putting away of the filth of the flesh, but the answer of *a good conscience toward God,*) by the resurrection of Jesus Christ.

Gal. 3, 26. 27: For ye are all the children of God by faith in Christ Jesus. For *as many* of you *as have been baptized* into Christ *have put on Christ.*

Matt. 26, 28: For *this is my blood* of the new testament, which is shed for many *for the remission of sins.*

9.

1 Pet. 3, 21: The like figure whereunto even *Baptism doth* also now *save us.*

Tit. 3, 5: Not by works of righteousness which we have done, but according to His mercy *He saved us by the washing of regeneration* and renewing of the Holy Ghost.

10.

Tit. 3, 5: Not by works of righteousness which we have done, but according to His mercy He saved us by the washing of regeneration and *renewing of the Holy Ghost.*

John 3, 5: Jesus answered, *Verily, verily,* I say unto thee, Except a man be born of water and of the Spirit, he cannot enter into the kingdom of God.

THE SACRAMENTS OF THE CHRISTIAN CHURCH.

§ 135. The sacraments of the Christian Church are Baptism and the Lord's Supper.

BAPTISM.

§ 136. The sacrament of Baptism is the act of sprinkling,[1] pouring,[2] or by immersion applying upon a living human person[3] water[4] in the name of the Father and of the Son and of the Holy Ghost,[5] the Triune God, who is Himself present with the water connected with the sacramental word,[6] and efficaciously offers the gifts of His grace,[7] and operates toward their acceptance, as in infants,[8] or toward perseverance in, and greater assurance of, their possession, as in adults who have been previously regenerated by the Word.[9]

1.

Hebr. 10, 22: Let us draw near with a true heart, in full assurance of faith, having our hearts *sprinkled* from an evil conscience, and our bodies *washed with pure water.*

1 Cor. 10, 2: And were all *baptized* unto Moses *in the cloud* and in the sea.

Exod. 24, 6—8: And Moses took half of the blood, and put it in basins; and half of the blood he *sprinkled* on the altar. And he took the Book of the Covenant, and read in the audience of the people: and they said, All that the Lord hath said will we do, and be obedient. And Moses took the blood, and *sprinkled* it on the people, and said, Behold the blood of the *covenant,* which the Lord hath made with you concerning all these words.

Hebr. 9, 19. 20: For when Moses had spoken every precept to all the people according to the Law, he took the blood of calves and of goats, with water, and scarlet wool, and hyssop, and *sprinkled* both the book and all the people, saying, This is the blood of the *testament* which God hath enjoined unto you.

Numb. 8, 7: And thus shalt thou do unto them, to *cleanse them:* *Sprinkle* water of purifying upon them, and let them shave all their flesh, and let them wash their clothes, and so make themselves clean.

Numb. 19, 18. 19: And a clean person shall take hyssop, and dip it in the water, and *sprinkle it* upon the tent, and upon all the *vessels,* and upon the *persons* that were there, and upon him that touched a bone, or one slain, or one dead, or a grave: and the clean person shall *sprinkle* upon the unclean on the third day, and on the seventh day: and on the seventh day he shall *purify* himself, and wash his clothes, and bathe himself in water, and shall be clean at even.

Mark 7, 4: And when they come from the market, except they *wash,* they eat not. And many other things there be which they have received to hold, as the *washing* of cups, and pots, brazen *vessels,* and of tables.

Luke 5, 14: And He charged him to tell no man: but go, and show thyself to the priest, and offer *for thy cleansing,* according as Moses commanded, for a testimony unto them.

Ezek. 36, 25: Then will I *sprinkle* clean water upon you, and ye shall be clean: from all your filthiness and from all your idols *will I cleanse you.*

Hebr. 9, 10: Which stood only in meats and drinks, and *divers washings,* and carnal ordinances, imposed on them until the time of reformation.

Acts 2, 41: Then they that gladly received his word were *bap-*

tized: and *the same day* there were added unto them about *three thousand* souls.

Acts 10, 47: Can any man *forbid water,* that these should not be *baptized?*

2.

Matt. 3, 11: I indeed *baptize* you with water unto repentance: but He that cometh after me is mightier than I, whose shoes I am not worthy to bear: He shall *baptize you with the Holy Ghost* and with fire.

Prov. 1, 23: Turn you at my reproof: behold, I will *pour out my Spirit* unto you, I will make known my words unto you.

Joel 2, 28: And it shall come to pass afterward that I will *pour out my Spirit* upon all flesh; and your sons and your daughters shall prophesy; your old men shall dream dreams; your young men shall see visions. Cf. Acts 2, 16. 17.

3.

Matt. 28, 19: Go ye therefore, and teach all *nations,* baptizing them in the name of the Father, and of the Son, and of the Holy Ghost.

Acts 8, 35—38: Then Philip opened his mouth, and began at the same scripture, and preached unto him Jesus. And as they went on their way, they came unto a certain water: and the eunuch said, See, here is water; what doth hinder me to be baptized? And Philip said, If thou believest with all thine heart, thou mayest. And he answered and said, I believe that Jesus Christ is the Son of God. And he commanded the chariot to stand still: and they went down both into the water, both Philip and the eunuch; and he baptized him.

John 3, 5. 6: Jesus answered, Verily, verily, I say unto thee, Except *a man* be born of water and of the Spirit, he cannot enter into the kingdom of God. That which is *born of the flesh* is flesh; and that which is born of the Spirit is spirit.

Mark 10, 14: But when Jesus saw it, He was much displeased, and said unto them, Suffer the *little children* to come unto me, and forbid them not; for of such is the kingdom of God.

Acts 2, 39: For the promise is unto *you,* and to *your children,* and to all that are afar off, even as many as the Lord, our God, shall call.

Acts 16, 15: And when *she* was baptized, and *her household,* she besought us, saying, If ye have judged me to be faithful to the Lord, come into my house, and abide there.

Acts 16, 33: And he took them the same hour of the night, and washed their stripes; and *was baptized, he* and *all his,* straightway.

Col. 2, 11. 12: In whom also ye are *circumcised* with the *circumcision made without hands,* in putting off the body of the sins of the flesh by the *circumcision of Christ:* buried with Him *in Baptism,* wherein also ye are risen with Him through the faith of the operation of God, who hath raised Him from the dead.

4.

John 1, 31: And I knew Him not: but that He should be made manifest to Israel, therefore am I come baptizing *with water.*

John 3, 5. 23: Jesus answered, Verily, verily, I say unto thee, Except a man be born of *water* and of the Spirit, he cannot enter into the kingdom of God. (23) And John also was baptizing in Aenon, near to Salim, because there was much *water* there: and they came and were *baptized.*

Acts 10, 47: Can any man forbid *water,* that these should not be *baptized,* which have received the Holy Ghost as well as we?

Acts 8, 38: And he commanded the chariot to stand still: and they went down both into *the water,* both Philip and the eunuch; and he *baptized* him.

5.

Matt. 28, 19: Go ye therefore, and teach all nations, *baptizing* them *in the name of the Father, and of the Son, and of the Holy Ghost.*

6.

Matt. 3, 16. 17: And *Jesus, when He was baptized,* went up straightway out of the water: and lo, the heavens were opened unto Him, and he saw the *Spirit of God* descending like a dove, and lighting upon Him: and lo, a voice from heaven, saying, This is MY *beloved Son,* in whom *I* am well pleased.

Matt. 28, 19: Go ye therefore, and teach all nations, baptizing them in the name of the *Father, and of the Son, and of the Holy Ghost.*

John 3, 5: Jesus answered, Verily, verily, I say unto thee, Except a man be born of water and of the *Spirit,* he cannot enter into the kingdom of God.

1 John 5, 6: This is He *that came by water* and blood, even *Jesus Christ;* not by water only, but by water and blood. And it is the *Spirit* that beareth witness, because the Spirit is truth.

Eph. 5, 26: That *He* might sanctify and cleanse it *with the washing of water by the Word.*

7.

Acts 22, 16: And now why tarriest thou? Arise, and *be baptized, and wash away thy sins,* calling on the name of the Lord.

Acts 2, 38: Then Peter said unto them, Repent, and *be baptized,* every one of you, in the name of Jesus Christ *for the remission of sins,* and ye shall receive the gift of the Holy Ghost.

Luke 3, 3: And he came into all the country about Jordan, preaching the *baptism* of *repentance* for *the remission of sins.*

Eph. 5, 26: That He might *sanctify and cleanse it* with the *washing of water by the Word.*

1 Pet. 3, 21: The like figure whereunto even *Baptism doth also now save us,* (not the putting away of the filth of the flesh, but *the answer of a good conscience* toward God,) by the resurrection of Jesus Christ.

8.

Gal. 3, 26. 27: For ye are all the *children of God by faith* in Christ Jesus. For *as many of you as have been baptized* into Christ *have put on Christ.*

Tit. 3, 5—7: Not by works of righteousness which we have done, but according to His mercy *He saved us by the washing of regeneration* and *renewing of the Holy Ghost,* which He shed on us abundantly through Jesus Christ, our Savior, that, *being justified by His grace,* we should be *made heirs according to the hope of eternal life.*

Rom. 6, 3. 4: Know ye not that so many of us as were *baptized* into Jesus Christ *were baptized into His death?* Therefore we are *buried with Him by baptism* into death, that, like as Christ was raised up from the dead by the glory of the Father, even so we also should walk in newness of life. Cf. Col. 2, 11. 12. See above sub **4.**

9.

Acts 8, 35—38: Then Philip opened his mouth, and began at the same scripture, and preached unto him Jesus. And as they went on their way, they came unto a certain water: and the eunuch said, See, here is water; *what doth hinder me to be baptized?* And Philip said, *If thou believest with all thine heart, thou mayest.* And he answered and said, *I believe* that Jesus Christ is the Son of God. And he commanded the chariot to stand still: and they went down both into the water, both Philip and the eunuch; and *he baptized him.*

THE LORD'S SUPPER.

§ 137. The sacrament of the Lord's Table,[1] or the Lord's Supper,[2] or the Eucharist,[3] is the divinely instituted act[4] of consecrating, by the word of institution,[5] the divinely prescribed visible elements, bread and wine,[6] of distributing[7] to the communicants[8] the consecrated elements, and of orally eating and drinking[9] in, with, and under the consecrated bread and wine the true body and blood of Christ,[10] who, being present in such act,[11] earnestly offers to all communicants[12] forgiveness of sins,[13] and efficaciously operates toward the acceptance of such gift,[14] and toward renewed assurance of its possession, and the effects of such assurance.[15]

1.

1 Cor. 10, 21: Ye cannot drink the cup of the Lord, and the cup of devils: ye cannot be partakers of the *Lord's Table,* and of the table of devils.

2.

1 Cor. 11, 20: When ye come together therefore into one place, this is not to eat the *Lord's Supper.*

3.

Matt. 26, 26: And as they were eating, Jesus took bread, and *blessed it,* and brake it, and gave it to the disciples, and said, Take, eat; this is my body.

1 Cor. 10, 16: The *cup of blessing which we bless,* is it not the communion of the blood of Christ? The bread which we break, is it not the communion of the body of Christ?

4.

Matt. 26, 26—28: And as they were eating, Jesus took bread, and blessed it, and brake it, and gave it to the disciples, and said, Take, eat; this is my body. And He took the cup, and gave thanks, and gave it to them, saying, Drink ye all of it; for this is my blood of the new testament, which is shed for many for the remission of sins.

1 Cor. 11, 24. 25: And when He had given thanks, He brake it, and said, Take eat; this is my body, which is broken for you: *this* DO in remembrance of me. After the same manner also He took the cup, when He had supped, saying, This cup is the new testament in my blood: *thiš* DO *ye,* as oft as ye drink it, in remembrance of me.

5.

Mark 14, 22—24: And as they did eat, Jesus took bread, and blessed, and brake it, and gave to them, *and said,* Take, eat; this is my body. And He took the cup, and when He had given thanks, He gave it to them: and they all drank of it. And He *said* unto them, This is my blood of the new testament, which is shed for many.

Luke 22, 19. 20: And He took bread, and gave thanks, and brake it, and *gave unto them, saying,* This is my body which is given for you: this do in remembrance of me. Likewise also the cup after supper, saying, This cup is the new testament in my blood, which is shed for you.

1 Cor. 11, 23—25: For I have received of the Lord that which also I delivered unto you, That the Lord Jesus in the same night in which He was betrayed took bread: and when He had given thanks, He brake it, *and said,* Take, eat; this is my body, which is broken for you: this do in remembrance of me. After the same manner also He took the cup, when He had supped, *saying,* This cup is the new testament in my blood: *this do ye,* as oft as ye drink it, in remembrance of me.

1 Cor. 10, 16: The *cup of blessing which we bless,* is it not the communion of the blood of Christ? The bread which we break, is it not the communion of the body of Christ?

6.

Matt. 26, 26. 29: And as they were eating, Jesus took *bread,* and blessed it, and brake it, and *gave it* to the disciples, and said, Take, eat; this is my body. (29) But I say unto you, I will not drink henceforth of *this fruit of the vine,* until that day when I drink it new with you in my Father's kingdom.

1 Cor. 11, 20. 21: When ye come together therefore into one place, this is not to eat the Lord's Supper. For in eating every one taketh before other his own supper: and one is hungry, and another *is drunken.* (Fermented wine.)

7.

Matt. 26, 26. 27: And as they were eating, Jesus took bread, and blessed it, and brake it, and gave it to the disciples, and said, Take, eat; this is my body. And He took the cup, and gave thanks, and gave it to them, saying, Drink ye all of it.

8.

Matt. 26, 26. 27: And as they were eating, Jesus took bread, and blessed it, and *brake it, and gave it to the disciples,* and said, Take, eat; this is my body. And He took the cup, and gave thanks, and *gave it to them,* saying, Drink ye all of it.

1 Cor. 11, 28. 29: But let a man examine himself, and so let him *eat of that bread,* and drink *of that cup.* For *he that eateth and drinketh unworthily* eateth and drinketh *damnation* to himself, not discerning the Lord's body.

Luke 22, 21: But, behold, the hand of him that betrayeth me is with me on the table.

Matt. 26, 26. 27. See below.

9.

Matt. 26, 26. 27: And *as they were eating,* Jesus took bread, and blessed it, and brake it, and gave it to the disciples, and said, *Take, eat;* this is my body. And He took the cup, and gave thanks, and gave it to them, saying, *Drink* ye all of it.

1 Cor. 11, 28: But let a man examine himself, and *so let him eat of that bread,* and *drink* of that *cup.*

10.

Matt. 26, 26—28: And as they were eating, Jesus took bread, and blessed it, and brake it, and gave it to the disciples, and said, Take, eat; *this is my body.* And He took the cup, and gave thanks, and gave it to them, saying, Drink ye all of it; for this is *my blood* of the new testament, *which is shed* for many for the remission of sins.

1 Cor. 10, 16: The *cup of blessing* which we bless, is it not the *communion of the blood of Christ?* The *bread* which we break, is it not *the communion of the body of Christ?*

1 Cor. 11, 27—29: Wherefore, whosoever shall *eat this bread,* and *drink this cup* of the Lord, unworthily, shall be guilty of *the body and blood of the Lord.* But let a man examine himself, and so let him *eat of that bread, and drink of that cup.* For he that eateth and drinketh unworthily eateth and drinketh damnation to himself, *not discerning the Lord's body.*

11.

Matt. 18, 20: For where two or three are gathered together in my name, there am I in the midst of them.

1 Cor. 10, 16: The cup of blessing *which we bless,* is it not the *communion of·the blood of Christ?* The bread *which we break,* is it not the *communion of the body of Christ?*

12.

1 Cor. 11, 27. 29: Wherefore, WHOSOEVER *shall eat this· bread, and drink this cup* of the Lord, *unworthily,* shall be *guilty of the body and blood of the Lord.* (29) For he that eateth and drinketh unworthily eateth and drinketh damnation to himself, *not discerning the Lord's body.*

Luke 22, 19—21: And He took bread, and gave thanks, and brake it, and *gave unto them,* saying, This is my body *which is given for you:* this do in remembrance of me. Likewise also the cup after supper, saying, This cup is the new testament in my blood, *which is shed for you.* But behold, the hand of *him* that *betrayeth* me *is with me on the table.*

13.

Matt. 26, 28: For this is my blood of the new testament, which is shed for many *for the remission of sins.*

14.

1 Cor. 11, 25: After the same manner also He took the cup, when He had supped, saying, This cup is *the new testament* in my blood: this do ye, as oft as ye drink it, *in remembrance of me.*

Luke 22, 20: Likewise also the cup after supper, saying, This cup is *the new testament* in my blood, *which is shed for you.*

15.

1 Cor. 11, 25. 26: This do ye, as oft as ye drink it, *in remembrance of me.* For as often.as ye eat this bread, and drink this cup, *ye do show the Lord's death till He come.*

EFFICACY AND RESISTIBILITY.

§ 138. The operations of God,[1] or, by appropriation, of the Holy Ghost,[2] performed through the means of grace,[3] though in all cases equally earnest and efficacious,[4] are in no case irresistible,[5] but the grace and power of God, as exerted through the means of grace, may be, and often actually is, frustrated by man's obstinate and continued resistance.[5]

1.

Phil. 2, 13: For it is *God* which *worketh* in you both *to will and to do* of His good pleasure.

Col. 2, 13: And you, being dead in your sins and the uncircumcision of your flesh, hath *He quickened* together with Him, having forgiven you all trespasses.

2.

1 Cor. 12, 3: Wherefore I give you to understand that no man speaking by the Spirit of God calleth Jesus accursed, and that no man can say that Jesus is the Lord *but by the Holy Ghost.*

3.

Rom. 10, 17: So, then, *faith cometh by hearing* and hearing by the Word of God.

James 1, 18: Of His own will *begat He us with the Word of Truth,* that we should be a kind of firstfruits of His creatures.

1 Pet. 1, 22: Seeing ye have purified your souls *in obeying the truth* through the Spirit unto unfeigned love of the brethren, see that ye love one another with a pure heart fervently.

Tit. 3, 5: Not by works of righteousness which we have done, but according to His mercy *He saved us by the washing of regeneration* and renewing of the Holy Ghost.

4.

Mark 16, 15: And He said unto them, Go ye into *all the world,* and preach the GOSPEL to *every creature.*

Rom. 1, 16: For I am not ashamed of the *Gospel* of Christ, for it is *the power of God unto salvation* to every one that believeth, to the *Jew* first, and also to *the Greek.*

Luke 10, 16: He that *heareth you heareth me,* and he that *despiseth you despiseth me;* and he that despiseth me *despiseth Him that sent me.*

Rom. 10, 16. 21: But they have not all obeyed the *Gospel.* For Esaias saith, Lord, *who hath believed our report?* (21) But to Israel He saith, *All day long I have stretched forth my hands* unto *a disobedient and gainsaying* people.

Matt. 23, 37: O Jerusalem, Jerusalem, thou *that killest the prophets,* and stonest them which *are sent unto thee,* how often *would I have gathered thy children together,* even as a hen gathereth her chickens under her wings, *and ye* would not!

Luke 19, 41. 42: And when He was come near, He beheld the city, and wept over it, saying, *If thou hadst known,* even thou, at least in this thy day, *the things which belong unto thy peace!* But now they are hid from thine eyes.

Acts 7, 51: Ye stiffnecked and uncircumcised in heart and ears, ye do always *resist the Holy Ghost;* as your fathers did, so do ye.

Rom. 2, 4: Or *despisest thou* the *riches of His goodness* and forbearance and longsuffering, not knowing that *the goodness of God leadeth thee to repentance?*

Is. 55, 10. 11: For as the rain cometh down, and the snow from heaven, and returneth not thither, but watereth the earth, and *maketh it bring forth* and bud, that it may give seed to the sower and bread to the eater, *so shall my Word be* that goeth forth out of my mouth: it *shall not return unto me void,* but it *shall accomplish* that which I please, and it *shall prosper* in the thing whereto I sent it.

5.

Rom. 10, 21: But to Israel He saith, *All day* long I have stretched forth my hands *unto a disobedient and gainsaying people.*

Matt. 23, 37: O Jerusalem, Jerusalem, thou that *killest the prophets,* and *stonest them which are sent unto thee, how often* would I have gathered thy children together, even as a hen gathereth her chickens under her wings, and *ye would not!*

Acts 7, 51: Ye *stiffnecked* and uncircumcised in heart and ears, ye do *always resist* the Holy Ghost; as your fathers did, so do ye.

Acts 13, 45. 46: But when the Jews saw the multitudes, they were *filled with envy,* and *spake against* those things which were spoken by Paul, *contradicting and blaspheming.* Then Paul and Barnabas waxed bold, and said, It was necessary that the *Word of God* should first have been spoken to you; but seeing *ye put it from you,* and *judge yourselves unworthy of everlasting life,* lo, we turn to the Gentiles.

Rom. 2, 5: But *after thy hardness and impenitent heart treasurest up unto thyself wrath* against the day of wrath and revelation of the righteous judgment of God.

John 3, 19—21: And this is the condemnation, that *light is come* into the world, and *men loved darkness rather than light,* because their deeds were evil. For every one that doeth evil *hateth the light, neither cometh to the light,* lest his deeds should be reproved. But he that doeth truth cometh to the light, that his deeds may be made manifest that they are wrought in God.

John 1, 5. 11: The light shineth in darkness; and the darkness *comprehended it not.* (11) He came unto His own, and His own *received Him not.*

OPERATIONS OF THE HOLY SPIRIT.

§ 139. The various operations of the Holy Spirit performed through the means of grace are the works of Vocation, Regeneration or Conversion, Renovation or Sanctification, and Preservation.

VOCATION.

§ 140. Vocation[1] is the act of God by which He, through the means of grace,[2] earnestly offers[3] to all who hear or read the Gospel,[4] or to whom the sacraments are administered,[5] the benefits of Christ's redemption,[6] truly and earnestly invites and exhorts them to accept and enjoy what is thus offered,[7] and endeavors to move and lead them by the power inherent in the means of grace[8] to such acceptance and enjoyment of the benefits of the redemption.[9]

1.

2 Tim. 1, 9: Who hath saved us, and *called us* with an holy *calling,* not according to our works, but according to His own purpose and grace, which was given us in Christ Jesus before the world began.

Matt. 11, 28: *Come unto me,* all ye that labor and are heavy laden, and I will give you rest.

Matt. 20, 16: So the last shall be first, and the first last; for *many be called,* but few chosen.

2.

2 Thess. 2, 14: Whereunto He *called* you *by our Gospel* to the obtaining of the glory of our Lord Jesus Christ.

3.

Luke 14, 17: And sent *his servant* at supper time to say to them that were bidden, *Come; for all things are now ready.*

Is. 55, 1: Ho, every one that thirsteth, *come ye* to the *waters,* and he that hath no money; *come ye,* buy, and *eat;* yea, *come, buy* wine and milk *without money and without price!*

4.

Acts 17, 30: And the times of this ignorance God winked at, but now commandeth *all men* everywhere to repent.

Matt. 22, 9. 10: Go ye therefore into the *highways;* and *as many as ye shall find, bid to the marriage.* So those servants went out into the highways, and gathered together *all as many as they found,* both bad and good: and the wedding was furnished with guests.

Col. 1, 28: Whom we preach, warning *every man,* and teaching *every man* in *all* wisdom, that we may present *every man* perfect in Christ Jesus.

Matt. 28, 19: Go ye therefore, and teach *all nations,* baptizing *them* in the name of the Father, and of the Son, and of the Holy Ghost.

Ezek. 2, 4. 5: For they are *impudent children* and *stiffhearted.* I do send thee *unto them,* and thou shalt say *unto them,* Thus saith the Lord God. And they, whether they will *hear, or whether they will forbear,* (for they are *a rebellious house,*) yet shall know that there hath been *a prophet among them.*

John 5, 39: *Search* the Scriptures; for in them ye think *ye have eternal life;* and they are they which testify of me.

5.

Acts 2, 38. 41: Then Peter said unto them, Repent, and *be baptized, every one of you,* in the name of Jesus Christ *for the remission of sins,* and ye shall receive the gift of the Holy Ghost. (41) Then they that gladly received his word *were baptized:* and the same day there were added unto them about three thousand souls.

6.

John 1, 16: And *of His fullness* have all we received, and grace for grace.

John 16, 15: All things that the Father hath are mine; therefore said I that *He shall take of mine,* and shall show it unto you.

1 Cor. 1, 9: God is faithful, by whom ye were *called unto the fellowship of His Son* Jesus Christ, our Lord.

Col. 1, 13. 14: Who hath *delivered* us from the power of darkness, and hath *translated* us into the kingdom of *His dear Son, in whom we have redemption* through His blood, even *the forgiveness of sins.*

1 Pet. 2, 9: But ye are a chosen generation, a royal priesthood, an holy nation, a peculiar people, that ye should show forth the praises of Him who hath *called you* out of darkness *into His marvelous light.*

1 Pet. 3, 7: Knowing that ye are *thereunto called,* that ye should *inherit a blessing.*

Eph. 1, 18: The eyes of your understanding being enlightened, that ye may know what is the *hope of His calling,* and what the *riches of the glory of His inheritance in the saints.*

Phil. 3, 14: I press toward the mark for *the prize of the high calling* of God *in Christ Jesus.*

1 Tim. 6, 12: Fight the good fight of faith, lay hold on *eternal life, whereunto thou art also called.*

7.

Matt. 22, 4: Again, he sent forth other servants, saying, *Tell them which are bidden,* Behold, *I have prepared my dinner:* my oxen *and my fatlings* are killed, and *all things are ready: come* unto the marriage!

8.

Rom. 1, 16: For I am not ashamed of the *Gospel* of Christ; for it *is the power of God* unto salvation to every one that believeth, to the Jew first, and also to the Greek.

Hebr. 4, 12: For the *Word of God* is *quick and powerful,* and sharper than any two-edged sword, piercing even to the dividing asunder of soul and spirit, and of the joints and marrow, and is a discerner of the thoughts and intents of the heart.

1 Pet. 1, 23: Being *born again,* not of corruptible seed, but of incorruptible, *by the Word of God,* which *liveth* and abideth forever.

9.

2 Cor. 5, 19. 20: To-wit, that *God was in Christ, reconciling the world unto Himself,* not imputing their trespasses unto them; and hath committed unto us the *word of reconciliation.* Now, then, we are ambassadors for Christ, as though God did beseech you by us: we pray you in Christ's stead, *Be ye reconciled to God!*

Luke 14, 21—23: So that servant came, and showed his lord these things. Then the master of the house, being angry, said to his servant, Go out quickly into the streets and lanes of the city, and bring in hither the poor, and the maimed, and the halt, and the blind. And the servant said, Lord, it is done as thou hast commanded, and yet there is room. And the lord said unto the servant, Go out into the highways and hedges, and compel them to come in *that my house may be filled.*

Acts 11, 14: Who shall tell thee *words whereby* thou and all thy house *shall be saved.*

EFFECTS OF THE CALL.

§ 141. By the divine power residing in the means of grace, and working through the same,[1] the calling grace of God effects regeneration[2] or conversion.[3] Wherever these effects are not attained, this is due to obstinate resistance on the part of man.[4]

1.

Rom. 1, 16: For I am not ashamed of the Gospel of Christ; for it is the *power of God unto salvation* to every one that believeth, to the Jew first, and also to the Greek.

1 Pet. 1, 3: Blessed be the God and Father of our Lord Jesus Christ, which according to His abundant mercy *hath begotten us again* unto a lively hope by the resurrection of Jesus Christ from the dead.

1 Cor. 1, 18: For the *preaching of the cross* is to them that perish foolishness, but *unto us which are saved it is the power of God.*

Hebr. 4, 12: For the Word of God is quick, and powerful, and sharper than any two-edged sword, piercing even to the dividing asunder of soul and spirit, and of the joints and marrow, and is a discerner of the thoughts and intents of the heart.

1 Pet. 1, 23: Being *born again,* not of corruptible seed, but of incorruptible, *by the Word of God,* which *liveth and abideth forever.*

2 Thess. 2, 14: Whereunto He *called you by our Gospel to the obtaining of the glory of our Lord Jesus Christ.*

1 Cor. 4, 15: In Christ Jesus I have *begotten you through the Gospel.*

2.

Cf. § 142.

3.

Cf. § 143.

4.

Luke 8, 5. 12: A sower went out to sow his seed: and as he sowed, some fell by the wayside; and it was *trodden down,* and the fowls of the air *devoured* it. (12) Those by the wayside are they that hear; then cometh the *devil,* and *taketh away the Word* out of their hearts, *lest they should believe and be saved.*

Luke 14, 18—20. 24: And they all with one consent began to *make excuse.* The first said unto him, I have bought a piece of ground, and I must needs go and see it: I pray thee have me excused. And another said, I have bought five yoke of oxen, and I go to prove them: I pray thee have me excused. And another said, I have married a wife, and therefore *I cannot come.* (24) For I say unto you, That *none of those men* which were bidden *shall taste of my supper.*

Acts 26, 28: Then Agrippa said unto Paul, *Almost* thou persuadest me to be a Christian.

Acts 24, 25: And as he reasoned of righteousness, temperance, and judgment to come, Felix trembled, and answered, *Go thy way for this time; when I have a convenient season,* I will call for thee.

John 3, 19—21: And this is the condemnation, that light is come into the world, and *men loved darkness rather than light,* because their deeds were evil. For every one that doeth evil *hateth the light,* neither cometh to the light, lest his deeds should be reproved. But he that doeth truth cometh to the light, that his deeds may be made manifest that they are wrought in God.

REGENERATION.

§ 142. Regeneration[1] is the act of divine grace[2] and power[3] by which man, born of the flesh,[4] void of all power to think,[5] to will,[6] or to do,[7] any good thing, and dead in sin,[8] is, through the means of grace,[9] raised from spiritual death,[10] born into a new spiritual life,[11] and endowed with spiritual power to know and understand[12] spiritual truths, to will and to do[13] what is spiritually good, and, especially, made to accept and enjoy the benefits of the redemption which is in Christ Jesus, the Savior of mankind.[14]

1.

Tit. 3, 5: Not by works of righteousness, which we have done, but according to His mercy He saved us by the washing of *regeneration* and renewing of the Holy Ghost.

1 Pet. 1, 3: Blessed be the God and Father of our Lord Jesus Christ, which according to His abundant mercy hath *begotten us again* unto a lively hope by the resurrection of Jesus Christ from the dead.

2.

2 Tim. 1, 9: Who hath saved us, and called us with an holy calling, not according to our works, but according to His own *purpose and grace,* which was given us in Christ Jesus before the world began.

Eph. 2, 6. 7: And hath *raised us up together,* and made us sit together in heavenly places in Christ Jesus, *that* in the ages to come

He might show the exceeding riches of His grace in His kindness toward us through Christ Jesus.

1 Pet. 1, 3: Blessed be the God and Father of our Lord Jesus Christ, which according to His abundant mercy hath begotten us again unto a lively hope by the resurrection of Jesus Christ from the dead.

Eph. 2, 4: But God, who is rich in mercy, for His great love wherewith He loved us.

Tit. 3, 5: Not by works of righteousness which we have done, but according to His *mercy* He *saved us* by the washing of *regeneration* and renewing of the Holy Ghost.

3.

John 1, 13: Which were born, not of blood, nor of the will of the flesh, nor of the will of man, *but of God.*

1 John 3, 9: Whosoever is *born of God* doth not commit sin; for His seed remaineth in him: and he cannot sin, because he is born of God.

2 Cor. 5, 17: Therefore if any man be *in Christ,* he is a *new creature.*

Eph. 2, 5. 6: Even when we were dead in sins, hath *quickened us* together with Christ, (by grace ye are saved;) and hath raised us up together, and made us sit together in heavenly places in Christ Jesus.

Eph. 1, 19: And what is the exceeding greatness of *His power* to *us-ward who believe,* according to *the working of His mighty power.*

4.

John 3, 6: That which is born of the flesh is flesh, and that which is born of the Spirit is spirit.

5.

2 Cor. 3, 5: Not that we are sufficient of ourselves to *think anything as of ourselves,* but our sufficiency is of God.

1 Cor. 2, 14: But the natural man receiveth not the things of the Spirit of God; for they are foolishness unto him, *neither can he know them,* because they are spiritually discerned.

Eph. 4, 18: Having the *understanding darkened,* being alienated from the life of God through the *ignorance* that is in them, because of the *blindness* of their heart.

Eph. 5, 8: For ye were sometimes *darkness,* but now are ye light in the Lord.

6.

Gen. 6, 5: And God saw that the wickedness of man was great in the earth, and that *every imagination* of the thoughts of his heart was *only evil continually.*

Gen. 8, 21: The imagination of man's heart is evil from his youth.

Rom. 8, 7: Because the carnal mind is *enmity against God;* for it is not subject to the Law of God, *neither indeed can be.*

12

7.

John 15, 5: Without me ye can do nothing.

Phil. 1, 6: Being confident of this very thing, that He which hath *begun* a good work in you will *perform* it until the day of Jesus Christ.

Rom. 7, 14: For we know that the Law is spiritual; but *I am carnal,* sold under sin.

Eph. 2, 3: Among whom also we all had our conversation in times past in the lusts of our flesh, *fulfilling the desires of the flesh* and of the mind; and were *by nature* the children of wrath, even as others.

8.

Col. 2, 13: And you, being *dead in your* sins and the uncircumcision of your flesh, hath He quickened together with Him.

Eph. 2, 1. 5: And you hath He quickened, *who were dead* in trespasses and sins. (5) Even when *we were dead* in sins, hath quickened us together with Christ, (by grace ye are saved).

9.

James 1, 18: Of His own will *begat* He us *with the Word of Truth,* that we should be a kind of firstfruits of His creatures.

1 Pet. 1, 23: Being *born again,* not of corruptible seed, but of incorruptible, *by the Word of God,* which liveth and abideth forever.

Tit. 3, 5: Not by works of righteousness which we have done, but according to His mercy He saved us by the *washing of regeneration* and renewing of the Holy Ghost.

John 3, 5: Jesus answered, Verily, verily, I say unto thee, Except a man be *born of water and of the Spirit,* he cannot enter into the kingdom of God.

1 Cor. 4, 15: For though ye have ten thousand instructors in Christ, yet have ye not many fathers; for in Christ Jesus I have *begotten you through the Gospel.*

Gal. 4, 19: My little children, of whom *I travail in birth* again until *Christ be formed in you.*

10.

Eph. 2, 5. 6: Even when we were *dead* in sins, hath *quickened* us together with Christ, (by grace ye are saved;) and hath *raised us up* together, and made us sit together in heavenly places in Christ Jesus.

Col. 2, 13: And you, being dead in your sins and the uncircumcision of your flesh, *hath He quickened* together with Him, having forgiven you all trespasses.

11.

1 Pet. 1, 23: Being *born again,* not of corruptible seed, but of incorruptible, by the Word of God, which *liveth and abideth forever.*

James 1, 18: Of His own will *begat He us* with the Word of Truth, that we should be a kind of *firstfruits of His creatures.*

12.

2 Cor. 3, 5: Not that we are sufficient of ourselves to *think* anything as of ourselves, but *our sufficiency is of God.*

Acts 26, 18: To *open their eyes,* and to turn them *from darkness to light,* and from the power of Satan unto God, that they may receive forgiveness of sins, and inheritance among them which are sanctified by faith that is in me.

13.

Phil. 2, 13: For it is *God* which *worketh* in you both *to will* and *to do* of His good pleasure.

14.

1 Pet. 1, 3: Blessed be the God and Father of our Lord Jesus Christ, which according to His abundant mercy hath *begotten us again* unto *a lively hope* by the resurrection of Jesus Christ from the dead.

Gal. 3, 26: For ye are all the *children of God by faith* in Christ Jesus.

Is. 53, 10: When Thou shalt make His soul an offering for sin, He shall *see His seed,* He shall prolong His days, *and the pleasure of the Lord shall prosper in His hand.*

CONVERSION.

§ 143. Conversion[1] in a stricter sense of the term is the work of God[2] by which man is, through the Gospel, transferred[3] from a state of sin and wrath and spiritual death, in which by nature all men are,[4] into a state of spiritual life and faith and grace[5] in which alone the sinner can enjoy the benefits of Christ's redemption.[6] — Conversion in a wider sense[7] is the process whereby man, being by the grace and power of God transferred from his carnal state of sin and wrath into a spiritual state of faith and grace, enters upon, and, under the continued influence of the Holy Spirit, continues in, a state of faith and spiritual life.[8]

1.

1 Pet. 2, 25: For ye were as sheep going astray, but are now *returned* unto the Shepherd and Bishop of your souls.

Jer. 31, 19: Surely, after that I was *turned,* I repented.

Acts 26, 18: To *turn* them from darkness to light and from the power of Satan unto God.

Acts 26, 20: That they should repent and turn to God.

2.

Jer. 31, 18: *Turn Thou me,* and I shall be turned; *for Thou art the Lord, my God.*

Col. 1, 12. 13: Giving thanks unto *the Father,* which hath *made us meet* to be partakers of the inheritance of the saints in light; *who hath delivered* us from the power of darkness, and hath *translated us* into the kingdom of His dear Son.

Acts 5, 31: *Him hath God exalted* with His right hand to be a Prince and a Savior, for *to give repentance* to Israel and forgiveness of sins.

John 6, 29: Jesus answered and said unto them, This is *the work of God,* that ye believe on Him whom He hath sent.

Col. 2, 12: Buried with Him in baptism, wherein also ye are risen with Him through the faith *of the operation of God,* who hath raised Him from the dead.

3.

Col. 1, 12. 13: Giving thanks unto the Father, which hath made us meet to be partakers of the inheritance of the saints in light; who hath delivered us from the power of darkness, and hath *translated* us into the kingdom of His dear Son.

Eph. 2, 6: And hath *raised us up* together, and *made us sit* together in heavenly places in Christ Jesus.

4.

Rom. 3, 9. 23: What then? are we better than they? No, in no wise; for we have before proved both Jews and Gentiles, that *they are all under sin.* (23) For *all have sinned, and come short of the glory of God.*

Job 15, 14: What is *man,* that he should be *clean?* and he which is *born of a woman,* that he should be *righteous?*

Ps. 14, 3: They are ALL *gone aside,* they are all together become filthy: there is *none* that doeth good, no, *not one.*

Eph. 2, 3: Among whom also *we all* had our conversation in times past in the *lusts of our flesh,* fulfilling the *desires of the flesh* and of the mind; and were *by nature* the children of wrath, *even as others.*

Col. 3, 5. 6: Mortify therefore your members which are upon the earth: fornication, uncleanness, inordinate affection, evil concupiscence, and covetousness, which is idolatry: for which things' sake the wrath of God cometh on the children of disobedience.

1 Pet. 2, 10: Which in time past *were not a people,* but are now the people of God; which *had not obtained mercy,* but now have obtained mercy.

Gal. 5, 24: And they that are Christ's have crucified the flesh with the affections and lusts.

1 Pet. 2, 25: For ye *were as sheep going astray,* but are now returned unto the Shepherd and Bishop of your souls.

Acts 26, 18: To open their eyes, and to turn them *from darkness* to light, and from the *power of Satan* unto God, that they may receive forgiveness of sins, and inheritance among them which are sanctified by faith that is in me.

Ezek. 18, 32: For I have no pleasure in the *death* of him that dieth, saith the Lord God: wherefore turn yourselves, and live ye!

Ezek. 33, 11: Say unto them, As I live, saith the Lord God, I have no pleasure in the death of the wicked, but that the wicked *turn from his way* and live: turn ye, *turn ye from your evil ways;* for why will ye die, O house of Israel?

5.

Gal. 4, 5: To redeem them that were under the Law, that we might receive *the adoption of sons.*

Acts 11, 21: And the hand of the Lord was with them; and a great number believed, and turned *unto the Lord.*

Acts 20, 21: Testifying both to the Jews, and also to the Greeks, repentance *toward God* and faith toward our Lord Jesus Christ.

Rom. 6, 14: For sin shall not have dominion over you; for ye are not under the Law, but *under grace.*

1 Pet. 2, 10: Which in time past were not a people, but *are now the people of God;* which had not obtained mercy, but *now have obtained mercy.*

1 Pet. 2, 25: For ye were as sheep going astray, but *are now returned unto the Shepherd and Bishop of your souls.*

John 1, 12: But as many as received Him, to them gave He power to *become the sons of God,* even to them that *believe* on His name.

Ezek. 11, 19: And I will give them one heart, and I will put *a new spirit* within you; and I will take the stony heart out of their flesh, and will *give them an heart of flesh.*

6.

Gal. 4, 5: To redeem them that were under the Law, *that we might receive the adoption of sons.*

1 Pet. 2, 10: Which in time past were not a people, but are now the people of God: which had not obtained mercy, but *now have obtained mercy.*

Acts 26, 18: To open their eyes, and to turn them from darkness to light, and from the power of Satan unto God, *that they may receive forgiveness of sins,* and *inheritance* among them which are sanctified by faith that is in me.

7.

Jer. 31, 18. 19: *Turn Thou me, and I shall be turned;* for Thou art the Lord, my God. Surely, after that I was turned, *I repented.*

Acts 26, 20: But showed first unto them of Damascus, and at Jerusalem, and throughout all the coasts of Judaea, and then to the Gentiles, that they should *repent and turn to God, and do works meet for repentance.*

8.

Acts 26, 20: But showed first unto them of Damascus, and at Jerusalem, and throughout all the coasts of Judaea, and then to the Gentiles, that they should repent and turn to God, and do works meet for repentance.

Jer. 31, 19: Surely, after that I was turned, I repented; and after that I was instructed, I smote upon my thigh. I was ashamed, yea, even confounded, because I did bear the reproach of my youth.

Deut. 30, 2: And shalt *return* unto the Lord, thy God, *and shalt obey His voice according to all that I command thee* this day, thou and thy children, *with all thine heart and with all thy soul.*

Rom. 12, 2: And be not conformed to this world, *but be ye transformed by the renewing of your mind,* that ye may prove what is that good, and acceptable, and perfect will of God.

Rom. 6, 17: But God be thanked that ye *were* the servants of sin, *but ye have obeyed from the heart* that form of doctrine which was delivered you.

Eph. 4, 13: Till we all come in the unity of the faith, and of the knowledge of the Son of God, *unto a perfect man,* unto the measure of the stature of the *fullness* of Christ.

Ps. 51, 12: Restore unto me the joy of Thy salvation; and uphold me with Thy free Spirit.

CONVERSION AND PREPARATORY OPERATIONS.

§ 144. Regeneration or Conversion in the stricter sense, being essentially the procreation of true and saving faith,[1] is an instantaneous act or process,[2] but is in adults preceded by preparatory operations, whereby the sinner is convicted of his sinful state and helpless condition under divine wrath by means of the Law[3] and led to a logical or historical understanding of the contents of the Gospel,[4] and which, with the outward use of the means of grace, in a measure, lie within the power and reach of irregenerate man.[5]

1.

John 1, 12. 13: But as many as received Him, to them gave He power to become the sons of God, even to them *that believe* on His name: *which were born,* not of blood, nor of the will of the flesh, nor of the will of man, but *of God.*

Gal. 3, 26: For ye are all the *children of God by faith* in Christ Jesus.

1 John 5, 1: Whosoever *believeth* that Jesus is the Christ *is born of God:* and every one that loveth Him that begat loveth him also that is begotten of Him.

John 6, 29: Jesus answered and said unto them, This is the work of God, *that ye believe* on Him whom He hath sent.

Col. 2, 12: Buried with Him in baptism, wherein also ye are *risen* with Him *through the faith of the operation of God,* who hath raised Him from the dead.

2.

Eph. 2, 5. 6: Even when we were dead in sins, hath *quickened* us together with Christ, (by grace ye are saved;) and hath *raised us up* together, and made us sit together in heavenly places in Christ Jesus.

3.

Rom. 5, 13: For until the *Law* sin was in the world: but sin is not imputed when there is no law.

Rom. 3, 20: Therefore by the deeds of the Law there shall no flesh be justified in His sight: for *by the Law is the knowledge of sin.*

Jer. 13, 18: Say unto the king and to the queen, Humble yourselves, sit down: for your principalities shall come down, even the crown of your glory.

4.

Matt. 13, 23: But he that received seed into the good ground is he that *heareth the Word, and understandeth it;* which also beareth fruit, and bringeth forth, some an hundredfold, some sixty, some thirty.

John 4, 39: And many of the Samaritans of that city believed on Him for the saying of the woman, which testified, He told me all that ever I did.

5.

James 2, 19: Thou believest that there is one God; thou doest well: the devils also believe, and tremble.

Acts 24, 25: And as he reasoned of righteousness, temperance, and judgment to come, Felix trembled, and answered, Go thy way for this time; when I have a convenient season, I will call for thee.

Luke 4, 16. 22: And He came to Nazareth, where He had been brought up: and as His custom was, He went into the synagogue on the Sabbath day, and stood up for to read. (22) And all bare Him witness, and wondered at the gracious words which proceeded out of His mouth. And they said, Is not this Joseph's son?

Acts 13, 44: And the next Sabbath day came almost the whole city together to hear the Word of God.

Acts 26, 26 ff.: For the king knoweth of these things, before whom also I speak freely; for I am persuaded that none of these things are hidden from him, for this thing was not done in a corner, etc.

CONVERSION PURELY THE WORK OF GOD.

§ 145. Inasmuch as regeneration or conversion is essentially the bestowal of faith,[1] it is wholly and exclusively a work of God,[2] wherein the person being regenerated or converted can in no wise or respect concur, but is merely the passive subject,[3] in which as in a rational being[4] the

salutary internal change is wrought by the grace and power
of God[5] through the means of grace.[6]

1.

John 1, 12. 13: But as many as received Him, to them gave He
power to become the sons of God, even to them that *believe* on His
name: *which were born,* not of blood, nor of the will of the flesh, nor
of the will of man, but *of God.*

1 John 5, 1: Whosoever *believeth* that Jesus is the Christ is
born of God.

Gal. 3, 26: For ye are all the *children of God by faith* in Christ
Jesus.

2.

John 6, 29: Jesus answered and said unto them, This is *the
work of God that ye believe* on Him whom He hath sent.

Col. 2, 12: Buried with Him in baptism, wherein also ye are
risen with Him through the *faith of the operation of God,* who hath
raised Him from the dead.

Hebr. 12, 2: Looking unto Jesus, the *Author and Finisher of
our faith,* who for the joy that was set before Him endured the cross,
despising the shame, and is set down at the right hand of the throne
of God.

1 Pet. 1, 21: Who *by Him do believe* in God, that raised Him up
from the dead, and gave Him glory, that your faith and hope might
be in God.

Eph. 6, 23: Peace be to the brethren, and love with *faith, from
God* the Father and the Lord Jesus Christ.

John 14, 6: Jesus saith unto him, I am the Way, the Truth,
and the Life: *no man cometh unto the Father but by me.*

Acts 11, 17. 18: Forasmuch, then, as *God gave them the like gift*
as He did unto us, *who believed* on the Lord Jesus Christ, what was
I that I could withstand God? When they heard these things, they
held their peace, and glorified God, saying, Then hath *God* also to
the Gentiles *granted repentance* unto life.

Hos. 13, 9: O Israel, thou hast destroyed thyself; but *in me is
thine help.*

3.

Eph. 2, 1. 5: And you hath He quickened, who *were dead* in trespasses and sins. (5) Even *when we were dead* in sins, hath quickened us together with Christ, (by grace ye are saved).

Col. 2, 13: And you *being dead* in your sins and the uncircumcision of your flesh, hath He quickened together with Him, having
forgiven you all trespasses.

Rom. 8, 7: Because the *carnal mind is enmity against God;* for
it is not subject to the Law of God, *neither indeed can be.*

Gal. 5, 17: For the flesh lusteth *against* the Spirit, and the Spirit
against the flesh; and these are *contrary* the one to the other, so
that ye cannot do the things that ye would.

John 3, 6: That which is born of the flesh is flesh, and that which is born of the Spirit is spirit.

Phil. 1, 29: For unto you it *is given* in the behalf of Christ not only *to believe* on Him, but also to suffer for His sake.

1 Cor. 2, 5: That your *faith* should not stand in the wisdom of men, but *in the power of God.*

4.

1 Cor. 12, 3: Wherefore I give you to understand that no man *speaking* by the Spirit of God calleth Jesus accursed, and that no man can *say* that Jesus is the Lord but by the Holy Ghost.

1 Cor. 1, 4—7: I thank my God always on your behalf for the grace of God which is *given you* by Jesus Christ, that in everything ye are *enriched* by Him, in all *utterance* and in all *knowledge,* even as the *testimony of Christ was confirmed in you,* so that ye come behind in no gift, waiting for the coming of our Lord Jesus Christ.

Rom. 10, 14: How, then, shall they *call on Him* in whom they have not *believed?* and how shall they *believe* in Him *of whom they have not heard?* and how shall they *hear* without a *preacher?*

John 17, 8: For I have *given* unto them the *words* which Thou gavest me; and they have *received* them, and have *known* surely that I came out from Thee, and they have *believed* that Thou didst send me.

John 6, 44. 45: No man can *come to me,* except the *Father* which hath sent me *draw him:* and I will raise him up at the last day. It it written in the prophets, And they shall be all *taught* of God. Every man therefore that hath *heard,* and hath *learned* of the Father, cometh unto me.

5.

Eph. 1, 19: And what is the exceeding greatness of His *power* to us-ward who believe, according to the *working of His mighty power.*

See also texts sub 2.

6.

Rom. 10, 17: So, then, faith cometh by hearing, and hearing by the *Word of God.*

John 17, 20: Neither pray I for these alone, but for them also which shall believe on me *through their word.*

1 Cor. 1, 21: For after that in the wisdom of God the world by wisdom knew not God, it pleased God *by the foolishness of preaching* to save them that believe.

2 Cor. 4, 6: For God, who commanded the light to shine out of darkness, hath *shined in our hearts,* to *give the light of the knowledge* of the glory of God in the face of Jesus Christ.

Tit. 3, 5: Not by works of righteousness which we have done, but according to His mercy He saved us by the *washing of regeneration* and renewing of the Holy Ghost.

1 Cor. 3, 5: Who, then, is Paul, and who is Apollos, but *ministers by whom ye believed,* even as the Lord gave to every man?

ACT OF FAITH.

§ 146. The act of saving faith is the acceptance[1] of the
benefits of Christ offered through the means of grace[2] by
knowledge of, assent to, and reliance on, the teachings and
promises of the Gospel[3] and, especially, confidence in Christ.[4]

1.

John 1, 12. 16: But as many as *received* Him, to them gave He
power to become the sons of God, even to them that *believe* on His
name. (16) And of His fullness have all we *received,* and grace for
grace.

John 17, 8: For I have *given* unto them the words which Thou
gavest me; and they have *received* them, and have *known* surely
that I came out from Thee, and they have *believed* that Thou didst
send me.

Acts 10, 43: To Him give all the prophets witness, that through
His name, whosoever *believeth* in Him, shall *receive* remission of sins.

Acts 26, 18: To open their eyes, and to turn them from darkness
to light, and from the power of Satan unto God, that they may *receive*
forgiveness of sins, and inheritance among them, which are sanctified by *faith* that is in me.

Col. 2, 6: As ye have therefore *received* Christ Jesus, the Lord,
so walk ye in Him. Cf. §§ 122. 123.

2.

John 4, 39—42: And many of the Samaritans of that city
believed on Him for the *saying* of the woman, which *testified,* He
told me all that ever I did. So when the Samaritans were come unto
Him, they besought Him that He would tarry with them: and He
abode there two days. And many more *believed* because of His own
word, and said unto the woman, Now *we believe,* not because of thy
saying; for we *have heard Him ourselves,* and *know* that this is indeed the Christ, the Savior of the world.

3.

Luke 1, 77: To give *knowledge of salvation* unto His people by
the remission of their sins.

Is. 53, 11: He shall see of the travail of His soul, and shall be
satisfied; *by His knowledge* shall my righteous Servant *justify many;*
for He shall bear their iniquities.

John 17, 3: And this *is life eternal,* that they might *know Thee*
the only true God, and Jesus Christ, whom Thou hast sent.

2 Pet. 1, 3: According as His divine power hath *given unto us all
things* that pertain unto life and godliness, *through the knowledge of
Him* that hath called us to glory and virtue.

Rom. 4, 20—22: He staggered not at the promise of God through
unbelief, but was strong in faith, giving glory to God, and being

fully persuaded that, what He had promised, He was able also to perform. And therefore it was imputed to him for righteousness.

John 17, 8: For I have given unto them the *words* which Thou gavest me; and they have *received* them, and have known surely that I came out from Thee, and they have *believed* that Thou didst send me.

Luke 8, 13: They on the rock are they, which, when they hear, *receive the Word with joy;* and these have no root, which for a while *believe,* and in time of temptation fall away.

Acts 8, 14: Now when the apostles which were at Jerusalem heard that Samaria had *received the Word* of God, they sent unto them Peter and John.

James 1, 21: Wherefore lay apart all filthiness and superfluity of naughtiness, and *receive with meekness* the engrafted *Word,* which is able to save your souls.

John 2, 22: When therefore He was risen from the dead, His disciples remembered that *He had said* this unto them; and *they believed the Scripture,* and the word which Jesus had said.

Phil. 1, 27: Only let your conversation be as it becometh the Gospel of Christ, that, whether I come and see you, or else be absent, I may hear of your affairs, that ye stand fast in one spirit, with one mind striving together for the *faith of the Gospel.*

Mark 1, 15: And saying, The time is fulfilled, and the kingdom of God is at hand; repent ye, and *believe the Gospel!*

John 20, 29. 31: Jesus saith unto him, Thomas, because thou hast seen me, thou hast believed. Blessed are they that have *not seen,* and *yet have believed.* (31) But these are *written, that ye might believe* that Jesus is the Christ, the Son of God, and that believing ye might have life through His name.

2 Cor. 3, 4: And such *trust* have we through Christ to God-ward.

2 Tim. 1, 12: For the which cause I also suffer these things; nevertheless I am not ashamed; for I know whom I have *believed,* and *am persuaded* that He is able to keep that which I have committed unto Him against that day.

Mark 4, 40: And He said unto them, Why *are ye so fearful?* How is it that ye *have no faith?*

4.

Gal. 2, 16—20: Knowing that a man is not justified by the works of the Law, but by the *faith of Jesus Christ,* even we have believed in Jesus Christ, that we might be justified by the *faith of Christ,* and not by the works of the Law; for by the works of the Law shall no flesh be justified. But if, while we seek to be justified by Christ, we ourselves also are found sinners, is therefore Christ the minister of sin? God forbid! For if I build again the things which I destroyed, I make myself a transgressor. For I through the Law am dead to the Law, that I might live unto God. I am crucified with Christ: nevertheless, I live; yet not I, but Christ liveth in me: and the life which I now live in the flesh I live by the *faith of the Son of God,* who loved me, and gave Himself for me.

Phil. 1, 29: For unto you it is given in the behalf of Christ, not only to *believe on Him,* but also to suffer for His sake.

1 Tim. 1, 16: Howbeit for this cause I obtained mercy, that in me first *Jesus Christ* might show forth all longsuffering, for a pattern to them which should hereafter *believe on Him* to life everlasting.

Rom. 9, 33: As it is written, Behold, I lay in Sion a stumbling-stone and rock of offense: and whosoever *believeth on Him* shall not be ashamed.

Acts 16, 31: And they said, *Believe on the Lord Jesus Christ,* and thou shalt be saved and thy house.

Rom. 3, 25: Whom God hath set forth to be a propitiation through *faith in His blood,* to declare His righteousness for the remission of sins that are past, through the forbearance of God.

John 20, 31: But these are written, that ye might *believe that Jesus is the Christ,* the Son of God, and that believing ye might have life through His name.

John 1, 12: But as many as received Him, to them gave He power to become the sons of God, even to them that *believe on His name.*

STATE OF FAITH.

§ 147. The state of saving faith[1] is the continued possession[2] of the benefits of Christ's sacrifice through an enduring confidence in Christ the Savior and the promises of the Gospel.[3]

1.

Luke 22, 32: But I have prayed for thee that *thy faith fail not.*

2 Cor. 13, 5: Examine yourselves, whether ye *be in the faith.*

1 Cor. 16, 13: Watch ye, *stand fast in the faith,* quit you like men, be strong!

Gal. 2, 20: I am crucified with Christ: nevertheless, I live; yet not I, but Christ liveth in me: and the life which I now live in the flesh *I live by the faith* of the Son of God, who loved me, and gave Himself for me.

Acts 16, 5: And so were the churches *established in the faith,* and increased in number daily.

Col. 2, 7: Rooted and built up in Him, and *established in the faith,* as ye have been taught, abounding therein with thanksgiving.

1 Tim. 2, 15: Notwithstanding she shall be saved in child-bearing, if they *continue in faith* and charity and holiness with sobriety.

2 Tim. 4, 7: I have fought a good fight; I have finished my course; I have *kept the faith.*

2 Cor. 10, 15: Not boasting of things without our measure, that is, of other men's labors, but having hope, when your *faith is increased,* that we shall be enlarged by you according to our rule abundantly.

1 Pet. 1, 7: That the *trial of your faith,* being much more precious than of gold that perisheth, though it be tried with fire, might be found unto praise and honor and glory at the appearing of Jesus Christ.

2.

Eph. 3, 12: In whom we *have* boldness and access with *confidence by the faith of Him.*

1 Pet. 1, 9: *Receiving the end of your faith,* even the salvation of your souls.

2 Tim. 1, 12: For the which cause I also suffer these things: nevertheless, *I am not ashamed;* for I know whom I have *believed,* and *am persuaded* that *He is able to keep that which I have committed unto Him* against that day.

Gal. 5, 4. 5: Christ is become of no effect unto you, whosoever of you are justified by the Law; *ye are fallen from grace.* For we through the Spirit wait for the hope of righteousness by faith.

1 Pet. 1, 5: Who are *kept* by the power of God *through faith unto salvation* ready to be revealed in the last time.

3.

2 Tim. 3, 14. 15: But *continue thou* in the things which thou hast learned and hast been assured of, knowing of whom thou hast learned them; and that from a child thou hast known the Holy Scriptures, which are able to make thee *wise unto salvation* through *faith which is in Christ Jesus.*

John 6, 68. 69: Then Simon Peter answered Him, Lord, to whom shall we go? Thou hast the words of eternal life. And we *believe and are sure* that Thou art that Christ, the Son of the living God.

JUSTIFICATION.

§ 148. The chief benefit of Christ's vicarious obedience is the perfect righteousness obtained by Christ for all mankind,[1] the acquisition of which God accepted as a reconciliation of the world to Himself,[2] imputing to mankind the merit of the Mediator[3] — general or objective justification —; and inasmuch as faith is the actual acceptance[4] of this imputation announced in the Gospel,[5] or of the righteousness imputed[6] and offered in the Gospel,[5] it is justifying faith,[7] and God in His judgment[8] graciously[9] and for Christ's sake[10] holds and pronounces[8] the believer[11] actually and by personal application fully absolved[12] from all guilt[13] and punishment[14] while in the state of faith[15] — individual or subjective justification.

1.

Cf. Christology, § 123.

2.

Cf. Christology, §§ 118. 123.

3.

2 Cor. 5, 19: To-wit, that God was in Christ, reconciling *the world* unto Himself, *not imputing their trespasses unto them;* and hath committed unto us the word of reconciliation.

Rom. 5, 18. 19: Therefore as by the offense of one judgment came upon all men to condemnation, even so by the righteousness of One the free gift came *upon all men unto justification of life.* For as by one man's disobedience many were made sinners, so by the obedience of One shall *many be made righteous.*

Is. 53, 11: He shall see of the travail of His soul, and shall be satisfied: by His knowledge shall my righteous servant *justify many; for He shall bear their iniquities.*

Rom. 4, 25: Who was delivered for our offenses, and was *raised again for our justification.*

1 Cor. 15, 17: And if Christ be not raised, your faith is vain; ye are yet in your sins.

4.

Cf. §§ 146. 147.

5.

Cf. §§ 132. 133.

Rom. 5, 19: For as by one man's disobedience many were made sinners, so by the obedience of One shall many be made righteous.

Rom. 3, 25: Whom God hath *set forth to be a propitiation through faith in His blood,* to. *declare* His righteousness for the *remission of sins* that are past, through the forbearance of God.

1 Cor. 1, 30: But of Him are ye in Christ Jesus, who of God is made unto us wisdom, *and righteousness,* and sanctification, and redemption.

Jer. 23, 6: In His days Judah shall be saved, and Israel shall dwell safely. And this is *His name* whereby He *shall be called, The Lord, Our Righteousness.*

2 Cor. 5, 18. 21: And all things are of God, who hath reconciled us to Himself by Jesus Christ, and hath given to us the *ministry of reconciliation.* (21) For He hath made Him to be sin for us who knew no sin, that *we might be made the righteousness of God in Him.*

John 15, 3: Now ye are. *clean through the word* which I have spoken unto you.

John 20, 23: Whosesoever *sins ye remit,* they *are remitted* unto them, and whosesoever sins ye retain, they are retained.

Luke 24, 47: And that repentance and *remission of sins should be preached* in *His name* among all nations, beginning at Jerusalem.

Gal. 3, 26: For ye are all the *children of God by faith in Christ Jesus.*

6.

Rom. 4, 3: For what saith the Scripture? Abraham *believed* God, and it was *counted unto him for righteousness.*

Rom. 4, 5. 6. 8—11. 22—24: But to him that worketh not, but believeth on Him that justifieth the ungodly, *his faith is counted for righteousness.* Even as David also describeth the blessedness of the man unto whom *God imputeth righteousness* without works. (8—11) Blessed is the man to whom the Lord will *not impute sin.* Cometh this blessedness, then, upon the circumcision only, or upon the uncircumcision also? for we say that *faith was reckoned to Abraham for righteousness.* How was it then reckoned? when he was in circumcision, or in uncircumcision? Not in circumcision, but in uncircumcision. And he received the sign of circumcision, a seal of the righteousness of the faith which he had yet being uncircumcised, that he might be the father of all them that believe, though they be not circumcised, that *righteousness might be imputed* unto them also. (22—24) And therefore it was *imputed to him for righteousness.* Now it was not written for his sake alone, that it was *imputed to him,* but for *us also,* to whom *it shall be imputed,* if we believe on Him that raised up Jesus, our Lord, from the dead.

Gal. 3, 6: Even as Abraham *believed* God, and it was *accounted to him for righteousness.*

7.

Rom. 3, 28: Therefore we conclude that a man is *justified by faith,* without the deeds of the Law.

Is. 53, 11: *By His knowledge* shall my righteous Servant *justify* many.

Rom. 4, 16: Therefore *it is of faith,* that it might be by grace, to the end the promise might be sure to all the seed, not to that only which is of the Law, but to that also which is of the faith of Abraham, who is the father of us all.

Rom. 5, 1: Therefore being *justified by faith,* we have peace with God through our Lord Jesus Christ.

Gal. 2, 16: Knowing that a man is not *justified* by the works of the Law, but *by the faith of Jesus Christ,* even we *have believed* in Jesus Christ, that we might *be justified by the faith of Christ,* and not by the works of the Law; for by the works of the Law shall no flesh be justified.

Gal. 3, 24: Wherefore the Law was our schoolmaster to bring us unto Christ, that we might be *justified by faith.*

8.

Rom. 8, 33. 34: Who shall *lay anything to the charge* of God's elect? It is *God that justifieth.* Who is he that *condemneth?* It is Christ that died, yea, rather, that is risen again, who is even at the right hand of God, who also maketh intercession for us.

Matt. 12, 37: For by thy words thou shalt be *justified,* and by thy words thou shalt be *condemned.*

Rom. 5, 16: And not as it was by one that sinned, so is the gift: for the *judgment* was by one *to condemnation,* but the free gift is of many offenses unto *justification.*

John 3, 18: He *that believeth* on Him is *not condemned;* but he that believeth not is condemned already, because he hath not believed in the name of the only-begotten Son of God.

John 5, 24: Verily, verily, I say unto you, He that heareth my word, and *believeth* on Him that sent me, hath everlasting life, and shall *not come into condemnation,* but is passed from death unto life.

9.

Rom. 3, 23. 24. 28: For all have sinned, and come short of the glory of God, being *justified freely by His grace,* through the redemption that is in Christ Jesus. (28) Therefore we conclude that a man is *justified* by faith, *without the deeds of the Law.*

Rom. 11, 6: And if *by grace,* then is it *no more of works;* otherwise grace is no more grace. But if it be of works, then is it no more grace; otherwise work is no more work.

Rom. 4, 16: Therefore it is of faith, that it might be *by grace.*

10.

Jer. 23, 6: This is His name whereby He shall be called, *The Lord, Our Righteousness.*

Is. 53, 11: By His knowledge shall my righteous Servant *justify* many; *for He shall bear their iniquities.*

Rom. 5, 19: So by the *obedience of One* shall many be made righteous.

Rom. 8, 34: *Who is he that condemneth?* It is *Christ that died.*

Rom. 3, 24: Being *justified* freely by His grace, *through the redemption that is in Christ Jesus.*

11.

Rom. 10, 10. 11: For with the heart man *believeth unto righteousness,* and with the mouth confession is made unto salvation. For the Scripture saith, Whosoever *believeth* on Him *shall not be ashamed.*

Rom. 3, 22. 26. 30: Even the *righteousness of God* which is *by faith* of Jesus Christ *unto all* and *upon all* them *that believe;* for there is no difference. (26) To declare, I say, at this time His righteousness, that He might be just, and the *Justifier of him which believeth in Jesus.* (30) Seeing it is one God, which shall *justify* the circumcision *by faith,* and uncircumcision *through faith.*

Rom. 4, 5. 6: But to him that worketh not, *but believeth* on Him that *justifieth the ungodly, his faith is counted for righteousness.* Even as David also describeth the blessedness of the man unto whom God imputeth righteousness without works.

Acts 10, 43: To Him give all the prophets witness, that through His name *whosoever believeth* in Him *shall receive remission of sins.*

12.

Col. 2, 13: And you, being dead in your sins and the uncircumcision of your flesh, hath He quickened together with Him, having *forgiven you all trespasses.*

Rom. 4, 7. 8: Saying, Blessed are they whose *iniquities are forgiven* and whose *sins are covered.* Blessed is the man to whom the Lord will *not impute sin.*

Acts 10, 43: To Him give all the prophets witness, that through His name whosoever *believeth* in Him shall receive *remission of sins.*

1 John 1, 7: The blood of Jesus Christ, His Son, *cleanseth us from all sin.*

Micah 7, 18. 19: Who is a God like unto Thee, that *pardoneth iniquity,* and passeth by the transgression of the remnant of His heritage? He retaineth not His anger forever, because He delighteth in mercy. He will turn again, He will have compassion upon us; He will subdue our iniquities; and Thou wilt *cast all their sins into the depths of the sea.*

Ps. 25, 18: Look upon mine affliction and my pain, and *forgive all my sins.*

Is. 38, 17: Behold, for peace I had great bitterness; but Thou hast in love to my soul delivered it from the pit of corruption, for Thou hast *cast* ALL *my sins behind Thy back.*

Ps. 85, 3. 4: Thou hast taken away all Thy wrath: Thou hast turned Thyself from the fierceness of Thine anger. Turn us, O God of our salvation, and cause Thine anger toward us to cease!

Ps. 103, 3: Who *forgiveth all thine iniquities;* who healeth all thy diseases.

13.

Rom. 8, 1: There is therefore now *no condemnation* to them which are in Christ Jesus, who walk not after the flesh, but after the Spirit.

Rom. 8, 31. 32. 34: What shall we then say to these things? If God be for us, who can be against us? He that spared not His own Son, but delivered Him up for us all, how shall He not with Him also freely give us all things? (34) *Who is He that condemneth?* It is Christ that died, yea, rather, that is risen again, who is even at the right hand of God, who also maketh intercession for us.

Matt. 18, 27. 32: Then the lord of that servant was moved with compassion, and loosed him, and *forgave him the debt.* (32) Then his lord, after he had called him, said unto him, O thou wicked servant, *I forgave thee all that debt,* because thou desiredst me.

Matt. 6, 12: And *forgive us our debts,* as we forgive our debtors.

13

14.

Is. 53, 5: But He was *wounded* for our transgressions, He was *bruised* for our iniquities: the *chastisement* of our peace was upon Him, and with His *stripes* we are *healed.*

Matt. 18, 27: Then the lord of that servant was moved with compassion, *and loosed him,* and forgave him the debt.

15.

Rom. 5, 1: Therefore, being justified by *faith,* we *have peace* with God through our Lord Jesus Christ.

Rom. 10, 10. 11: For with the heart man *believeth unto righteousness,* and with the mouth confession is made unto salvation. For the Scripture saith, Whosoever believeth on Him shall not be ashamed.

Rom. 3, 26. 30: To declare, I say, at this time His righteousness, that He might be just, and the justifier of him *which believeth in Jesus.* (30) Seeing it is one God, which shall justify the circumcision *by faith,* and uncircumcision *through faith.*

Rom. 4, 5. 6: But to him that worketh not, but *believeth* on Him that justifieth the ungodly, his faith is counted for righteousness. Even as David also describeth the blessedness of the man unto whom God imputeth righteousness without works.

Rom. 3, 28: Therefore we conclude that a man is justified *by faith.*

CONSEQUENCES OF JUSTIFICATION.

§ 149. The consequences of justification are peace with God,[1] a good conscience,[2] comfort and consolation under the cross,[3] and hope of life everlasting.[4]

1.

Is. 59, 2: But your iniquities have separated between you and your God, and your sins have hid His face from you, that He will not hear.

Rom. 5, 1. 2: Therefore being *justified* by faith, *we have peace with God* through our Lord Jesus Christ: by whom also we have access by faith into this grace wherein we stand, and rejoice in hope of the glory of God.

2.

Rom. 8, 15: For ye have *not* received the spirit of bondage *again to fear,* but ye have received the Spirit of adoption, whereby we cry, *Abba, Father!*

Eph. 3, 12: In whom we have boldness and access with confidence by the faith of Him.

Rom. 5, 11: And not only so, but we also joy in God through our Lord Jesus Christ, by whom we have now received the atonement.

3.

Rom. 5, 3—5: And not only so, but we glory in tribulations also: knowing that tribulation worketh patience; and patience, experience; and experience, hope: and hope maketh not ashamed; because the love of God is shed abroad in our hearts by the Holy Ghost which is given unto us.

4.

Tit. 3, 7: That, being justified by His grace, we should be made heirs according to the hope of eternal life.

Rom. 5, 2. 21: By whom also we have access by faith into this grace wherein we stand, and rejoice in hope of the glory of God. (21) That as sin hath reigned unto death, even so might grace reign through righteousness unto eternal life by Jesus Christ, our Lord.

Rom. 8, 30: Moreover, whom He did predestinate, them He also called: and whom He called, them He also justified: and whom He justified, them He also glorified.

ACTIVITY OF FAITH.

§ 150. From the moment when justifying faith has been wrought by the Holy Spirit in the act of regeneration or conversion, the same Spirit of God also actuates such living faith in the divine work of renovation or sanctification.

1 Cor. 1, 30: But of Him are ye in Christ Jesus, who of God is made unto us wisdom, and *righteousness,* and *sanctification,* and redemption.

1 Pet. 1, 22: Seeing ye have *purified* your souls in obeying the truth through the Spirit unto unfeigned love of the brethren, *see that ye love one another* with a pure heart fervently.

Eph. 4, 22—24: That ye put off concerning the former conversation the old man, which is corrupt according to the deceitful lusts; and be *renewed* in the Spirit of your mind; and that ye put on the new man, which after God is created in righteousness and true holiness.

Col. 3, 10: And have put on the new man, which is *renewed* in knowledge after the image of Him that created him.

2 Tim. 2, 21: If a man therefore purge himself from these, he shall be a vessel unto honor, sanctified, and meet for the master's use, and prepared unto every good work.

1 John 3, 3: And every man that hath this hope in Him purifieth himself, even as He is pure.

2 Cor. 7, 1: *Having* therefore *these promises,* dearly beloved, *let us cleanse ourselves* from all filthiness of the flesh and spirit, perfecting holiness in the fear of God.

Acts 15, 9: And put no difference between us and them, purifying their hearts by faith.

Gal. 5, 6: For in Jesus Christ neither circumcision availeth anything, nor uncircumcision, but *faith which worketh by love.*

2 Pet. 1, 5: And beside this, giving all diligence, add to your faith virtue.

Eph. 3, 20: Now unto Him that is able to do exceeding abundantly above all that we ask or think, according to the power that worketh in us.

Col. 1, 29: Whereunto *I also labor,* striving *according to His working,* which *worketh in me mightily.*

James 5, 16: Confess your faults one to another, and pray one for another, that ye may be healed. The effectual fervent prayer of a righteous man availeth much.

RENOVATION OR SANCTIFICATION.

§ 151. Renovation,[1] or sanctification,[2] is the restitution of the divine image[3] in the regenerate[4] by the operation of the Holy Spirit,[5] through the means of grace,[6] and in the exertion of the spiritual energies[7] engendered in the act of regeneration[8] and sustained, strengthened, and actuated by the power of God.[9]

1.

Eph. 4, 23: And *be renewed* in the spirit of your mind.

2.

1 Cor. 1, 30: But of Him are ye in Christ Jesus, who of God is made unto us wisdom, and righteousness, and *sanctification,* and redemption.

1 Thess. 4, 3: For this is the will of God, even your *sanctification,* that ye should abstain from fornication.

3.

Col. 3, 10: And have put on the new man, which is *renewed* in knowledge *after the image of Him that created him.*

Eph. 4, 24: And that ye put on the *new man,* which *after God is created* in righteousness and true holiness.

1 Pet. 1, 15: But *as He which hath called you* is holy, *so be ye holy* in all manner of conversation.

4.

Col. 2, 6: As ye have therefore received Christ Jesus, the Lord, so walk ye in Him.

Eph. 5, 8: Now are ye light in the Lord: walk as children of light!

Rom. 6, 22: Now being made free from sin, and become servants to God, ye have your fruit unto holiness.

1 Thess. 5, 23: And the very *God of peace sanctify you* wholly;

and I pray God your whole spirit and soul and body be preserved blameless unto the coming of our Lord Jesus Christ.

2 Cor. 7, 1: *Having* therefore *these promises,* dearly beloved, *let us cleanse ourselves* from all filthiness of the flesh and spirit, perfecting holiness in the fear of God.

See also texts below sub 8.

5.

1 Thess. 5, 23: And the very God of peace sanctify you wholly; and I pray God your whole spirit and soul and body be preserved blameless unto the coming of our Lord Jesus Christ.

Rom. 8, 14: For as many as are led by the Spirit of God, they are the sons of God.

6.

Tit. 3, 5: Not by works of righteousness which we have done, but according to His mercy He saved us by the *washing* of regeneration and *renewing of the* Holy Ghost.

John 17, 17: *Sanctify* them *through Thy truth:* Thy Word is the truth.

2 Tim. 3, 16. 17: All Scripture is given by inspiration of God, and is profitable for doctrine, for reproof, for correction, for *instruction in righteousness,* that the man of God may be perfect, *throughly furnished unto all good works.*

Rom. 12, 1: *I beseech you* therefore, brethren, *by the mercies of God,* that ye present your bodies a living sacrifice, holy, acceptable unto God, which is your reasonable service.

7.

Gal. 5, 6: For in Jesus Christ neither circumcision availeth anything, nor uncircumcision, but *faith* which *worketh* by love.

Gal. 5, 16: This I say, then, Walk in the Spirit, and ye shall not fulfill the lust of the flesh.

Gal. 5, 25: If we *live* in the Spirit, let us also *walk* in the Spirit.

Eph. 5, 8. 9: For ye were sometimes darkness, but now are ye *light* in the Lord: *walk as children of light!* (For the *fruit of the Spirit* is in all goodness and righteousness and truth.)

2 Pet. 1, 5: And beside this, *giving all diligence,* add to your faith virtue; and to virtue, knowledge.

8.

1 John 3, 9: Whosoever is *born of God* doth not commit sin; for *His seed remaineth in him:* and he *cannot sin, because he is born of God.*

Rom. 6, 2: God forbid! How shall we, that are dead to sin, live any longer therein?

Eph. 2, 10: For we are His workmanship, *created* in Christ Jesus *unto good works,* which God hath before ordained that we should walk in them.

1 John 5, 4. 5: For whatsoever is *born of God overcometh the world:* and this is the victory that overcometh the world, *even our faith.* Who is he that *overcometh the world,* but he that *believeth* that Jesus is the Son of God?

See also texts above sub 4.

9.

2 Cor. 9, 8: And *God is able* to make all grace abound toward you, that ye, always having all sufficiency in all things, *may abound to every good work.*

2 Cor. 12, 9: And He said unto me, *My grace is sufficient* for thee; for my strength is made perfect in weakness. Most gladly therefore will I rather glory in my infirmities, that the power of Christ may rest upon me.

Phil. 4, 13: I can *do all things through Christ* which *strengtheneth* me.

John 15, 5: I am the Vine, ye are the branches. He that abideth in me, and I in him, the same bringeth forth much fruit; for without me ye can do nothing.

MODE OF SANCTIFICATION.

§ 152. The restitution of the image of God is effected in the putting off of the old man[1] with his evil propensities and works, of which a Christian must ever anew be reminded by the mirror of the Law,[2] and in the putting on of the new man,[3] who walks before God in newness of life.[4]

1.

Col. 3, 9: Lie not one to another, seeing that ye have *put off the old man* with his deeds.

Eph. 4, 22. 25: That ye *put off* concerning the former conversation *the old man,* which is corrupt according to the deceitful lusts. (25) Wherefore putting away lying, speak every man truth with his neighbor; for we are members one of another.

2.

Rom. 3, 20: Therefore by the deeds of the Law there shall no flesh be justified in His sight; for *by the Law is the knowledge of sin.*

Rom. 7, 7: What shall we say, then? Is the Law sin? God forbid! Nay, *I had not known sin but by the Law;* for I had not *known* lust, except the *Law* had said, Thou shalt not covet.

3.

Col. 3, 10: And have *put on the new man,* which is renewed in knowledge after the image of Him that created him.

Eph. 4, 24: And that ye *put on the new man,* which after God is created in righteousness and true holiness.

4.

Rom. 6, 4. 11: Therefore we are buried with Him by baptism into death, that, like as Christ was raised up from the dead by the glory of the Father, even so we also should *walk in newness of life.* (11) Likewise reckon ye also yourselves to be *dead indeed unto sin,* but *alive unto God* through Jesus Christ, our Lord.

PROGRESSIVE SANCTIFICATION.

§ 153. The development and growth of the new man consists in the progressive enlightenment of the understanding[1] toward a more extensive and intensive knowledge of divine truth,[2] a continued renewal of the will toward its original rectitude and energy for good,[3] and an increasing sanctification of the appetites and affections toward their primeval purity.[4]

1.

Eph. 1, 17. 18: That the God of our Lord Jesus Christ, the Father of glory, may give unto you the *Spirit of wisdom* and revelation in the *knowledge* of Him, the *eyes of your understanding being enlightened,* that ye may *know* what is the hope of His calling, and what the riches of the glory of His inheritance in the saints.

Col. 1, 9. 11: For this cause we also, *since the day* we heard it, do *not cease* to pray for you, and to desire *that ye might be filled with the knowledge* of His will in *all wisdom* and spiritual *understanding.* (11) *Strengthened* with all might, according to His glorious power, unto all patience and longsuffering with joyfulness.

2 Pet. 3, 18: But *grow* in grace, and *in the knowledge* of our Lord and Savior Jesus Christ. To Him be glory both now and forever! Amen.

2.

1 Cor. 1, 5: That in everything ye are enriched by Him, in all utterance, and in *all knowledge.*

Eph. 4, 13. 14: Till we all come in the unity of the faith, and of *the knowledge of the Son of God,* unto a perfect man, unto the measure of the stature of the fullness of Christ, that we henceforth *be no more children,* tossed to and fro, and carried about with every wind of *doctrine,* by the sleight of men, and cunning craftiness, whereby they lie in wait to deceive.

Hebr. 5, 12—14: For when for the time ye *ought to be teachers,* ye have need that one teach you again which be the first principles of the oracles of God; and are become such as have need of milk and not of strong meat. For every one that useth milk is unskillful in the word of righteousness; for he is a babe. But *strong meat* belongeth to them that are *of full age,* even those who by reason of use have *their senses exercised* to discern both good and evil.

Rom. 12, 2: And be not conformed to this world; but be ye transformed by the renewing of your mind, that ye may prove what is that good, and acceptable, and perfect will of God.

Phil. 1, 9: And this I pray, that your love may abound yet more and more in *knowledge* and in all judgment.

Eph. 1, 17: That the God of our Lord Jesus Christ, the Father of glory, may give unto you the Spirit of wisdom and revelation in the *knowledge* of Him.

3.

Phil. 2, 13: For it is God which worketh in you both *to will* and to do of His good pleasure.

Rom. 7, 15. 16. 18. 19. 21. 22. 25: For that which I do I allow not; for what I would, that do I not, but what I hate, that do I. If, then, I do that which I would not, I consent unto the Law that it is good. (18. 19) For I know that in me (that is, in my flesh,) dwelleth no good thing; for to will is present with me, but how to perform that which is good I find not. For the good that I would I do not, but the evil which I would not, that I do. (21. 22) I find, then, a law, that, when I would do good, evil is present with me. For I delight in the Law of God after the inward man. (25) I thank God through Jesus Christ, our Lord. So, then, with the mind I myself serve the Law of God, but with the flesh the law of sin.

Gal. 5, 17: For the flesh lusteth against the Spirit, and the Spirit against the flesh: and these are contrary the one to the other, so that ye cannot do the things that ye would.

Rom. 6, 12—14: Let not sin therefore reign in your mortal body, that ye should obey it in the lusts thereof. Neither yield ye your members as instruments of unrighteousness unto sin; but yield yourselves unto God, as those that are alive from the dead, and your members as instruments of righteousness unto God. For sin shall not have dominion over you; for ye are not under the Law, but under grace.

4.

1 Pet. 2, 11: Dearly beloved, I beseech you as strangers and pilgrims, abstain from fleshly lusts, which war against the soul.

2 Tim. 2, 22: Flee also youthful lusts; but follow righteousness, faith, charity, peace, with them that call on the Lord out of a pure heart.

Gal. 5, 16. 24: This I say, then, Walk in the Spirit, and ye shall not fulfill the lusts of the flesh. (24) And they that are Christ's have crucified the flesh with the affections and lusts.

Acts 17, 16: Now while Paul waited for them at Athens, his *spirit was stirred* in him, when he saw the city wholly given to idolatry.

Phil. 4, 4: *Rejoice in the Lord* always: and again I say, *Rejoice!*

Ps. 119, 162: I *rejoice at Thy Word,* as one that findeth great spoil.

John 15, 10. 11: If ye keep my commandments, ye shall abide in my love, even as I have kept my Father's commandments, and abide in His love. These things have I spoken unto you, that my joy might remain in you, and *that your joy might be full.*

Luke 6, 36: Be ye therefore *merciful,* as your *Father* also is merciful.

GOOD WORKS.

§ 154. The restitution of the image of God in the regenerate is necessarily[1] productive of good works[2] in accordance with the will of God[3] expressed in His commandments,[4] the rule of Christian life, and in the imitation of the example of Christ.[5]

1.

Matt. 7, 17. 18: Even so *every* good tree bringeth forth good fruit; but a corrupt tree bringeth forth evil fruit. A good tree *cannot* bring forth evil fruit, neither can a corrupt tree bring forth good fruit.

Matt. 12, 35: A *good* man out of the *good* treasure of the *heart* bringeth forth *good* things: and an evil man out of the evil treasure bringeth forth evil things.

Rom. 6, 2—12: God forbid! *How shall we,* that are *dead* to sin, *live* any longer therein? Know ye not that so many of us as were baptized into Jesus Christ were baptized into His death? Therefore we are buried with Him by baptism into death, that, like as Christ was raised up from the dead by the glory of the Father, even so we also should *walk in newness of life.* For if we have been planted together in the likeness of His *death,* we shall be also in the likeness of His *resurrection,* knowing this, that our *old* man is *crucified* with Him, that the *body of sin* might be *destroyed,* that henceforth we should *not serve sin.* For he that is *dead* is *freed* from sin. Now if we be *dead* with Christ, we believe that we shall also *live with Him,* knowing that Christ, being raised from the dead, dieth no more; death hath no more dominion over Him. For in that He died, He died unto sin once; but in that He liveth, He liveth unto God. Likewise reckon ye also yourselves to be *dead* indeed unto *sin,* but *alive* unto *God* through Jesus Christ, our Lord. Let not sin therefore reign in your mortal body, that ye should obey it in the lusts thereof.

2.

Eph. 2, 10: For we are His workmanship, *created* in Christ Jesus, *unto good works,* which God hath before *ordained* that we *should walk in them.*

Col. 1, 10: That ye might walk worthy of the Lord unto all pleasing, being *fruitful* in *every good work,* and increasing in the knowledge of God.

Tit. 2, 14: Who gave Himself for us, that He might redeem us from all iniquity, and purify unto Himself a peculiar people, *zealous of good works.*

3.

Rom. 12, 2: And be not conformed to this world; but be ye *transformed* by the *renewing* of your mind, that ye may prove what is *that good,* and *acceptable,* and *perfect will of God.*

Eph. 5, 10: Proving what is acceptable unto the Lord.

1 Thess. 4, 3: For this is the *will of God,* even your *sanctification,* that ye should abstain from fornication.

Ps. 119, 32: I will run the way of Thy commandments, when *Thou shalt enlarge my heart.*

4.

John 14, 15: If ye love me, *keep my commandments.*

Ps. 119, 32: I will run *the way of Thy commandments,* when Thou shalt enlarge my heart.

John 15, 10: If ye *keep my commandments,* ye shall abide in my love, even as I have kept my Father's commandments, and abide in His love.

Rom. 13, 9. 10: For this, Thou shalt not commit adultery, Thou shalt not kill, Thou shalt not steal, Thou shalt not bear false witness, Thou shalt not covet; and *if there be any other commandment,* it is briefly comprehended in this saying, namely, Thou shalt love thy neighbor as thyself. Love worketh no ill to his neighbor; therefor *love* is *the fulfilling of the Law.*

Eph. 6, 1. 2: Children, obey your parents in the Lord; for this is right. Honor thy father and mother, which is the first *commandment* with promise.

1 John 2, 3. 4: And hereby we do know that we know Him, if we *keep His commandments.* He that saith, I know Him, and keepeth not His *commandments,* is a liar, and the truth is not in him.

1 John 3, 24: And he that *keepeth His commandments* dwelleth in Him, and He in him. And hereby we know that He abideth in us, by the Spirit which He hath given us.

1 John 5, 3: For this is the love of God, that we *keep His commandments:* and His commandments are not grievous.

5.

1 John 2, 6: He that saith he abideth in Him ought himself also so to *walk, even as He walked.*

John 13, 34: A new commandment I give unto you, That ye love one another; *as I have loved you,* that ye *also love* one another.

John 15, 12: This is my commandment, That ye love one another, *as I have loved you.*

Phil. 2, 5: Let *this mind* be in you, which was *also in Christ Jesus.*

John 13, 15: For I have given you an *example,* that ye should *do as I have done to you.*

IMPUTED AND INHERENT RIGHTEOUSNESS COMPARED.

§ 155. While Christ's vicarious obedience constitutes the righteousness imputed to us[1] and accepted by our faith,[2] and is a necessary cause of our salvation,[3] our own obedience constitutes a righteousness inherent in us,[4] and is a necessary fruit[5] and evidence[6] of our faith, but in no wise a cause of, or necessary for, our salvation.[7]

1.

Cf. § 148.

2.

Cf. §§ 146. 147.

3.

Acts 4, 12: Neither is there salvation in any other; for there is none other name under heaven given among men whereby we must be saved.

Cf. Christology, § 124, g.

4.

Rom. 6, 22: But now being made free from sin, and become servants to God, ye have *your fruit* unto holiness, and the end everlasting life.

Eph. 4, 22. 23: That ye put off concerning the former conversation the old man, which is corrupt according to the deceitful lusts; and be *renewed* in the *spirit of your mind.*

5.

Tit. 3, 8. 14: This is a faithful saying, and these things I will that thou affirm constantly, that they which have believed in God might be careful to maintain good works. These things are good and profitable unto men. (14) And let ours also learn to maintain good works for necessary uses, that they be not unfruitful.

Matt. 7, 17. 18: Even so *every* good tree *bringeth forth good fruit;* but a corrupt tree bringeth forth evil fruit. A good tree *cannot* bring forth evil fruit, neither can a corrupt tree bring forth good fruit.

Matt. 12, 35: A *good* man out of the *good* treasure of the heart bringeth forth *good* things: and an evil man out of the evil treasure bringeth forth evil things.

6.

James 2, 18: Yea, a man may say, Thou hast faith, and I have works: *show me thy faith* without thy works, and I *will show thee my faith by my works.*

Gal. 5, 6: For in Jesus Christ neither circumcision availeth anything, nor uncircumcision, but faith which worketh by love.

John 13, 35: *By this* shall all men *know* that ye are my disciples, if ye have *love* one to another.

7.

Tit. 3, 5: *Not by works of righteousness* which *we have done,* but according to *His mercy* He saved us by the washing of regeneration and renewing of the Holy Ghost.

Eph. 2, 8. 9: For *by grace* are ye *saved* through faith; and that *not of yourselves:* it is the *gift* of God: *not of works,* lest any man should boast.

Rom. 3, 28: Therefore we conclude that a man is justified by faith, *without the deeds of the Law.*

SANCTIFICATION IMPERFECT IN THIS LIFE.

§ 156. While Christ's obedience imputed to us constitutes a perfect[1] righteousness in the sight of God, our own obedience, or the righteousness inherent in us, must, on account of the residue of sinful flesh still active within us,[2] remain imperfect in this life[3] — *justitia inchoata* —, the beginning only[4] of the restitution of the divine image in the regenerate being made in this temporal life.[5]

1.

Cf. § 148, 12. 13. 14.

2.

Rom. 7, 18: For I know that *in me* (that is, *in my flesh,*) dwelleth *no good thing;* for to will is present with me, but how to perform that which is good I find not.

Hebr. 12, 1: Wherefore, seeing we also are compassed about with so great a cloud of witnesses, let us *lay aside* every weight, and the *sin which doth so easily beset us,* and let us run with patience the race that is set before us.

Rom. 7, 21. 23—25: I find, then, a law, that, when I would do good, *evil is present with me.* (23—25) But I see *another law in my members,* warring *against* the law of my mind, and bringing me into captivity to *the law of sin which is in my members.* O wretched man that I am! who shall *deliver me* from the body of this death? I thank God through Jesus Christ, our Lord. So, then, with the mind I myself serve the Law of God, but *with the flesh the law of sin.*

Gal. 5, 16. 17: This I say, then, Walk in the Spirit, and ye shall not fulfill the lust of the flesh. For *the flesh lusteth against the Spirit,* and the Spirit against the flesh: and these are *contrary* the one to the other, so that *ye cannot do the things that ye would.*

1 John 1, 8: If we *say that we have no sin,* we deceive ourselves, and *the truth is not in us.*

Matt. 6, 12: And forgive us *our debts,* as we forgive our debtors.

James 3, 2: For in *many* things *we offend all.* If any man offend not in word, the same is a perfect man, and able also to bridle the whole body.

Rom. 6, 12. 14: Let not *sin* therefore *reign* in your mortal body, that ye should obey it in *the lusts thereof.* (14) For sin shall not have *dominion* over you; for ye are not under the Law, but under grace.

Is. 64, 6: But *we are all as an unclean thing,* and all our righteousnesses are as filthy rags; and we all do fade as a leaf; and *our iniquities,* like the wind, have taken us away.

3.

Is. 64, 6: But we are all as an unclean thing, and all *our righteousnesses* are *as filthy rags;* and we all do fade as a leaf; and our iniquities, like the wind, have taken us away.

Matt. 6, 12: And forgive us *our debts,* as we forgive our debtors.

1 John 1, 8: If we say that we have no sin, we deceive ourselves, and the truth is not in us.

4.

Phil. 1, 6: Being confident of this very thing, that He which hath *begun* a good work in you will perform it until the day of Jesus Christ.

Phil. 3, 12: Not as though I had *already attained,* either were *already perfect,* but I follow after, if that I may apprehend that for which also I am apprehended of Christ Jesus.

Eph. 4, 13: Till *we all come* in the unity of the faith, and of the knowledge of the Son of God, *unto a perfect man,* unto the measure of the stature of the *fullness* of Christ.

2 Cor. 4, 16: For which cause we faint not; but though our outward man perish, yet the inward man is *renewed day by day.*

2 Cor. 7, 1: Having therefore these promises, dearly beloved, let us *cleanse ourselves* from all filthiness of the flesh and spirit, *perfecting holiness* in the fear of God.

5.

1 John 3, 2. 3: Beloved, now are we the sons of God, and it doth *not yet appear* what *we shall be;* but we know that, when He shall appear, *we shall be like Him;* for we shall see Him as He is. And every man that hath this *hope* in Him *purifieth himself,* even as He is pure.

INVISIBLE CHURCH.

§ 157. The community of the regenerate, or of all those who believe in Christ and are justified by faith,[1] is the invisible[2] Church of Christ on earth, the one holy catholic church,[3] in the proper sense of the word, the spiritual body of Christ,[4] of which Christ is the only spiritual Head,[5] the spiritual house and temple of God,[6] of which Christ is the sole Foundation;[7] and this is the Church which is to endure forever and against which the gates of hell shall not prevail.

1.

Eph. 2, 19—22: Now therefore ye are no more strangers and foreigners, but *fellow-citizens with the saints,* and of the *household of God;* and are built upon the foundation of the apostles and prophets, Jesus Christ Himself being the chief corner-stone; in whom all the building fitly *framed together* groweth *unto an holy temple in the Lord;* in whom ye also are builded together for an habitation of God through the Spirit.

Eph. 5, 25—27: Husbands, love your wives, even as Christ also loved *the Church,* and gave Himself for it, that He might *sanctify and cleanse it* with the washing of water by the Word, that He might present it to Himself a glorious *Church,* not having spot, or wrinkle, or any such thing, but that it should be *holy and without blemish.*

1 Pet. 2, 9: But ye are a *chosen generation,* a *royal priesthood,* an *holy nation,* a *peculiar people,* that ye should show forth the praises of Him who hath *called you out of darkness into His marvelous light.*

Eph. 1, 1: Paul, an apostle of Jesus Christ by the will of God, to *the saints* which are *at Ephesus,* and to *the faithful in Christ Jesus.*

Phil. 1, 1: Paul and Timotheus, the servants of Jesus Christ, to *all the saints* in Christ Jesus which are *at Philippi,* with the bishops and deacons.

Col. 1, 2: To the *saints and faithful brethren* in Christ which are *at Colosse:* Grace be unto you, and peace, from God, our Father, and the Lord Jesus Christ.

John 10, 26. 27: But ye believe not, because ye are not of *my sheep,* as I said unto you. *My sheep hear my voice,* and I know them, and *they follow me.*

2.

Hebr. 11, 1: Now faith is the substance of things hoped for, the evidence of things not seen.

2 Tim. 2, 19: Nevertheless, the foundation of God standeth sure, having this seal, *The Lord knoweth them that are His.* And, Let every one that nameth the name of Christ depart from iniquity.

Luke 17, 20. 21: And when He was demanded of the Pharisees, when the kingdom of God should come, He answered them and said, The *kingdom of God* cometh *not with observation;* neither shall they say, Lo here! or, lo there! For, behold, the kingdom of God *is within you.*

1 Kings 19, 14. 18: And he said, I have been very jealous for the Lord God of hosts; because the children of Israel have forsaken Thy covenant, thrown down Thine altars, and slain Thy prophets with the sword; and I, even *I only, am left;* and they seek my life, to take it away. (18) Yet, *I have left me seven thousand* in Israel, all the knees which have not bowed unto Baal, and every mouth which hath not kissed him.

3.

Eph. 4, 3—6: Endeavoring to keep the *unity* of the Spirit in the bond of peace. There is *one body,* and *one Spirit,* even as ye are called in one hope of your calling; *one* Lord, *one* faith, *one* baptism, *one* God and Father *of all,* who is above *all,* and through *all,* and *in you all.*

1 Cor. 12, 13: For by *one Spirit* are we *all* baptized into *one body,* whether we be Jews or Gentiles, whether we be bond or free; and have been all made to drink into *one Spirit.*

Rom. 12, 4. 5. 12: For as we have *many members* in *one body,* and all members have not the same office, so *we, being many,* are *one body in Christ,* and every one members one of another. (12) Rejoicing in hope; patient in tribulation; continuing instant in prayer.

John 10, 16: And ôther sheep I have, which are not of this fold: them also I must bring, and they shall *hear my voice;* and there shall be *one fold,* and one Shepherd.

Rev. 5, 9. 10: And they sung a new song, saying, Thoû art worthy to take the book, and to open the seals thereof; for Thou wast slain, and hast redeemed us to God by Thy blood *out of every kindred, and tongue, and people, and nation,* and hast made us unto our God kings and priests: and we shall reign on the earth.

4.

Eph. 1, 23: Which is *His body,* the fullness of Him that filleth all in all.

Rom. 12, 4. 5: For as we have many members in one body, and all members have not the same office, so we, being many, are *one body in Christ,* and every one members one of another.

Eph. 4, 12: For the perfecting of the saints, for the work of the ministry, for the edifying of *the body of Christ.*

5.

Eph. 1, 22: And hath put all things under His feet, and gave Him to be the *Head over all things to the Church.*

Eph. 4, 15: But speaking the truth in love, may grow up into Him in all things, which is *the Head, even Christ.*

Eph. 5, 23: For the husband is the head of the wife, even as *Christ is the Head of the Church:* and He is the Savior of the body.

Col. 1, 18: And *He is the Head of the body, the Church:* who is the beginning, the Firstborn from the dead, that in all things He might have the preeminence.

6.

Eph. 2, 21. 22: In whom all the building fitly framed together groweth unto *an holy temple in the Lord,* in whom *ye are also builded together* for an *habitation of God* through the Spirit.

2 Cor. 6, 16: And what agreement hath the temple of God with idols? *For ye are the temple of the living God,* as God hath said, I will dwell in them, and walk in them; and I will be their God, and they shall be my people.

7.

Eph. 2, 20: And we are built upon *the foundation of the apostles and prophets, Jesus Christ* Himself being the chief *corner-stone.*

1 Cor. 3, 11: For other *foundation* can no man lay than that is laid, which is *Jesus Christ.*

1 Pet. 2, 6: Wherefore also it is contained in the Scripture, Behold, I lay in Sion a *chief corner-stone,* elect, precious: and he that believeth on Him shall not be confounded.

8.

Matt. 16, 18: And I say also unto thee, That thou art Peter, and upon this rock I will build *my Church;* and *the gates of hell shall not prevail against it.*

John 10, 27. 28: My sheep hear my voice, and I know them, and they follow me: and I give unto them eternal life; and they shall *never perish, neither shall any man pluck them out of my hand.*

VISIBLE CHURCHES.

§ 158. In a tropical sense all those who have and hear the Gospel and profess the Christian religion, true believers and hypocrites together,[1] are called the visible church, and in the same synecdochical sense every particular community or local congregation gathered about the means of grace and professing the Christian faith is termed a visible Christian church,[2] since, wherever the Gospel of Christ is preached and His sacraments are administered, the Holy Spirit is active, works regeneration, builds and preserves the invisible Church of God.[3]

1.

Matt. 13, 47. 48: Again, the *kingdom of heaven* is like unto a net that was cast into the sea and gathered of *every kind,* which, when it was full, they drew to shore, and sat down, and gathered the *good* into vessels, but cast the *bad* away.

Matt. 25, 1. 2: Then shall the *kingdom of heaven* be likened unto *ten virgins,* which took their lamps, and went forth to meet the bridegroom. And *five* of them were *wise,* and *five* were *foolish.*

Matt. 22, 2. 11: The *kingdom of heaven* is like unto a certain king which made a marriage for his son. (11) And when the king came in to see the guests, he saw there a man *which had not on a wedding garment.*

2.

Gal. 1, 2: And all the brethren which are with me, unto the *churches of Galatia.*

Matt. 18, 17: And if he shall neglect to hear them, *tell it unto the church;* but if he neglect to hear the church, let him be unto thee as an heathen man and a publican.

3 John 9. 10: I *wrote unto the church;* but Diotrephes, who loveth to have the preeminence among them, receiveth us not. Wherefore, if I come, I will remember his deeds which he doeth, prating against us with malicious words: and not content therewith, neither doth he himself receive the brethren, and forbiddeth them that would, and casteth them *out of the church.*

Rev. 3, 13—18: He that hath an ear, let him hear what the Spirit saith *unto the churches.* And unto the angel of the *church of the Laodiceans* write: These things saith the Amen, the faithful and true Witness, the beginning of the creation of God: I know thy works, that thou art *neither cold nor hot:* I would thou wert cold or hot. So, then, because thou art lukewarm, and neither cold nor hot, I will spue thee out of my mouth. Because thou sayest, I am rich, and increased with goods, and have need of nothing, and *knowest not that thou art wretched,* and miserable, and poor, and blind, and naked: I counsel thee to buy of me gold tried in the fire, that thou mayest be rich; and white raiment, that thou mayest be clothed, and that the *shame of thy nakedness* do not appear; and anoint thine eyes with eyesalve, that thou mayest see.

3.

Is. 55, 10. 11: For as the rain cometh down, and the snow from heaven, and returneth not thither, but watereth the earth, and maketh it bring forth and bud, that it may give seed to the sower and bread to the eater, so shall *my Word* be that goeth forth out of my mouth: it shall *not return unto me void,* but it shall *accomplish* that which I please, and it shall *prosper* in the thing whereto I sent it.

Luke 8, 11—15: Now the parable is this: The seed is the Word of God. Those by the wayside are they that hear; then cometh the devil, and taketh away the Word out of their hearts, lest they should believe and be saved. They on the rock are they, which, when they hear, receive the Word with joy; and these have no root, which for a while believe, and in time of temptation fall away. And that which fell among thorns are they, which, when they have heard, go forth, and are choked with cares and riches and pleasures of this life, and bring no fruit to perfection. But that on the good ground are they, which in an honest and good heart, having heard the Word, keep it, and bring forth fruit with patience.

MARKS OF THE CHURCH.

§ 159. Since, wherever the Gospel is preached and the sacraments are administered,[1] the invisible Church of Christ is sure to be,[2] the preaching of the Gospel and the administra-

14

tion of the sacraments are the unfailing marks of the existence of the invisible Church.

1.

Acts 2, 42: And they continued steadfastly in the apostles' doctrine and fellowship, and in breaking of bread, and in prayers.

2.

Is. 55, 10. 11: For as the rain cometh down, and the snow from heaven, and returneth not thither, but watereth the earth, and maketh it bring forth and bud, that it may give seed to the sower and bread to the eater, so shall *my Word* be that goeth forth out of my mouth: it shall *not return unto me void,* but it shall *accomplish* that which I please, and it shall *prosper* in the thing whereto I sent it.

Mark 16, 15. 16: And He said unto them, Go ye into all the world, and *preach the Gospel* to every creature. He that believeth and is *baptized* shall be saved; but he that believeth not shall be damned.

ORTHODOX CHURCH.

§ 160. The preaching, teaching, and profession, of divine truth in all its purity, and the administration of the sacraments in full accordance with their divine institution, are the criteria of the true or orthodox visible church of Christ on earth.

John 8, 31. 32: Then said Jesus to those Jews which believed on Him, *If ye continue in my Word,* then are ye *my disciples indeed;* and ye shall know the truth, and the truth shall make you free.

Matt. 28, 20: *Teaching* them to *observe all* things *whatsoever* I have commanded you: and, lo, *I am with you* alway, even unto the end of the world. Amen.

RIGHTS OF THE CHURCH WHERE VESTED.

§ 161. The invisible Church of Christ is endowed with certain spiritual rights, privileges, and powers,[1] all of which are vested in every local congregation of believers.[2]

1.

Matt. 16, 15—19: He saith unto *them,* But whom say *ye* that I am? And *Simon Peter answered* and said, Thou art the Christ, the Son of the living God. And Jesus answered and said unto him, Blessed art thou, Simon Bar-jona; for flesh and blood hath not revealed it unto thee, but my Father which is in heaven. And I say also unto thee, That thou art Peter, and upon this rock I will build my Church; and the gates of hell shall not prevail against it. And I will give unto thee the *keys of the kingdom of heaven:* and whatsoever thou shalt *bind* on earth shall be bound in heaven: and whatsoever thou shalt *loose* on earth shall be loosed in heaven.

Matt. 18, 15—18: Moreover, if thy brother shall trespass against thee, go and tell him his fault between thee and him alone: if he shall hear thee, thou hast gained thy brother. But if he will not hear thee, then take with thee one or two more, that in the mouth of two or three witnesses every word may be established. And if he shall neglect to hear them, tell it unto the *church;* but if he neglect to hear the *church,* let him be unto thee as an heathen man and a publican. Verily, I say unto you, Whatsoever *ye shall bind* on earth shall be bound in heaven; and whatsoever *ye shall loose* on earth shall be loosed in heaven.

John 20, 22. 23: And when He had said this, He breathed on them, and saith unto them, *Receive ye the Holy Ghost:* whosesoever sins *ye remit,* they are remitted unto them, and whosesoever sins *ye retain,* they are retained.

1 Cor. 3, 21—23: Therefore let no man glory in men; for *all things are yours:* whether Paul, or Apollos, or Cephas, or the world, or life, or death, or things present, or things to come; *all are yours;* and ye are Christ's; and Christ is God's.

1 Pet. 2, 9: But *ye* are a *chosen generation,* a *royal priesthood,* an holy nation, a peculiar people, that *ye should show forth* the praises of Him who hath *called you* out of darkness into His marvelous light.

2.

Matt. 18, 17. 18: And if he shall neglect to hear them, *tell it unto the church;* but if he neglect to hear the church, let him be unto thee as an heathen man and a publican. Verily, I say unto you, Whatsoever *ye* shall bind on earth shall be bound in heaven; and whatsoever *ye* shall loose on earth shall be loosed in heaven.

Matt. 16, 19. 20: And I will give unto thee the keys of the kingdom of heaven; and whatsoever thou shalt bind on earth shall be bound in heaven: and whatsoever thou shalt loose on earth shall be loosed in heaven.

1 Cor. 1, 2: Unto the *church of God* which is *at Corinth,* to them that are sanctified in Christ Jesus, called to be saints, with all that *in every place* call upon the name of Jesus Christ, our Lord, both theirs and ours.

Gal. 1, 2: And all the brethren which are with me, unto the *churches of Galatia.*

1 Thess. 1, 1: Paul, and Silvanus, and Timotheus, unto the *church of the Thessalonians* which is in God the Father and in the Lord Jesus Christ: Grace be unto you, and peace, from God, our Father, and the Lord Jesus Christ.

RIGHTS AND POWERS OF THE CHURCH.

§ 162. The rights and powers of the Church of Christ and of every local congregation are those of preaching the Gospel, the administration of the sacraments, especially the application of the keys of heaven, by loosing and binding in the name of God.

Matt. 16, 19: And I will give unto thee the *keys of the kingdom of heaven:* and whatsoever thou *shalt bind* on earth shall be bound in heaven: and whatsoever thou shalt *loose* on earth shall be loosed in heaven.

Matt. 18, 15—18: Moreover, if thy brother shall trespass against thee, go and tell him his fault between thee and him alone: if he shall hear thee, thou hast gained thy brother. But if he will not hear thee, then take with thee one or two more, that in the mouth of two or three witnesses every word may be established. And if he shall neglect to hear them, tell it *unto the church;* but if he neglect to *hear the church,* let him be unto thee as an heathen man and a publican. Verily, I say unto you, Whatsoever *ye shall bind* on earth shall be bound in heaven: and whatsoever *ye shall loose* on earth shall be loosed in heaven.

Mark 16, 15. 16: And He said unto them, *Go ye* into all the world, and *preach the Gospel* to every creature. He that believeth and is *baptized* shall be saved; but he that believeth not shall be damned.

John 20, 22. 23: And when He had said this, He breathed on them, and saith unto them, *Receive ye the Holy Ghost:* whosesoever sins *ye remit,* they are remitted unto them, and whosesoever sins *ye retain,* they are retained.

1 Cor. 5, 13: But them that are without God judgeth. Therefore put away from among yourselves that wicked person.

See § 128 and texts.

MINISTERIAL OFFICE.

§ 163. For the public performance of the privileges and duties of the Church in preaching the Gospel and administering the sacraments Christ has instituted the ministerial office in the Church.

1 Cor. 12, 29: Are all apostles? are all prophets? are all teachers?

Rom. 10, 15: And how shall they *preach,* except they *be sent?* as it is written, How beautiful are the feet of them that preach the Gospel of peace, and bring glad tidings of good things!

2 Cor. 5, 18: And all things are of God, who hath reconciled us to Himself by Jesus Christ, and hath *given to us the ministry of reconciliation.*

Matt. 28, 19. 20: *Go ye* therefore, and teach all nations, baptizing them in the name of the Father, and of the Son, and of the Holy Ghost, *teaching them* to observe all things whatsoever I have commanded you: and, lo, I am with you alway, even *unto the end of the world.*

Eph. 4, 11: And *He gave* some, apostles; and some, prophets; and some, evangelists; and some, pastors and teachers.

Acts 20, 28: Take heed therefore unto yourselves, and to all the flock, over which *the Holy Ghost* hath *made you overseers,* to feed the Church of God.

John 20, 21. 23: Then said Jesus to them again, Peace be unto you! As my Father hath sent me, even *so send I you.* (23) Whosesoever sins ye remit, they are remitted unto them; and whosesoever sins ye retain, they are retained.

1 Pet. 5, 2: *Feed the flock of God* which is among you, *taking the oversight thereof,* not by constraint, but willingly; not for filthy lucre, but of a ready mind.

MINISTRY HOW CONFERRED.

§ 164. The ministerial office[1] is conferred upon its incumbents by God,[2] by the Holy Spirit,[3] by Christ,[4] the Head and Archbishop of His Church,[5] through the congregations,[6] which, by the call extended through them,[7] delegate or transfer upon the men[8] thus called the public exercise of those functions of the priesthood of all believers[9] which, by virtue of such call, the ministers of Christ[10] and of the Church[11] perform in the name of the congregation and of Christ, who mediately called them through the congregation.

1.

1 Cor. 3, 5: Who, then, is Paul, and who is Apollos, but *ministers* by whom ye believed, even as the Lord gave to every man?

1 Cor. 4, 1: Let a man so account of us as of the *ministers of Christ* and stewards of the mysteries of God.

2.

1 Cor. 12, 28: And *God hath set* some in the Church, first apostles, secondarily prophets, thirdly *teachers,* after that miracles, then gifts of healings, helps, governments, diversities of tongues.

3.

Acts 20, 17. 28: And from Miletus he sent to Ephesus, and called the elders of the church. (28) Take heed therefore unto yourselves, and to all the flock, over the which the *Holy Ghost* hath *made you overseers,* to feed the Church of God, which He hath purchased .with His own blood.

Acts 13, 2: As they ministered to the Lord, and fasted, the *Holy Ghost* said, *Separate me* Barnabas and Saul *for the work whereunto I have called them.*

4.

Eph. 4, 11: And *He gave* some, apostles; and some, prophets; and some, evangelists; and some, *pastors and teachers.*

1 Pet. 5, 1. 2. 4: The *elders* which are among you I exhort, who am also an elder, and a witness of the sufferings of Christ, and also a partaker of the glory that shall be revealed: *Feed the flock of God which is among you,* taking the oversight thereof, not by constraint, but willingly; not for filthy lucre, but of a ready mind. (4) And when the *Chief Shepherd* shall appear, ye shall receive a crown of glory that fadeth not away.

5.

1 Pet. 5, 4: And when the *Chief Shepherd* shall appear, ye shall receive a crown of glory that fadeth not away.

1 Pet. 2, 25: For ye were as sheep going astray, but are now returned unto *the Shepherd and Bishop* of your souls.

Hebr. 13, 20: Now the God of peace, that brought again from the dead our Lord Jesus, *that great Shepherd of the sheep,* through the blood of the everlasting covenant.

Eph. 4, 15: But speaking the truth in love, may grow up into Him in all things, which is *the Head, even Christ.*

Is. 40, 11: *He shall feed His flock* like a *shepherd;* He shall gather the lambs with His arm, and carry them in His bosom, and shall gently lead those that are with young.

6.

Acts 6, 1—6: And in those days, when the number of the disciples was multiplied, there arose a murmuring of the Grecians against the Hebrews, because their widows were neglected in the daily ministration. Then the twelve called the *multitude of the disciples* unto them, and said, It is not reason that we should leave the Word of God and serve tables. Wherefore, brethren, *look ye out* among you seven men of honest report, full of the Holy Ghost and wisdom, whom we may appoint over this business. But we will give ourselves continually to prayer and to the ministry of the Word. And the saying pleased the whole multitude: and *they chose* Stephen, a man full of faith and of the Holy Ghost, and Philip, and Prochorus, and Nicanor, and Timon, and Parmenas, and Nicolas, a proselyte of Antioch: whom *they set* before the apostles. And when they had prayed, they laid their hands on them.

Acts 14, 23: And when they had ordained them elders in every church, and had prayed with fasting, they commended them to the Lord, on whom they believed.

7.

Acts 13, 2. 4: As they ministered to the Lord, and fasted, the Holy Ghost said, *Separate me* Barnabas and Saul for the work whereunto *I have called them.* (4) So they, *being sent forth by the Holy Ghost,* departed unto Seleucia; and from thence they sailed to Cyprus.

8.

1 Cor. 14, 34: Let your women keep silence in the churches; for it is not permitted unto them to speak; but they are commanded to be under obedience, as also saith the Law.

1 Tim. 2, 12: But I suffer not a woman to teach, nor to usurp authority over the man, but to be in silence.

9.

1 Pet. 2, 9: But ye are a chosen generation, *a royal priesthood,* an holy nation, a peculiar people, that *ye should show forth* the praises of Him who hath called you out of darkness into His marvelous light.

Matt. 18, 17—20: And if he shall neglect to hear them, tell it *unto the church;* but if he neglect to hear *the church,* let him be unto thee as an heathen man and a publican. Verily, I say unto you, Whatsoever *ye shall bind* on earth shall be bound in heaven: and whatsoever *ye shall loose* on earth shall be loosed in heaven. Again I say unto you, That if two of you shall agree on earth as touching anything that they shall ask, it shall be done for them of my Father which is in heaven. For *where two or three are gathered together in my name,* there am I in the midst of them.

10.

1 Cor. 4, 1: Let a man so account of us as of the *ministers of Christ* and stewards of the mysteries of God.

Rom. 1, 1: Paul, *a servant of Jesus Christ,* called to be an apostle, *separated unto the Gospel of God.*

Gal. 1, 1: Paul, an apostle, (not *of* men, neither *by* man, but *by Jesus Christ,* and God the Father, who raised Him from the dead).

11.

2 Cor. 4, 5: For we preach not ourselves, but Christ Jesus the Lord, and ourselves *your servants* for Jesus' sake.

1 Cor. 3, 21—23: Therefore let no man glory in men; for *all things are yours,* whether *Paul,* or *Apollos,* or *Cephas,* or the world, or life, or death, or things present, or things to come: *all are yours;* and ye are Christ's; and Christ is God's.

ORDINATION.

§ 165. The ministerial office being conferred through the call of the congregation, the ecclesiastical rite of ordination is but a public acknowledgment of that call and of its accept-ance, and of the fitness of the person called for the proper performance of the duties of the office conferred upon him.

Acts 13, 3: And when they had fasted and prayed, and *laid their hands on them,* they sent them away.

Acts 6, 6: Whom they set before the *apostles:* and when they had prayed, they *laid their hands* on them.

1 Tim. 5, 22: *Lay hands* suddenly on no man, neither be par-taker of other men's sins. Keep thyself pure!

1 Tim. 4, 14: Neglect not the gift that is in thee, which was given thee by prophecy, with *the laying on of the hands* of the *presbytery.*

2 Tim. 1, 6: Wherefore I put thee in remembrance that thou stir up the gift of God which is in thee by *the putting on of my hands.*

QUALIFICATIONS FOR THE MINISTRY.

§ 166. The qualifications prescribed by the Head of the Church for those men[1] who are to be called to the ministerial office are soundness of doctrine, aptness to teach, blameless-ness of life, and a good and honest report of them that are without.[2]

1.

1 Cor. 14, 34: Let your women keep silence in the churches; for it is not permitted unto them to speak; but they are commanded to be under obedience, as also saith the Law.

1 Tim. 2, 12: But I suffer not a woman to teach, nor to usurp authority over the man, but to be in silence.

2.

1 Tim. 3, 2. 3: A bishop, then, must be *blameless,* the husband of one wife, vigilant, sober, of good behavior, given to hospitality, *apt to teach;* not given to wine, no striker, not greedy of filthy lucre; but patient, not a brawler, not covetous.

1 Tim. 3, 4—7: One that ruleth well his own house, having his children in subjection with all gravity: (for if a man know not how to rule his own house, how shall he take care of the Church of God?) not a novice, lest, being lifted up with pride, he fall into the con-demnation of the devil. Moreover, he must have *a good report of them which are without,* lest he fall into reproach and the snare of the devil.

Tit. 1, 6—9: If any be *blameless,* the husband of one wife, hav-ing faithful children not accused of riot or unruly. For a bishop must be *blameless,* as the steward of God; not self-willed, not soon angry, not given to wine, no striker, not given to filthy lucre; but a lover of hospitality, a lover of good men, sober, just, holy, temperate, holding fast the faithful Word as he hath been taught, that he may be able by *sound doctrine* both to exhort and to convince the gainsayers.

Acts 6, 3: Wherefore, brethren, look ye out among you seven men of *honest report,* full of the Holy Ghost and wisdom, whom we may appoint over this business.

EQUALITY OF MINISTERS.

§ 167. The incumbents of the ministerial office, either in one congregation or in different congregations, are equal in rank among themselves, no degrees in the ministry having been established by the Head of the Church.

Matt. 23, 8: One is your Master, even Christ; and all ye are brethren.

Acts 20, 17. 28: And from Miletus he sent to Ephesus, and called the *elders* of the church. (28) Take heed therefore unto yourselves, and to all the flock, over the which the Holy Ghost hath made you *overseers,* to feed the Church of God, which He hath purchased with His own blood.

Tit. 1, 5. 7: For this cause left· I thee in Crete, that thou shouldest set in order the things that are wanting, and ordain *elders* in every city, as I had appointed thee. (7) *For a bishop* must be blameless, as the steward of God; not self-willed, not soon angry, not given to wine, no striker, not given to filthy lucre.

1 Pet. 5, 1—3: The *elders* which are among you I exhort, who am also an elder, and a witness of the sufferings of Christ, and also a partaker of the glory that shall be revealed: Feed the flock of God which is among you, taking the *oversight* thereof, not by constraint, but willingly; not for filthy lucre, but of a ready mind; *neither as being lords* over God's heritage, but being ensamples to the flock.

ASSISTANT FUNCTIONARIES IN THE CHURCH.

§ 168. Though the ministerial office in the Church is but one, yet by the will of the congregations and with the consent of the incumbents of the whole ministerial office certain functions of this office may be delegated to assistant functionaries in the service of the congregations.

Acts 6, 2—6: Then the twelve called the multitude of the disciples unto them, and said, It is not reason that we should leave the *Word of God,* and *serve tables.* Wherefore, brethren, look ye out among you seven men of honest report, full of the Holy Ghost and wisdom, whom we may appoint *over this business.* But *we* will give ourselves continually to prayer and to the *ministry of the Word.* And the saying pleased the whole multitude: and they chose Stephen, a man full of faith and of the Holy Ghost, and Philip, and Prochorus, and Nicanor, and Timon, and Parmenas, and Nicolas, a proselyte of Antioch: whom they set before the apostles: and when they had prayed, they laid their hands on them.

1 Tim. 3, 8: Likewise must the *deacons* be grave, not double-tongued, not given to much wine, not greedy of filthy lucre.

1 Tim. 5, 17: Let the *elders* that rule well be counted worthy of double honor, *especially* they who *labor in the Word and doctrine.*

1 Cor. 12, 5. 29: And there are *differences of administrations,* but the same Lord. (29) Are all apostles? are all prophets? are all teachers? are all workers of the miracles?

Rom. 12, 7. 8: Or ministry, let us wait on *our ministering;* or he that *teacheth,* on teaching; or he that *exhorteth,* on exhortation; he that *giveth,* let him do it with simplicity; he that *ruleth,* with diligence; he that showeth mercy, with cheerfulness.

VALIDITY OF MINISTERIAL FUNCTIONS.

§ 169. Inasmuch as all those to whom the ministerial office or certain functions thereof have been delegated or conferred are, in the performance of their official duties, servants of Christ[1] and functionaries of the invisible Church,[2] and since the means of grace administered by them have their efficacy in themselves,[3] the functions of the ministers of the Church are valid, and the means of grace administered by them are efficacious, irrespective of the faith or unbelief of the functionaries by whom the duties of the ministry are performed.[4]

1.

1 Cor. 4, 1: Let a man so account of us as of the *ministers of Christ* and *stewards* of the mysteries of *God.*

Rom. 1, 1: Paul, a *servant of Jesus Christ,* called to be an apostle, separated unto the Gospel of God.

2.

2 Cor. 4, 5: For we preach not ourselves, but Christ Jesus the Lord, and ourselves *your servants* for Jesus' sake.

1 Cor. 3, 21—23: Therefore let no man glory in men. For *all things are yours:* whether *Paul,* or *Apollos,* or *Cephas,* or the world, or life, or death, or things present, or things to come; *all are yours;* and ye are Christ's; and Christ is God's.

1 Cor. 5, 4: In the name of our Lord Jesus Christ, *when ye are gathered together,* and my spirit, with the power of our Lord Jesus Christ.

3.

Cf. §§ 133—137.

4.

2 Cor. 2, 10: To whom *ye forgive* anything, *I forgive* also; for if
I forgave anything, to whom I forgave it, for *your sakes forgave I it*
in the person of Christ.

Matt. 23, 2: Saying, The scribes and the Pharisees *sit in
Moses' seat.*

1 Cor. 5, 3—5: For I verily, as absent in body, but *present in
spirit,* have *judged* already, *as though I were present,* concerning him
that hath so done this deed, in the name of our Lord Jesus Christ,
when ye are gathered together, and my spirit, with the power of our
Lord Jesus Christ, to deliver such an one unto Satan for the destruction of the flesh, that the spirit may be saved in the day of the Lord
Jesus.

ERRING CHURCHES.

§ 170. Since an erring church, or a church contaminated
with erroneous doctrine, is still a church[1] as long as it has
and sets into operation the essentials of the Gospel,[2] the
ministers called by such church are still ministers of Christ
and of the Church of God,[3] and their official acts are valid
as far as their performance is an administration of the means
of grace.[4]

1.

Gal. 1, 2: comp. with Gal. 3, 1; 4, 10. 11; 5, 4. 9: —

Gal. 1, 2: And all the brethren which are with me, unto the
churches of Galatia.

Gal. 3, 1: O *foolish Galatians,* who hath *bewitched you,* that ye
should *not obey the truth,* before whose eyes Jesus Christ hath been
evidently set forth, crucified among you?

Gal. 4, 10. 11: *Ye observe days,* and months, and times, and
years. I am afraid of you, lest I have bestowed upon you *labor
in vain.*

Gal. 5, 4. 9: Christ is become *of no effect unto you,* whosoever of
you are justified by the Law; ye are *fallen from grace.* (9) A little
leaven leaveneth the whole lump.

2.

Cf. § 159.

3.

Rev. 3, 1—3: And unto the *angel of the church in Sardis* write:
These things saith He that hath the seven Spirits of God, and the
seven stars: I know thy works, that thou hast a name that *thou*

livest, and art dead. .Be watchful, and *strengthen* the things which
remain, that are *ready to die;* for I have not found thy works perfect before God. Remember therefore how thou hast received and
heard, and *hold fast,* and *repent.* If therefore thou shalt not watch,
I will come on thee as a thief, and thou shalt not know what hour
I will come upon thee.

Rev. 3, 14—18: And unto the *angel of the church of the Laodiceans* write: These things saith the Amen, the faithful and true Witness, the beginning of the creation of God: I know thy works, that
thou art neither cold nor hot: I would thou wert cold or hot. So,
then, because thou art lukewarm, and neither cold nor hot, I will
spue thee out of my mouth. Because thou *sayest, I am rich,* and
increased with goods, and have need of nothing, and knowest not that
thou art wretched, and miserable, and poor, and blind, and naked:
I counsel thee to buy of me gold tried in the fire, that thou mayest
be rich, and white raiment, that thou mayest be clothed, and that the
shame of thy nakedness do not appear; and anoint thine eyes with
eyesalve, that thou mayest see.

4.

Cf. § 169.

END AND AIM OF THE MINISTRY.

§ 171. The end and aim of the ministerial office and of
the performance of its functions is the upbuilding and ex-
tension of the Church of God[1] by the regeneration and conversion of sinners,[2] an inward spiritual growth of all its
members in faith and Christian graces,[3] and their preservation
unto life everlasting.[4]

1.

Eph. 4, 11. 12: And He gave some, apostles; and some, prophets;
and some, evangelists; and some, pastors and teachers, *for the perfecting of the saints,* for the *work of the ministry,* for the *edifying of
the body of Christ.*

1 Cor. 9, 19—22: For though I be free from all men, yet have I
made myself servant unto all, *that I might gain the more.* And unto
the Jews I became as a Jew, that I might *gain the Jews;* to them
that are under the Law, as under the Law, that I might *gain them that
are under the Law;* to them that are without Law, as without Law,
(being not without Law to God, but under the Law to Christ,) that
I might *gain them that are without Law.* To the weak became I as
weak, that I might *gain the weak.* I am made all things to all men,
that I might by all means *save some.*

2.

1 Cor. 4, ·15: For though ye have ten thousand instructors in Christ, yet have ye not many fathers; for in Christ Jesus I have *begotten you through the Gospel.*

Gal. 4, 19: My little children, of whom *I travail in birth again* until Christ be formed *in you.*

3.

Eph. 4, 13—16: Till we all come in the unity of the faith, and of the knowledge of the Son of God, unto a perfect man, unto the measure of the stature of the fullness of Christ, that we henceforth be no more children, tossed to and fro, and carried about with every wind of doctrine, by the sleight of men, and cunning craftiness, whereby they lie in wait to deceive, but speaking the truth in love, may grow up into Him in all things, which is the Head, even Christ, from whom the whole body fitly joined together and compacted by that which every joint supplieth, according to the effectual working in the measure of every part, maketh increase of the body unto the edifying of itself in love.

4.

1 Tim. 4, 16: Take heed unto thyself and unto the doctrine; continue in them; for in doing this thou shalt both *save thyself,* and *them that hear thee.*

1 Cor. 1, 21: For after that in the wisdom of God the world by wisdom knew not God, it pleased God *by the foolishness of preaching* to *save* them that believe.

CHURCH MILITANT AND TRIUMPHANT.

§ 172. Inasmuch as the ministers of the Church and all its members are enlisted in continual warfare against the devil,[1] the world,[2] and the flesh,[3] as against enemies ever bent upon frustrating the accomplishment of the ends and aims of the Gospel, the Church of Christ on earth is, and shall at all times remain, a church militant[4] until, with the consummation of all things, the entire Church will enter into her state of glory as the church triumphant.[5]

1.

Eph. 6, 10. 11: Finally, my brethren, *be strong* in the Lord and in the power of His might. Put on the *whole armor* of God, that ye may be able to *stand against* the wiles of the *devil.*

1 Pet. 5, 8. 9: Be sober, be vigilant; because your adversary, the *devil,* as a roaring lion, walketh about, seeking whom he may devour: whom resist steadfast in the faith, knowing that the same afflictions are accomplished in·your brethren that are in the world.

2.

1 John 5, 4: For whatsoever is born of God *overcometh the world:* and this is the victory that *overcometh the world,* even our faith.

James 4, 4: Ye adulterers and adulteresses, know ye not that the friendship of the *world* is enmity with God?

John 16, 33: These things I have spoken unto you, that in me ye might have peace. In *the world* ye shall have *tribulation;* but be of good cheer; I have *overcome the world.*

John 15, 18—21: If the *world hate you,* ye know that it hated me before it hated you. If ye were of the world, the world would love his own; but because ye are not of the world, but I have chosen you out of the world, therefore *the world hateth you.* Remember the word that I said unto you, The servant is not greater than his lord. If they have persecuted me, they *will also persecute you;* if they have kept my saying, they will keep yours also. But all these things will they do unto you for my name's sake, because they know not Him that sent me.

3.

Rom. 7, 14—16: For we know that the Law is spiritual: but *I am carnal,* sold under sin. For that which I do I allow not; for what I would, that do I not, but what I hate, that do I. If, then, I do that which I would not, I consent unto the Law that it is good.

Gal. 5, 17—20: For *the flesh* lusteth *against the Spirit,* and the *Spirit against the flesh:* and these are contrary the one to the other, so that ye cannot do the things that ye would. But if ye be led of the Spirit, ye are not under the Law. Now the works of the flesh are manifest, which are these, Adultery, fornication, uncleanness, lasciviousness, idolatry, witchcraft, hatred, variance, emulations, wrath, strife, seditions, heresies.

4.

Cf. supra 1—3.

5.

Cf. Eschatology § 185.

PREDESTINATION AND THE SALVATION OF THE ELECT.

§ 173. The entire work of leading those who shall constitute the church triumphant from a state of sin and wrath and spiritual death, through a state of faith and grace and spiritual life, to a state of glory and eternal life, is the divine execution of that eternal decree[1] whereby God, before the foundation of the world,[2] and prompted only by His grace[3] in Christ Jesus,[4] purposed to call,[5] enlighten, and sanctify,[6] keep and preserve,[7] by the means of grace,[8] according to the

counsel of His will,[9] all those[10] whom, by eternal election of
grace in Christ,[11] the Redeemer of the world,[12] He had chosen
from fallen mankind[13] and predestinated to eternal glory.[14]

1.

See § 51.

2.

2 Tim. 1, 9: According to His own purpose and grace, which was
given us in Christ Jesus *before the world began.*

Eph. 3, 11: According to the *eternal purpose* which He purposed
in Christ Jesus, our Lord.

3.

2 Tim. 1, 9: Who hath saved us . . . *not according to our works,*
but according to His own purpose and *grace, which was given us* in
Christ Jesus *before the world began.*

Rom. 9, 11: That the *purpose of God* according to election might
stand, *not of works,* but of Him that calleth.

Eph. 1, 5: Having predestinated us unto the adoption of children
by Jesus Christ to Himself, *according to the good pleasure of His will.*

Jer. 31, 3: I have loved thee with *an everlasting love;* therefore
with loving-kindness have I drawn thee.

Eph. 2, 5: By grace ye are saved.

4.

Eph. 3, 11: According to the eternal purpose which He purposed
in Christ Jesus, our Lord.

2 Tim. 1, 9: Who hath saved us . . . according to His own purpose and grace, which was given us *in Christ Jesus* before the world
began.

Eph. 1, 3. 4: Who hath blessed us with *all* spiritual blessings in
heavenly places *in Christ,* according as He hath chosen us *in Him.*

5.

Rom. 9, 11: That the *purpose* of God according to election might
stand, not of works, but of Him *that calleth.*

2 Tim. 1, 9: Who hath saved us, and *called us* with an *holy calling* . . . *according to His own purpose and grace.*

Rom. 8, 30: Whom He did predestinate, them He also *called.*

Rom. 8, 28: To them who are the *called according to His purpose.*

6.

Acts 13, 48: And as many as were ordained to everlasting life
believed.

Eph. 1, 5: Having predestinated us *unto the adoption of children
by Jesus Christ* to Himself. Cf. Gal. 3, 26: Ye are all the *children
of God by faith* in Christ Jesus.

Rom. 8, 30: Whom He did predestinate, them He also called: and whom He called, them He also *justified.* — Cf. Rom. 3, 26: . . . the Justifier of him which *believeth* in Jesus.

1 Pet. 1, 2: Elect according to the foreknowledge of God the Father, through *sanctification* of the Spirit, *unto obedience and sprinkling of the blood of Jesus Christ.*

Eph. 1, 4: According as He hath chosen us in Him before the foundation of the world, that we should be *holy and without blame* before Him.

7.

2 Thess. 2, 13: God hath from the beginning *chosen you to salvation.*

Acts 13, 48: As many as were *ordained to eternal life* believed.

Eph. 1, 11. 12: Being predestinated according to the purpose of Him who *worketh all things* after the counsel of His own will, *that we should be to the praise of His glory,* who first trusted in Christ.

2 Tim. 2, 10: Therefore I endure all things for *the elect's* sakes, that they may *also obtain the salvation* which is in Christ Jesus.

Rom. 8, 28: We know that *all things work together for good to them that love God,* to them who are the called according to His purpose.

Mark 13, 22: False Christs and false prophets shall rise, and shall show signs and wonders, to seduce, *if it were possible,* even *the elect.*

8.

2 Thess. 2, 13. 14: God hath from the beginning *chosen you to salvation* through sanctification of the Spirit and belief of *the truth, whereunto He called you by our Gospel* to the obtaining of the glory of our Lord Jesus Christ.

Tit. 1, 1: Paul, a servant of God and an *apostle* of Jesus Christ, *according to the faith of God's elect.*

Eph. 1, 9: Having *made known unto us the mystery of His will,* according to His good pleasure which He hath *purposed in Himself.*

9.

Eph. 1, 11: In whom also we have obtained an inheritance, being *predestinated* according to *the purpose* of Him who *worketh all things after the counsel of His own will.*

10.

Matt. 20, 16: *Many* be called, but *few* chosen. Cf. 22, 14.

John 13, 18: I know whom I have chosen.

1 Pet. 1, 2: Elect according to the *foreknowledge* of God.

Rom. 8, 29: For whom He *did foreknow* He also did predestinate to be conformed to the image of His Son.

Acts 13, 48: *As many* as were ordained to eternal life believed.

11.

Rom. 11, 5: Even so, then, at this present time also there is a remnant according to *the election of grace.*

Rom. 9, 11: That the purpose of God according to election might stand, *not of works.*

Eph. 1, 4: According as He hath chosen us *in Him* before the foundation of the world.

12.

Cf. §§ 50 and 123.

13.

John 15, 19: Ye are not of the world, but I have *chosen you out of the world.*

Eph. 1, 4: According as He hath *chosen* us in Him before the foundation of the world, *that we should be* holy and without blame before Him.

Rom. 9, 23. 24: That He might make known the riches of His glory on the *vessels of mercy,* which *He had afore prepared unto glory,* even us, whom He hath called, not *of the Jews* only, but also *of the Gentiles.*

Rom. 11, 7: The *election* hath obtained it, and the *rest* were blinded.

14.

Rom. 8, 29. 30: Whom He did foreknow He also did *predestinate* to be *conformed to the image of His Son,* that He might be the First-born among many brethren. Moreover, whom He did *predestinate,* them He also called: and whom He called, them He also justified: and whom He justified, them He also *glorified.* — Cf. 2 Tim. 2, 10: *"with eternal glory."*

ESCHATOLOGY.

DEFINITION.

§ 174. Eschatology is the doctrine of Holy Scripture concerning the end of temporal life, the second advent of Christ, the resurrection of the dead, final judgment, the consummation of all things, the everlasting damnation of the wicked, and the eternal bliss of the just in the world to come.

TEMPORAL DEATH.

§ 175. Temporal death is the termination of man's temporal life by the separation[1] of his immortal soul[2] from his mortal body.[3]

15

1.

Luke 12, 20: But God said unto him, Thou fool, this night thy *soul shall be required of thee.*

2 Tim. 4, 6: I am now ready to be offered, and the time of my *departure* is at hand.

Phil. 1, 23: I am in a strait betwixt two, having a desire to *depart* and to be with Christ, which is far better.

2 Cor. 5, 1. 4. 8: We know that if our earthly house of this tabernacle were *dissolved,* we have a building of God, an house not made with hands, eternal in the heavens. (4) For we that are in this tabernacle do groan, being burdened: not for that we would be *unclothed,* but clothed upon, that mortality might be swallowed up of life. (8) We are confident, I say, and willing rather to be absent *from the body,* and to be present with the Lord.

2.

Matt. 10, 28: Fear not them which kill the body, but are *not able to kill the soul.*

Matt. 22, 32: I am the God of Abraham, and the God of Isaac, and the God of Jacob. God is not the God of the dead, but of *the living.*

3.

Rom. 8, 11: He that raised up Christ from the dead shall also quicken your *mortal bodies.*

1 Cor. 15, 35: But some man will say, How are the *dead raised up?*

1 Cor. 15, 44: It is sown a natural body; it is raised a spiritual body.

Matt. 10, 28: And fear not them which *kill the body,* but are not able to kill the soul; but rather fear Him which is able to destroy both soul and body in hell.

DEATH OF THE WICKED.

§ 176. The temporal death of the wicked is a consequence[1] and punishment[2] of sin, and the transition of the soul spiritually dead into eternal death.[3]

1.

Rom. 5, 12: By one man sin entered into the world, and death by sin; and so death passed upon all men, for that all have sinned.

Rom. 5, 17: By one man's offense death reigned by one.

Rom. 5, 21: Sin hath reigned unto death.

2.

Rom. 6, 23: The *wages* of sin is death; but the gift of God is eternal life.

Ezek. 18, 20. 26: The soul that *sinneth,* it shall *die.* The son shall not bear the iniquity of the father, neither shall the father bear the iniquity of the son. (26) *For his iniquity* that he hath done *shall he die.*

Ezek. 33, 18: When the righteous turneth from his righteousness, and committeth iniquity, he shall even *die thereby.*

3.

1 Pet. 3, 19. 20: By which also He went and preached unto the *spirits in prison,* which sometime were disobedient, when once the longsuffering of God waited in the days of Noah.

Luke 16, 23: And *in hell* he lifted up his eyes, being *in torments,* and seeth Abraham *afar off,* and Lazarus in his bosom.

Prov. 11, 7: When a *wicked* man *dieth,* his *expectation shall perish:* and the *hope of unjust men perisheth.*

Eccl. 11, 3: If the tree fall toward the south, or toward the north, in the place where the tree falleth, *there it shall be.*

DEATH OF BELIEVERS.

§ 177. Though the temporal death of believers is also a consequence of sin,[1] it is no longer a punishment of sin,[2] but rather the cessation from sinning,[3] and a transition from a spiritual life of faith and hope[4] into an eternal life of perfect bliss with God.[5]

1.

Rom. 5, 12. 15: Wherefore, as by one man sin entered into the world, and *death by sin;* and so death passed upon *all men,* for that all have sinned. (15) But not as the offense, so also is the free gift. For if *through the offense* of one *many be dead,* much more the *grace of God,* and the gift by grace, which is by one man, Jesus Christ, hath *abounded unto many.*

2 Cor. 5, 4: For we that are in this tabernacle do *groan,* being *burdened; not* for that we would be *unclothed, but clothed upon,* that mortality might be swallowed up of life.

Rom. 8, 10: And if Christ be in you, the *body is dead because of sin;* but the Spirit is life because of righteousness.

2.

Is. 53, 5: But He was *wounded* for *our transgressions,* He was *bruised for our iniquities:* the *chastisement* of our peace was *upon Him;* and with His stripes we are healed.

1 Pet. 2, 24: Who *His own self bare our sins* in His own body on the tree, that we, being dead to sins, should *live unto righteousness;* by whose stripes ye were healed.

Phil. 1, 21. 23: For to me to live is Christ, and *to die is gain.* (23) For I am in a strait betwixt two, having a *desire to depart,* and to be with Christ, which is *far better.*

2 Cor. 5, 4: For we that are in this tabernacle do groan, being burdened; not for that we would be unclothed, but clothed upon, that mortality might be swallowed up of life.

Luke 2, 29: Lord, now lettest Thou Thy servant *depart in peace,* according to Thy word.

3.

Rom. 7, 23. 24: But I see another law in my members, warring against the law of my mind, and bringing me into captivity to the law of sin which is in my members. O wretched man that I am! who shall *deliver me from the body of this death?*

4.

Rom. 8, 24. 25: For we are *saved by hope.* But hope that is seen is not hope; for what a man seeth, why doth he yet hope for? But if we hope for that we see not, then do we with patience *wait for it.*

2 Cor. 5, 7: For we walk by *faith, not by sight.*

5.

Rev. 14, 13: And I heard a voice from heaven saying unto me, Write, *Blessed are the dead which die in the Lord from henceforth.* Yea, saith the Spirit, that they may *rest* from their labors; and their works do follow them.

Luke 23, 43: And Jesus said unto him, Verily, I say unto thee, To-day shalt thou be *with me in paradise.*

2 Cor. 5, 2. 8: For in this we groan, earnestly desiring to be clothed upon with our house which is from heaven. (8) We are confident, I say, and willing rather to be absent from the body, and to be *present with the Lord.*

Phil. 1, 23: For I am in a strait betwixt two, having a *desire to depart,* and to *be with Christ,* which is far better.

Acts 7, 59: And they stoned Stephen, calling upon God, and saying, *Lord Jesus, receive my spirit!*

Eccl. 12, 7: Then shall the dust return to the earth as it was: and the *spirit shall return unto God* who gave it.

THE LAST GENERATION.

§ 178. Temporal death is not the future lot of all mankind, inasmuch as a generation of men will live[1] to witness the second coming of Christ.[2]

1.

1 Thess. 4, 15. 17: For this we say unto you by the word of the Lord that we which are alive *and remain unto the coming of the Lord* shall not prevent them which are asleep. (17) Then we which are *alive and remain* shall be caught up together with them in the clouds to meet the Lord in the air; and so shall we ever be with the Lord.

1 Cor. 15, 51: Behold, I show you a mystery: *We shall not all sleep,* but we shall all be changed.

Matt. 24, 30: And then shall appear the sign of the Son of Man in heaven: and then shall all the tribes of the earth mourn, and *they shall see the Son of Man coming* in the clouds of heaven with power and great glory.

2.

Hebr. 9, 28: So Christ was once offered to bear the sins of many; and unto them that look for Him shall He *appear the second time* without sin unto salvation.

Acts 1, 11: Which also said, Ye men of Galilee, why stand ye gazing up into heaven? This same Jesus which is taken up from you into heaven *shall so come* in like manner as ye have seen Him go into heaven.

SIGNS OF THE LAST TIMES.

§ 179. The predicted[1] second visible[2] advent of Christ may be expected at any time,[3] since all the signs which are to remind us of His coming[4] have been fulfilled or are still in process of fulfillment,[5] Antichrist is come and has been revealed in the Roman pontiff,[6] and the last times are doubtless upon the world.[7]

1.

Matt. 26, 64: *Hereafter* shall ye see the *Son of Man* sitting on the right hand of power, and *coming* in the clouds of heaven.

Acts 1, 11: Which also said, Ye men of Galilee, why stand ye gazing up into heaven? *This same Jesus* which is taken up from you into heaven *shall so come* in like manner as ye have seen Him go into heaven.

Matt. 25, 31: When the *Son of Man shall come* in His glory, and all the holy angels with Him, then shall He sit upon the throne of His glory.

Matt. 24, 30: Then *shall appear the sign of the Son of Man* in heaven: and then shall all the tribes of the earth mourn, and they shall see *the Son of Man coming* in the clouds of heaven with power and great glory.

Mark 13, 26: And then shall they see *the Son of Man coming* in the clouds with great power and glory.

1 Thess. 4, 16: For *the Lord* Himself *shall descend* from heaven with a shout, etc.

1 Cor. 1, 7: So that ye come behind in no gift, *waiting for the coming of our Lord Jesus Christ.*

Tit. 2, 13: Looking for that blessed hope, and the glorious *appearing of the great God* and our Savior *Jesus Christ.*

2.

Rev. 1, 7: Behold, *He cometh* with clouds; and every eye *shall see Him,* and they also which pierced Him.

John 19, 37: And again another scripture saith, *They shall look on Him* whom they pierced.

Luke 21, 27: And then *shall they see* the Son of Man coming in a cloud with power and great glory.

Matt. 26, 64: Jesus saith unto him, Thou hast said: nevertheless, I say unto you, Hereafter *shall ye see* the Son of Man sitting on the right hand of power, and *coming* in the clouds of heaven.

Acts 1, 11: Which also said, Ye men of Galilee, why stand ye gazing up into heaven? This same Jesus which is taken up from you into heaven shall so *come in like manner as ye have seen Him* go into heaven.

3.

Mark 13, 32: But of that day and *that hour* knoweth no man, no, not the angels which are in heaven, neither the Son, but the Father.

Matt. 24, 36. 42: But of that *day and hour* knoweth no man, no, not the angels of heaven, but my Father only. (42) *Watch therefore;* for ye know not what *hour* your Lord doth come.

Luke 12, 40: *Be ye therefore ready also;* for the Son of Man cometh at an hour when ye think not.

Luke 21, 36: *Watch ye therefore,* and pray *always,* that ye may be accounted worthy to escape all these things that shall come to pass, and to stand before the Son of Man.

1 Cor. 1, 7: So that ye come behind in no gift, *waiting* for the coming of our Lord Jesus Christ.

Tit. 2, 13: *Looking for* that blessed hope, and the glorious appearing of the great God and our Savior Jesus Christ.

2 Pet. 3, 12: *Looking for* and hastening unto the coming of the day of God, wherein the heavens, being on fire, shall be dissolved, and the elements shall melt with fervent heat.

Phil. 3, 20: For our conversation is in heaven, from whence also *we look for* the Savior, the Lord Jesus Christ.

4.

Matt. 24, 3. 33: Tell us, when shall these things be? and what shall be the *sign of Thy coming* and of the end of the world? (33) So likewise ye, when ye shall *see all these things, know that it is near, even at the doors.*

Mark 13, 29: So ye in like manner, when ye shall see these things come to pass, know that it is nigh, even at the doors.

Luke 21, 25: And there shall be *signs in the sun,* and in the *moon,* and in the *stars;* and *upon the earth* distress of nations, with perplexity, the *sea* and the waves roaring.

5.

Luke 21, 26: Men's hearts failing them for fear, and for looking after those things which are coming on the earth.

Mark 13, 22: For *false Christs* and *false prophets* shall rise, and shall show signs and wonders, to seduce, if it were possible, even the elect.

Matt. 24, 24: For there shall arise *false Christs,* and *false prophets,* and shall show great signs and wonders, inasmuch that, if it were possible, they shall deceive the very elect.

Matt. 24, 37—39: But as *the days of Noe* were, so shall also *the coming of the Son of Man be.* For as in the days that were before the flood they were eating and drinking, marrying and giving in marriage, until the day that Noe entered into the ark, and knew not until the flood came, and took them all away, *so* shall also *the coming of the Son of Man be.*

1 Tim. 4, 1: Now the Spirit speaketh expressly that in the latter times some shall *depart from the faith,* giving heed to *seducing spirits* and doctrines of devils.

Luke 21, 24. 25: And they shall fall by the edge of the sword, and shall be led away captive into all nations: and *Jerusalem* shall be *trodden down of the Gentiles,* until the times of the Gentiles be fulfilled. And there shall be *signs* in the sun, and in the moon, and in the stars; and upon the earth distress of nations, with perplexity, the sea and the waves roaring.

Matt. 24, 14. 34: And this *Gospel* of the kingdom shall be *preached in all the world* for a witness unto all nations; and then shall the end come. (34) Verily, I say unto you, *This generation shall not pass,* till all these things be fulfilled.

6.

1 John 2, 18: Little children, it is the last time: and as ye have heard that *Antichrist* shall come, even now are there many antichrists: *whereby we know that it is the last time.* — Cf. 4, 3.

2 Thess. 2, 3. 4. 8—11: *That day* shall not come, except there come a falling away first, and that *man of sin* be revealed, the *son of perdition,* who *opposeth and exalteth himself* above all that is called *God,* or that *is worshiped,* so that he *as God sitteth in the temple of God,* showing himself that he is God. (8—11) And then shall that Wicked be revealed, whom the Lord shall consume with the spirit of His mouth, and shall destroy *with the brightness of His coming:* even him, whose coming is after the *working of Satan* with all *power* and *signs* and *lying wonders,* and with all *deceivableness of unrighteousness* in them that perish, because they received not the love of the truth, that they might be saved. And for this cause God shall send them *strong delusion,* that they should believe a lie.

Cf. Dan. 11, 36—45. Rev. 17. 18.

7.

1 John 2, 18: Little children, it is *the last time:* and as ye have heard that *Antichrist* shall come, even now are there many antichrists: whereby we know that it is *the last time.*

Luke 18, 8: I tell you that He will .avenge them speedily. Nevertheless, when the Son of Man cometh, shall He find faith on the earth?

1 Cor. 10, 11: Now all these things happened unto them for en-samples: and they are written for our admonition, upon whom *the ends of the world are come.*

1 Pet. 4, 7: But *the end of all things is at hand.* Be ye therefore sober, and watch unto prayer!

PURPOSE OF THE SECOND ADVENT.

§ 180. The purpose of the second coming of Christ is not the establishment of a millennial kingdom on earth,[1] but the resurrection of all the dead,[2] the final judgment,[3] and the consummation of all things.[4]

1.

1 Cor. 15, 50: Now this I say, brethren, that *flesh and blood* cannot inherit the kingdom of God; neither doth corruption inherit incorruption. Cf. Matt. 25, 34.

John 16, 33: These things I have spoken unto you, that in me ye might have peace. *In the world ye shall have tribulation:* but be of good cheer; I have overcome the world.

1 Thess. 4, 16. 17: For *the Lord Himself shall descend from heaven* with a shout, with the voice of the archangel, and with the trump of God: and *the dead in Christ shall rise* first. Then we which are alive and remain shall be caught up together with them in the clouds *to meet the Lord in the air:* and so shall we ever be with the Lord.

Hebr. 9, 28: So Christ was once offered to bear the sins of many; and unto them that look for Him shall He *appear the second time* without sin *unto salvation.*

2 Tim. 4, 8: *Henceforth* there is laid up for me a crown of righteousness, which the Lord, the righteous Judge, shall give me *at that day,* and not to me only, but unto *all them also that love His appearing.*

Phil. 3, 20: For our conversation is in heaven, from whence also we look for the Savior, the Lord Jesus Christ.

2.

Cf. § 181.

3.

Cf. § 182.

4.

Cf. § 183.

RESURRECTION OF ALL THE DEAD.

§ 181. The first[1] act of Christ on. His second advent[2] and of the Holy Trinity,[3] at the last day,[4] will be the quickening or resuscitation of all the dead,[5] whose souls will then be reunited with the same[6] bodies from which they were separated in temporal death,[7] but which will be adapted to a future state,[8] those of the wicked to a state of everlasting shame and torment,[9] those of the righteous to an everlasting state of celestial glory.[10]

1.

1 Thess. 4, 16: For the Lord Himself shall descend from heaven with a shout, with the voice of the archangel, and with the trump of God: and *the dead in Christ shall rise first.*

1 Cor. 15, 52: In a moment, in the twinkling of an eye, at the last trump; for the trumpet shall sound, and the dead shall be raised incorruptible, and we shall be changed.

2.

1 Thess. 4, 16: For *the Lord Himself* shall *descend* from heaven with a shout, with the voice of the archangel, and with the trump of God: and the dead in Christ shall rise first.

Matt. 25, 31. 32: When *the Son of Man shall come* in His glory, and all the holy angels with Him, then shall He sit upon the throne of His glory: and before Him shall be gathered all nations.

3.

John 5, 21: For as *the Father raiseth up the dead* and quickeneth them, even so the Son quickeneth whom He will.

John 6, 40. 54: And this is *the will of Him that sent me,* that every one which seeth the Son, and believeth on Him, may have everlasting life: and *I will raise him up* at the last day. (54) Whoso eateth my flesh, and drinketh my blood, hath eternal life; and I will raise him up at the last day.

Rom. 8, 11: But if *the Spirit of Him* that raised up Jesus from the dead dwell in you, *He that raised up Christ* from the dead *shall also quicken your mortal bodies by His Spirit* that dwelleth in you.

4.

John 6, 40. 54: And this is the will of Him that sent me, that every one which seeth the Son, and believeth on Him, may have everlasting life: and *I will raise him up at the last day.* (54) Whoso eateth my flesh, and drinketh my blood, hath eternal life; and *I will raise him up at the last day.*

5.

John 5, 21: For as the Father raiseth up the dead and *quickeneth* them, even so the Son *quickeneth* whom He will.

John 5, 28. 29: Marvel not at this; for the hour is coming in the which all that are in the graves shall hear His voice, and shall come forth: they that have done good, unto the *resurrection of life;* and they that have done evil, unto the *resurrection of damnation.*

Matt. 25, 32: And before Him shall be gathered *all nations:* and He shall separate them one from another, as a shepherd divideth his sheep from the goats.

2 Cor. 5, 10: For we must *all* appear before the judgment seat of Christ, that *every one* may receive the things done in his body, according to that he hath done, whether it be good or bad.

Acts 24, 15: And have hope toward God, which they themselves also allow, that there shall be a resurrection of the dead, *both of the just and unjust.*

6.

Rom. 8, 11: But if the Spirit of Him that raised up Jesus from the dead dwell in you, He that raised up Christ from the dead shall also *quicken your mortal bodies* by His Spirit that dwelleth in you.

Phil. 3, 21: Who shall change *our vile body,* that it may be fashioned like unto His glorious body, according to the working whereby He is able even to subdue all things unto Himself.

2 Cor. 5, 10: For we must all appear before the judgment seat of Christ, that every one may receive the things done *in his body,* according to that he hath done, whether it be good or bad.

Job 19, 26: Yet *in my flesh* shall I see God.

1 Cor. 15, 44. 53: It is sown *a natural body;* it is *raised a spiritual body.* There is a natural body, and there is a spiritual body. (53) For *this corruptible* must *put on incorruption,* and *this mortal* must *put on immortality.*

John 5, 28: Marvel not at this; for the hour is coming in the which all *that are in the graves* shall hear His voice.

Rev. 20, 12: And I saw *the dead,* small and great, stand before God; and the books were opened: and another book was opened, which is the book of life: and *the dead* were judged out of those things which were written in the books, according to their works.

7.

Cf. § 175.

8.

John 5, 29: And shall come forth: they that have done good, *unto the resurrection of life;* and they that have done evil, *unto the resurrection of damnation.*

1 Cor. 15, 50: Flesh and blood cannot inherit the kingdom of God; neither doth corruption inherit incorruption.

9.

Dan. 12, 2: And many of them that sleep in the dust of the earth shall awake, some to everlasting life, and *some to shame and everlasting contempt.*

Matt. 25, 41. 46: Then shall He say also unto them on the left hand, Depart from me, ye cursed, *into everlasting fire,* prepared for the devil and his angels! (46) And these shall go away *into everlasting punishment,* but the righteous into life eternal.

John 5, 29: And shall come forth: they that have done good, unto the resurrection of life; and they that have done evil, unto the *resurrection of damnation.*

10.

Dan. 12, 1. 2: And at that time shall Michael stand up, the great prince which standeth for the children of thy people: and there shall be a time 'of trouble, such as never was since there was a nation even to that same time: and at that time *thy people shall be delivered,* every one that shall be found written in the book. And many of them that sleep in the dust of the earth shall awake, some *to everlasting life,* and some to shame and everlasting contempt.

John 5, 29: And shall come forth: they that have done good, unto the *resurrection of life;* and they that have done evil, unto the resurrection of damnation.

1 Cor. 15, 52: In a moment, in the twinkling of an eye, at the last trump; for the trumpet shall sound, and the dead shall be *raised incorruptible,* and we shall be changed.

1 Cor. 15, 42—44. 49. 50. 53: So also is the resurrection of the dead. It is sown in corruption; it is *raised in incorruption.* It is sown in dishonor; it is *raised in glory:* it is sown in weakness; it is *raised in power:* it is sown a natural body; it is *raised a spiritual body.* There is a natural body, and there is a spiritual body. (49. 50) And as we have borne the image of the earthy, we shall also *bear the image of the heavenly.* Now this I say, brethren, that flesh and blood cannot inherit the kingdom of God; neither doth corruption inherit incorruption. (53) For this corruptible must *put on incorruption,* and this mortal must *put on immortality.*

Phil. 3, 21: Who shall change our vile body, that it may be fashioned *like unto His glorious body,* according to the working whereby He is able even to subdue all things unto Himself.

Matt. 13, 43: Then shall the righteous *shine forth as the sun* in the kingdom of their Father. Who hath ears to hear, let him hear!

Rev. 7, 16: They shall *hunger no more, neither thirst any more;* neither shall the sun light on them, nor any heat.

FINAL JUDGMENT.

§ 182. After the resurrection of all the dead,[1] and the change of those who shall have lived to see the second advent of Christ,[2] all nations shall be gathered before Him,[3] and He will separate the righteous from the wicked,[4] and will, in public judgment,[5] by the testimony of their works,[6] the good works[7] of the righteous in evidence of their faith,[8] and the evil works of the wicked[9] in evidence of their unbelief, reveal to angels and men[10] the righteousness of His judgment[11] and of the final sentence pronounced by God through Jesus Christ,[12] which will be just damnation to everlasting punishment for the wicked[13] and gracious assignment to life everlasting for the righteous.[14]

1.

Cf. § 181.

2.

1 Cor. 15, 51. 52: Behold, I show you a mystery: We shall not all sleep, but *we shall all be changed,* in a moment, in the twinkling of an eye, at the last trump; for the trumpet shall sound, and the dead shall be raised incorruptible, and *we shall be changed.*

1 Thess. 4, 15. 17: We which are alive and *remain unto the coming of the Lord* shall not prevent them which are asleep. (17) Then we which are *alive and remain* shall be caught up together with them in the clouds.

3.

Matt. 25, 32: And before Him shall be gathered all nations.

Rom. 14, 10: For we shall all stand before the judgment seat of Christ.

John 5, 22: For the Father judgeth no man, but hath committed *all judgment* unto the Son.

Acts 17, 31: Because He hath appointed a day in the which He will judge *the world* in righteousness by that Man whom He hath ordained.

Rev. 1, 7: Behold, He cometh with clouds; and *every eye shall see Him,* and they also which pierced Him.

4.

Matt. 25, 32: And before Him shall be gathered all nations: and He shall *separate them* one from another, as a shepherd divideth his sheep from the goats.

Mark 16, 16: He that *believeth* and is baptized *shall be saved;* but he that *believeth not* shall be *damned.*

5.

2 Cor. 5, 10: For we must all *appear* before the judgment seat of Christ.

1 Cor. 4, 5: Therefore judge nothing before the time, until the Lord come, who both will *bring to light* the hidden things of darkness, and will *make manifest* the counsels of the hearts.

Rom. 2, 5. 16: But after thy hardness and impenitent heart treasurest up unto thyself wrath against the *day* of wrath and *revelation of the righteous judgment of God.* (16) In the day when God shall *judge* the secrets of men by Jesus Christ, according to my Gospel.

6.

Rom. 2, 6: Who will render to every man *according to his deeds.*

2 Cor. 5, 10: For we must all appear before the judgment seat of Christ, that every one may receive the things done in his body, *according to that he hath done,* whether it be *good or bad.*

Matt. 25, 35. 36. 42. 43: For I was an hungred, and ye gave me meat: I was thirsty, and ye gave me drink: I was a stranger, and ye took me in: naked, and ye clothed me: I was sick, and ye visited me: I was in prison, and ye came unto me. (42. 43) For I was an hungred, and ye gave me no meat: I was thirsty, and ye gave me no drink: I was a stranger, and ye took me not in: naked, and ye clothed me not: sick, and in prison, and ye visited me not.

7.

Is. 43, 25: I, even I, am He that *blotteth out thy transgressions* for mine own sake, and will *not remember thy sins.*

Ezek. 18, 22: All *his transgressions* that he hath committed, *they shall not be mentioned* unto him.

1 John 2, 28: And now, little children, abide in Him, that, when He shall appear, we may have confidence, and *not be ashamed* before Him *at His coming.*

Matt. 25, 35: See sub **6.**

8.

Matt. 25, 34. 35: Come, ye *blessed* of my Father, *inherit* the kingdom *prepared for you* from the foundation of the world. (35, above sub **6.**)

John 3, 16. 18: For God so loved the world that He gave His only-begotten Son, that whosoever *believeth* in Him should not perish, but have everlasting life. (18) He that *believeth* on Him *is not condemned.*

John 3, 36: He that *believeth* on the Son *hath* everlasting life.

Rev. 14, 13: Blessed are the dead which die *in the Lord* from henceforth. Yea, saith the Spirit, that they may rest from their labors; and their works do follow them.

Gal. 5, 6: For in Jesus Christ neither circumcision availeth anything nor uncircumcision, but *faith which worketh by love.*

John 13, 35: By this shall all men *know* that ye are *my disciples,* if ye have *love* one to another.

9.

Matt. 25, 42: For I was an hungred, and ye gave me no meat.

Matt. 7, 17. 18: Even so every good tree bringeth forth good fruit; but a *corrupt tree* bringeth forth *evil fruit.* A *good* tree *cannot* bring forth *evil fruit,* neither can a *corrupt* tree bring forth *good fruit.*

John 3, 18. 36: But he that *believeth not* is *condemned* already, *because he hath not believed* in the name of the only-begotten Son of God. (36) And he that *believeth not* the Son *shall not see life,* but the wrath of God abideth on him.

10.

Luke 9, 26: For whosoever shall be ashamed of me and of my words, of him shall the Son of Man be ashamed when He shall come in His own glory, and in His Father's, and of the holy angels.

Matt. 25, 31. 32: When the Son of Man shall come in His glory, and *all the holy angels* with Him, then shall He sit upon the throne of His glory. And before Him shall be gathered *all nations.*

11.

Rom. 2, 5: But after thy hardness and impenitent heart treasurest up unto thyself wrath against the day of wrath and *revelation* of the *righteous judgment of God.*

Acts 17, 31: Because He hath appointed a day in the which He will judge the world *in righteousness* by that Man whom He hath ordained.

12.

Acts 17, 31: He will judge the world in righteousness *by that Man whom He hath ordained.*

Rom. 2, 16: In the day when God shall judge the secrets of men *by Jesus Christ,* according to my Gospel.

13.

Matt. 25, 41. 46: Then shall He say also unto them on the left hand, *Depart from me,* ye cursed, *into everlasting fire,* prepared for the devil and his angels! (46) And these shall go away into *everlasting punishment,* but the righteous into life eternal.

14.

Matt. 25, 34. 46: Then shall the King say unto them on His right hand, *Come,* ye blessed of my Father, *inherit the kingdom* prepared for you from the foundation of the world! (46) And these shall go away into everlasting punishment, but the righteous into *life eternal.*

END OF THE WORLD.

§ 183. The day of the resurrection of all the dead[1] will also be the last day,[2] the day of the end of the world,[3] when earth and heaven shall come to ruin[4] and pass away,[5] consumed in fire,[6] and God will create a new heaven and a new earth.[7]

1.

Cf. § 181.

2.

John 6, 40. 44: And this is the will of Him that sent me, that every one which seeth the Son, and believeth on Him, may have everlasting life: and I will raise him up at *the last day.* (44) No man can come to me, except the Father which hath sent me draw him: and I will raise him up at *the last day.*

John 11, 24: Martha saith unto Him, I know that he shall rise again in the resurrection at *the last day.*

3.

Matt. 24, 3. 14: Tell us, when shall these things be? and what shall be the sign of Thy coming, and of the *end of the world?* (14) And this Gospel of the kingdom shall be preached in all the world for a witness unto all nations; and then shall *the end* come.

Matt. 13, 39: The enemy that sowed them is the devil; the harvest is the *end of the world.*

1 Cor. 15, 24: Then cometh *the end,* when He shall have delivered up the kingdom to God, even the Father, when He shall have put down all rule and all authority and power.

4.

Matt. 24, 29: Immediately after the tribulation of those days shall the *sun be darkened,* and the *moon shall not give her light,* and the *stars shall fall from heaven,* and the *powers of the heavens shall be shaken.* Cf. Mark 13, 24—26.

5.

2 Pet. 3, 10: But the day of the Lord will come as a thief in the night, in the which *the heavens shall pass away with a great noise,* and the *elements* shall melt with fervent heat, the earth also and the works that are therein shall be burned up.

Luke 21, 33: Heaven and earth shall *pass away;* but my words shall not pass away. Cf. Matt. 24, 35.

Matt. 5, 18: For, verily, I say unto you, Till *heaven and earth pass,* one jot or one tittle shall in no wise pass from the Law, till all be fulfilled.

Ps. 102, 26. 27: They shall *perish,* but Thou shalt endure: yea, all of them shall wax old like a garment; as a vesture shalt Thou change them, and they shall be changed. But Thou art the same, and Thy years shall have no end.

Hebr. 1, 11: *They shall perish;* but Thou remainest; and they all shall wax old as doth a garment.

Rev. 20, 11: And I saw a great white throne, and Him that sat on it, from whose face the earth and the heaven fled away; and there was found *no place* for them.

Rev. 21, 1: And I saw a new heaven and a new earth; for the first heaven and the first earth *were passed away;* and there *was no more sea.*

6.

2 Pet. 3, 7. 10. 12: But the heavens and the earth, which are now, by the same word are kept in store, reserved *unto fire* against the day of judgment and perdition of ungodly men. (10) But the day of the Lord will come as a thief in the night, in the which the

heavens shall pass away with a great noise, and the *elements shall melt with fervent heat;* the earth also and the works that are therein shall be *burned up.* (12) Looking for and hasting unto the coming of the day of God, wherein the *heavens, being on fire,* shall be *dissolved,* and the elements shall melt with fervent heat.

7.

Is. 65, 17: For, behold, *I create new heavens and a new earth:* and the former shall not be remembered, nor come into mind.

Is. 66, 22: For as the *new heavens* and the *new earth,* which I *will make,* shall remain before me, saith the Lord, so shall your seed and your name remain.

2 Pet. 3, 13: Nevertheless, we, according to His promise, look for *new heavens* and a *new earth,* wherein dwelleth righteousness.

Rev. 21, 1: And I saw *a new heaven* and *a new earth;* for the first heaven and the first earth were passed away; and there was no more sea.

ETERNAL DAMNATION.

§ 184. The punishment of the damned, after the consummation, will be everlasting shame[1] and torment[2] of body and soul[3] with the devil and his angels[4] in the fire of hell;[5] but while the punishment of all will be endless[6] and severe,[7] the degrees of torment will differ with different degrees of guilt in different individuals.[8]

1.

Dan. 12, 2: And many of them that sleep in the dust of the earth shall awake: some to everlasting life, and some to *shame and everlasting contempt.*

2.

Luke 16, 23—25: And *in hell* he lifted up his eyes, being *in torments,* and seeth Abraham afar off, and Lazarus in his bosom. And he cried and said, Father Abraham, have mercy on me, and send Lazarus, that he may dip the tip of his finger in water, and cool my tongue; for *I am tormented in this flame.* But Abraham said, Son, remember that thou in thy lifetime receivedst thy good things, and likewise Lazarus evil things; but now he is comforted, and *thou art tormented.*

Matt. 8, 12: But the children of the kingdom shall be cast out into *outer darkness:* there shall be *weeping* and *gnashing of teeth.*

Rev. 20, 10: And the devil that deceived them was cast into the lake of *fire and brimstone,* where the beast and the false prophet are, and shall be *tormented day and night for ever and ever.*

Is. 66, 24: And they shall go forth, and look upon the carcasses of the men that have transgressed against me; for *their worm shall not die, neither* shall *their fire be quenched;* and they shall be *an abhorring* unto all flesh.

Rev. 14, 10. 11: The same shall drink of *the wine of the wrath of God,* which is poured out *without mixture* into the cup of His indignation; and he shall be *tormented* with fire and brimstone in the presence of the holy angels, and in the presence of the Lamb: and the *smoke of their torment* ascendeth up *for ever and ever:* and they have *no rest* day nor night, who worship the beast and his image, and whosoever receiveth the mark of his name.

3.

Matt. 10, 28: And fear not them which kill the body, but are not able to kill the soul; but rather fear Him which is able to *destroy both soul and body in hell.*

4.

Matt. 25, 41: Then shall He say also unto them on the left hand, Depart from me, ye cursed, into everlasting fire, prepared for *the devil and his angels!*

5.

Matt. 25, 41: See above sub 4.
Luke 16, 23. 24: See above sub 2.

6.

Matt. 25, 41. 46: Then shall He say also unto them on the left hand, Depart from me, ye cursed, into *everlasting fire,* prepared for the devil and his angels! (46) And these shall go away into *everlasting* punishment, but the righteous into life eternal.

2 Thess. 1, 9: Who shall be punished with *everlasting* destruction from the presence of the Lord, and from the glory of His power.

Dan. 12, 2: And many of them that sleep in the dust of the earth shall awake: some to everlasting life, and some to shame and *everlasting* contempt.

Mark 9, 43. 45. 48: And if thy hand offend thee, cut it off: it is better for thee to enter into life maimed, than having two hands to go into hell, into the fire that *never shall be quenched.* (45) And if thy foot offend thee, cut it off: it is better for thee to enter halt into life, than having two feet to be cast into hell, into the fire that *never shall be quenched.* (48) Where their *worm dieth not,* and the *fire is not quenched.*

Matt. 26, 24: It had been good for that man if he had not been born.

7.

James 2, 13: For he shall have judgment *without mercy* that hath showed no mercy; and mercy rejoiceth against judgment.

Rev. 14, 10. 11: The same shall drink of the wine of the *wrath* of God, which is poured out *without mixture* into the cup of His indignation; and he shall be tormented with *fire and brimstone* in the presence of the holy angels, and in the presence of the Lamb: and the smoke of their torment ascendeth up for ever and ever: and they have *no rest* day nor night.

16

8.

Matt. 10, 15: Verily, I say unto you, It shall be *more tolerable for the land of Sodom and Gomorrha* in the day of judgment *than for that city.*

Matt. 11, 22. 23: But I say unto you, It shall be *more tolerable for Tyre and Sidon* at the day of judgment *than for you.* And thou, *Capernaum,* which art exalted unto heaven, shalt be brought down to hell; for if the mighty works which have been done in thee had been done in Sodom, it would have remained until this day.

Luke 10, 12: But I say unto you, that it shall be more tolerable in that day for Sodom than for that city.

Matt. 23, 13: *Woe* unto you, *scribes and Pharisees,* hypocrites! for ye shut up the kingdom of heaven against men; for ye neither go in yourselves, neither suffer ye them that are entering to go in.

Luke 12, 47. 48: And that servant, which knew his lord's will, and prepared not himself, neither did according to his will, shall be beaten with *many stripes.* But he that knew not, and did commit things worthy of stripes, shall be beaten with *few stripes.* For unto whomsoever *much* is given, of him shall be *much* required: and to whom men have committed much, of him they will ask the more.

ETERNAL LIFE.

§ 185. The state of the elect, after the consummation, will be a state of eternal life[1] with God[2] and His angels[3] in glory[4] and bliss[5] of body and soul[6] unmarred by sin,[7] pain,[8] death,[9] or the possibility of apostasy;[10] and while the bliss of all the heirs of salvation[11] will be perfect[12] and their glory great,[13] there will be degrees of glory,[14] as God will graciously reward[15] in the kingdom of glory[16] the works performed by those who were faithful stewards[17] in the kingdom of grace. Then shall the glory of the righteous redound to the glory of Him to whose cross we shall owe our crowns and whom with immortal lips we shall forever praise, our Savior and our God.[18]

1.

Matt. 25, 46: And these shall go away into everlasting punishment, but the righteous into *life eternal.*

Tit. 3, 7: That, being justified by His grace, we should be made heirs according to the hope of *eternal life.*

Rom. 6, 23: But the gift of God is *eternal life* through Jesus Christ, our Lord.

John 3, 15. 16: That whosoever believeth in Him should not perish, but have *eternal life.* For God so loved the world that He gave

His only-begotten Son, that whosoever believeth in Him should not perish, but have *everlasting life.*

1 John 2, 25: And this is the promise that He hath promised us, even *eternal life.*

2.

1 John 3, 2: We know that, when He shall appear, we shall be like Him; for we shall *see Him as He is.*

1 Thess. 4, 17: And so shall we ever *be with the Lord.*

Job 19, 26: Yet in my flesh shall I *see God.*

Matt. 5, 8: Blessed are the pure in heart; for they shall *see God.*

John 17, 24: Father, I will that they also, whom Thou hast given me, *be with me* where I am.

Rev. 21, 3: And *God* Himself *shall be with them,* and be their God.

Phil. 1, 23: Having a desire to depart, and to *be with Christ,* which is far better.

3.

Hebr. 12, 22: But ye are come unto Mount Sion, and unto the city of the living God, the heavenly Jerusalem, and to an innumerable company of angels.

Matt. 18, 10: Take heed that ye despise not one of these little ones; for I say unto you, That in heaven their angels do always behold the face of my Father which is in heaven.

2 Thess. 1, 7: And to you who are troubled, rest with us, when the Lord Jesus shall be revealed from heaven with His mighty angels.

4.

2 Tim. 2, 10: For the elect's sakes, that they may also obtain the salvation which is in Christ Jesus *with eternal glory.*

Rev. 3, 5: He that overcometh, the same shall be *clothed in white raiment.*

5.

1 Pet. 5, 10: But the God of all grace, who hath *called us unto His eternal glory* by Christ Jesus, after that ye have suffered awhile, make you perfect, stablish, strengthen, settle you!

2 Cor. 4, 17: For our light affliction, which is but for a moment, worketh for us a far more exceeding and *eternal weight of glory.*

Rom. 8, 17. 18: If so be that we suffer with Him, that we may be also glorified together. For I reckon that the sufferings of this present time are not worthy to be compared with the glory which shall be revealed in us.

Rom. 8, 30: Whom He justified, them He also glorified.

Ps. 16, 11: In Thy presence is *fullness of joy;* at Thy right hand there are pleasures for evermore.

Is. 35, 10: And the ransomed of the Lord shall return, and come to Zion with songs and *everlasting joy upon their heads:* they shall obtain *joy and gladness,* and sorrow and sighing shall flee away.

6.

John 5, 29: And shall *come forth:* they that have done good, unto the *resurrection of life,* and they that have done evil, unto the resurrection of damnation.

1 Cor. 15, 42: So also is the resurrection of the *dead.* It is *sown* in corruption; it is *raised in incorruption.*

7.

2 Tim. 4, 8: Henceforth there is laid up for me a crown of *righteousness.*

1 Pet. 1, 4: To an inheritance incorruptible, and *undefiled,* and that fadeth not away, reserved in heaven for you.

Hebr. 12, 23: And to God, the Judge of all, and to the spirits of *just men made perfect.*

8.

Is. 25, 8: He will swallow up death in victory; and the Lord God will *wipe away tears* from off all faces.

Is. 35, 10: They shall obtain joy and gladness, *and sorrow and sighing shall flee away.*

Is. 60, 20: For the Lord shall be thine everlasting light, and the days of thy *mourning shall be ended.*

Is. 49, 10: They shall *not hunger nor thirst;* neither shall the *heat* nor sun smite them.

Rev. 7, 16. 17: They shall *hunger no more, neither thirst* any more; neither shall the sun light on them, *nor any heat.* And God shall *wipe away all tears* from their eyes.

Rev. 21, 4: And God shall *wipe away all tears* from their eyes; and there shall be no more death, *neither sorrow,* nor *crying, neither* shall there be *any more pain;* for the former things are passed away.

9.

Rom. 7, 24: O wretched man that I am! Who shall *deliver me from the body of this death?*

Is. 25, 8: He will *swallow up death* in victory.

1 Cor. 15, 26. 54: The last enemy that shall be *destroyed* is *death.* (54) So when this corruptible shall have put on incorruption, and this mortal shall have put on immortality, then shall be brought to pass the saying that is written, *Death is swallowed up* in victory.

Rev. 21, 4: And there shall be *no more death.*

Rev. 20, 14: And *death* and hell were cast into the lake of fire.

Luke 20, 36: *Neither* can *they die any more;* for they are equal unto the angels, and are the children of God, being *the children of* the *resurrection.*

10.

1 Thess. 4, 17: And so shall we *ever be with the Lord.*

Rev. 3, 5. 12: And I will *not blot out his name out* of the book of life. (12) Him that overcometh will I make a pillar in the temple of my God, and *he shall go no more out.*

11.

Acts 20, 32: And now, brethren, I commend you to God, and to the Word of His grace, which is able to build you up, and to give you an *inheritance* among all them which are sanctified.

Hebr. 1, 14: Are they not all ministering spirits, sent forth to minister for them who shall be *heirs of salvation?*

Hebr. 9, 15: That . . . they which are called might receive the promise of *eternal inheritance.*

Eph. 1, 14: Which is the earnest of *our inheritance.*

1 Pet. 5, 9: Whom resist steadfast in the faith, knowing that the same afflictions are accomplished in your brethren that are in the world.

1 Pet. 1, 4: To an *inheritance* incorruptible.

12.

1 Cor. 13, 10. 12: But *when that which is* PERFECT *is come,* then that which is in part shall be done away. (12) For now we see through a glass, darkly; but then face to face: *now* I know *in part;* but then shall I know even as also I am known.

2 Tim. 4, 18: The Lord shall *deliver* me from EVERY *evil work.*

13.

2 Cor. 12, 2. 4: I knew a man in Christ above fourteen years ago, (whether in the body, I cannot tell; or whether out of the body, I cannot tell: God knoweth;) such an one caught up to the third heaven. (4) How that he was caught up into paradise, and heard *unspeakable words,* which it is not lawful for a man to utter.

Matt. 13, 43: Then shall the righteous shine forth *as the sun* in the kingdom of their Father.

14.

1 Cor. 15, 41. 42: There is one glory of the sun, and another glory of the moon, and another glory of the stars; for one star differeth from another star in glory. So also is the resurrection of the dead.

15.

Matt. 25, 14—23. (Parable of the talents.)

Rev. 14, 13: Blessed are the dead which die in the Lord from henceforth. Yea, saith the Spirit, that they may rest from their labors; and *their works do follow them.*

Rev. 22, 12: And, behold, I come quickly; and *my reward is with me.* to give every man according as his work shall be.

Matt. 10, 42: And whosoever shall give to drink unto one of these little ones a cup of cold water only in the name of a disciple, *verily,* I say unto you, *he shall in no wise lose his reward.*

Matt. 19, 29: And every one that hath forsaken houses, or brethren, or sisters, or father, or mother, or wife, or children, or lands, for my name's sake, *shall receive an hundredfold,* and shall inherit everlasting life.

Mark 9, 41: For whosoever shall give you a cup of water to drink in my name, because ye belong to Christ, verily, I say unto you, *he shall not lose his reward.*

2 Cor. 9, 6: But this I say, He which *soweth sparingly* shall *reap* also *sparingly;* and he which *soweth bountifully* shall *reap* also *bountifully.*

16.

See CHRISTOLOGY on the royal office of Christ, §§ 126—129.

17.

Matt. 25, 14—23. (Parable of the talents.)

2 Tim. 4, 7. 8: I have *fought a good fight,* I have *finished my course,* I have kept the faith: henceforth there is laid up' for me a crown of righteousness, which the Lord, the *righteous Judge,* shall *give me* at that day, and not to me only, but *unto all them also that love His appearing.*

18.

Ps. 126, 2. 3: Then was our mouth filled with laughter, and our tongue with singing: then said they among the heathen, The Lord hath done great things for them. The Lord hath done great things for us, whereof we are glad.

Rev. 4, 10. 11: The four and twenty elders fall down before Him that sat on the throne, and worship Him that liveth for ever and ever, and cast their crowns before the throne, saying, Thou art worthy, O Lord, to receive glory and honor and power; for Thou hast created all things, and for Thy pleasure they are and were created.

Rev. 5, 8—12: And when He had taken the book, the four beasts and four and twenty elders fell down before the Lamb, having every one of them harps, and golden vials full of odors, which are the prayers of saints. And they sung a new song, saying, Thou art worthy to take the book, and to open the seals thereof; for Thou wast slain, and hast redeemed us to God by Thy blood out of every kindred, and tongue, and people, and nation; and hast made us unto our God kings and priests: and we shall reign on earth. And I beheld, and I heard the voice of many angels round about the throne and the beasts and the elders: and the number of them was ten thousand times ten thousand, and thousands of thousands, saying with a loud voice, Worthy is the Lamb that was slain to receive power, and riches, and wisdom, and strength, and honor, and glory, and blessing.

INDEX.

www.ingramcontent.com/pod-product-compliance
Lightning Source LLC
Chambersburg PA
CBHW020402100426
42812CB00001B/169

*9 7 8 0 7 5 8 6 1 8 1 2 2 *